The Language of Houses

THE LANGUAGE OF HOUSES
Copyright © 2014 by Alison Lurie

First Edition

Jacket and interior design by Greg Mortimer

Library of Congress Cataloging-in-Publication Data is available on request.

Chapters 7, 9 and 10 of this book originally appeared in the *New York Review of Books*.

ISBN 978-1-88-328560-9

14 15 16 17 18   RRD 10 9 8 7 6 5 4 3 2 1

The Language *of* Houses

HOW BUILDINGS SPEAK TO US

Alison Lurie

Illustrations by Karen Sung

DELPHINIUM BOOKS
Harrison, New York • Encino, California

For my sister Jennifer

CONTENTS

CHAPTER I

What Buildings Say

A building is an inanimate object, but it is not an inarticulate one. Even the simplest house always makes a statement, one expressed in brick and stone and plaster, in wood and metal and glass, rather than in words—but no less loud and obvious. When we see a rusting trailer surrounded by weeds and derelict cars, or a brand-new mini-mansion with a high, spike-topped wall, we instantly get a message. In both of these cases, though in different accents, it is "Stay Out of Here."

It is not only houses, of course, that communicate with us. All kinds of buildings—churches, museums, schools, hospitals, restaurants, hotels, stores, and offices—speak to us silently. Sometimes the statement is deliberate. A store or restaurant can be designed so that it welcomes mostly low-income or high-income customers; a church or temple can announce that God is a friendly neighbor, a stern judge, or a remote and inaccessible spirit. Buildings tell us what to think and how to act, though we may not register their messages consciously.

In this sense, architecture is a kind of language, one that most designers, builders, and decorators speak, sometimes fluently and sometimes clumsily, and that all of us hear. In many ways it is a more universal language than words, since it uses three-dimensional shapes, colors, and textures rather than words. We may be at a loss to understand what is said in most foreign languages, but almost every building conveys information, though we may not understand all of it. And, like spoken and written languages, architecture may be formal or casual, simple or complex.

FORMAL AND INFORMAL

Formal speech is weighty, balanced, without hesitations, interruptions, or incomplete sentences: we hear it in a written and rehearsed political oration or public lecture. Formal public buildings, from an early Greek temple to the latest state capitol, have been carefully planned. They tend to be bilaterally symmetrical from a front or rear view: one side is a mirror image of the other. Any internal asymmetry (the placement of bathrooms and closets, for instance) is invisible from outside. Many grand private homes, including most great European and American mansions of the sixteenth to the nineteenth centuries, were bilaterally symmetrical. The formal regularity of their façades, both front and rear, suggested that what went on within them was equally formal and well regulated.

Buildings that look symmetrical only from in front are more common. The town hall and the library, as well as the classic Southern mansion, Cape Cod cottage, or Colonial Revival house, with their central doorways flanked by identical windows, all suggest formality, especially when there is a front walk with matching trees or flower beds on either side. Seeing such a building, we assume (not always correctly) that life inside it will be well ordered and perhaps rather conventional. Often, however, in the back of these structures there will be uneven additions—as well as sheds, garages, porches, and decks—that suggest a more complex private life.

Informal speech is colloquial, often impetuous, and fragmentary. Informal architecture also usually seems casual and unplanned—as if it just grew, which is often the case. Most people who buy a house eventually make alterations if they can afford it. As a result, over the years the original structure of a building may have been altered many times. Wings may have been extended, a bay window pushed out, a porch added or removed. Most buildings don't stand still over time: they grow and shrink; different tenants move in, and as they do, meanings change. When my grown son and I went to look at my parents' former summer house on the ocean in Maine, we were sad and even rather angry to see that the big screened porch where we all used to sit had been enclosed and turned into just another room. The house was larger and more impressive now, but less open and welcoming.

SIMPLE AND COMPLEX

Like speech, architecture can be simple or complex. Simple speech favors short words and sentences, with few adjectives and adverbs and similes. Simple architecture, too, is largely unadorned. The basic nineteenth-century American farmhouse, shotgun cabin, or little country church recalls the simple songs and ballads of an earlier time and the traditionally laconic speech of the frontier. Their minimalism may have been unplanned, the result of a shortage of money and time, or it may have been consciously chosen, like Shaker architecture. Today, the deliberate choice of simple construction is common among people who favor a back-to-the-land or green lifestyle; occasionally, however, their apparently basic buildings have in fact been expensive to build and heat and light, though the hope is always that they will save money over time as well as reducing the strain on our natural resources. Some owners may also try to create the look of a supposedly simpler and more "authentic" past in their brand-new houses. They use old bricks and boards that in fact cost more than new ones, and may even have fresh paint scratched and scraped to create a "distressed" look.

In most of Europe and America there seems to have always been an instinctive propensity toward constructing simple rectangular buildings with sloping roofs that shed rain and snow easily. This basic pattern even appears in children's drawings. The French architectural historian Gaston Bachelard speaks of the picture so often drawn by children, and known to psychologists as the "Happy

House." It is usually a square one- or two-story home with a peaked roof, a central door, and two or more symmetrically placed windows. There is often a chimney from which smoke rises, implying that the building is warm and inhabited. Frequently the Happy House is surrounded by simple lollipop-shaped trees and/or outsize flowers, and a big round yellow sun shines in the sky, which is indicated by a strip of bright blue at the top of the drawing.

Unhappy or disturbed children will sometimes produce a version of this picture in which the strip of sky is black, and there is no sun. Their houses often have no windows, or only black squares, implying that nobody can see in or out; bad things presumably go on in such a building. In extreme cases, the Happy House may collapse entirely. *The New York Times*, in an article about the aftermath of Hurricane Katrina, reported that many children who had lived through the storm drew not an entire house but simply a triangle representing its roof and attic, possibly the only part that remained above water: windows and stick figures sometimes appeared inside this triangle.

Simple buildings, whether large or small, are reassuring because we readily understand them. Their shapes are uncomplicated, and they have few and regularly placed doors and windows, so that it is easy to visualize their interiors. The houses of our primitive ancestors were often simply round or rectangular, partly because such basic shapes are easier to construct and heat and defend: for one thing, they have proportionately less exterior wall space. An irregularly shaped building is not only harder to build and protect against enemies; if it is also irregular inside it can lead to trouble. Blurry boundaries within a house can cause clashes between family members; in a public building they are often the source of confusion and annoyance, as when library patrons become lost in oddly arranged stacks or customers blunder into staff washrooms. The same thing is true on a larger historical and geographical scale, where ill-defined boundaries between countries and states traditionally lead to conflict.

Though primitive houses were often round, in contemporary

America circular buildings are rare, like unusual or eccentric speech. If small and private, like the yurts built by hippies in the 1960s and 1970s, they recall the teepees and domed houses of Native Americans. If large and formal, they may remind us of the public buildings of classical Rome and Washington, D.C., and (like the Parthenon and the Jefferson Memorial) have an aura of moral uplift and commemoration. Less formal circular and oval buildings may also make us think of circus tents or football stadiums, and thus of entertainment and sports.

Rectangular buildings sometimes disguise circular spaces: the interior of many traditional theatres, churches, and lecture halls often takes the shape of a half circle or two-thirds circle. While there is no suggestion of athletic competition, the associations of both entertainment and moral or cultural value remain. There is also a sense of formal order, since the space is open and intelligible at a glance, and the seats are usually arranged in parallel rows.

Circular plans may, however, be disturbing. The elegant snail shape of the Guggenheim Museum in New York depends on the flexibility of metal and concrete and presumably suggests that viewing art is natural and fun. However, after nearly seventy-five years, some art lovers refuse to visit the Guggenheim, claiming that it makes them feel dizzy and ill because of the low interior walls, the sloping floor, and the vertiginous view down to the bottom of the spiral walkway.

Complex speech favors elaboration: long words and sentences, striking metaphors and similes, and intricate grammatical constructions. Complex architecture tends to involve intricate shapes and elaborate decoration. The result may be attractive or hideous, depending on the skill of the architect and our own taste. The architecture of late Victorian Europe and America, heavy with ornamentation, sometimes recalls the romantic lushness of late-nineteenth-century poetry. Private houses of the period were often complex in design and ornamentation, with bow windows, elaborate porches and verandas, canopies over the front door, towers, romantic balconies, and lacy wooden trim. They can be wonderfully original and charming, like the famous "painted ladies" of San Francisco, where windows and doors and gables are outlined in brilliant complementary colors. They can also be ostentatious and oppressive, especially when very large, as in some of the Newport, Rhode Island, chateau-style "cottages" built by the tycoons of the Gilded Age.

But just as the great nineteenth-century poets inspired hundreds of untalented and melodramatic imitators, so did less talented practitioners of Victorian styles in architecture sometimes produce monstrosities. These are the haunted houses of contemporary cartoons and film, with their spiky wrought-iron trim and their elaborate, sometimes nonfunctional towers, pillars, balconies, gables, dormers, and verandas.

For the founders of modern architecture, such houses were truly haunted, but by an evil cultural past; their complex exterior design and elaborate interiors seemed to suggest artistic immorality or dishonesty. To committed modernists, all decoration was superfluous, and thus unsightly. Only unadorned simplicity was considered beautiful and good. As Alain de Botton puts it in *The Architecture of Happiness*, "a structure was correct and honest in so far as it performed its mechanical functions efficiently, and false and immoral in so far as it was burdened with non-supporting pillars, decorative statues, frescos or carvings."

The conscious preference for apparent simplicity in the early-twentieth-century modernist movement in prose and poetry was echoed in what is known as the International Style of architecture. The new literature avoided archaic words, elaborate images, grammatical inversions, and sometimes even meter and rhyme—a rose was a rose was a rose. In the same way, one of the basic principles of early modernist architecture was that every part of a building must be functional, without any unnecessary protuberances or fancy trimmings. Most

International Style architecture aggressively banned moldings, cornices, and sometimes even window and door frames. Like the prose of Hemingway or Samuel Beckett, it proclaimed, and sometimes proved, that less was more. But, just as with the many less talented imitators of Hemingway and Beckett, second-rate modern architects often produced buildings that were simple without being inspiring or original. Instead they were boring and often unpleasant to live in.

Some modern architects, unfortunately, designed buildings that looked simple and elegant but didn't in fact function very well: their flat roofs leaked in wet climates, their plaster disintegrated, and their metal railings and window frames rusted. Occasionally these buildings also made people psychologically or physically uncomfortable. Anyone who has ever tried to descend a floating staircase without risers or an effective handrail, or sat through a dinner party in a chair designed by an artist with no knowledge of ergonomics, will recognize these sensations.

Absolute simplicity, in most cases, remained an ideal rather than a reality, and in the early twentieth century complex architectural decorations continued to adorn many private and public buildings. During those years the façade of almost every new apartment house of any pretension in a major American or European city was deliberately ornamented in some way. Often the ground floors were faced with marble or granite blocks; luxury buildings had exterior nonfunctional columns and statuary and elaborate entrances and balconies; even less expensive ones might have classical trim on the lower floors and low-relief plaster garlands around the main door.

As time passed, some modernist architects, rather than opting for total functionalism, incorporated what were seen as up-to-date decorative styles. The columns and garlands were replaced with Art Deco designs that suggested science and technology, motion and speed. Statues and flowers were out: squares and zigzags and parallel lines were in. The middle years of the twentieth century also saw the proliferation of nonfunctional tailfins for automobiles, and jazzy patterns on carpets, curtains, and clothing. Toasters and clocks that were not going anywhere and could therefore never profit from reduced wind resistance were "streamlined." Even today, modernist decorations have still not been totally phased out in new construction and design, though they sometimes express a self-conscious postmodern nostalgia and irony.

After World War II many builders (perhaps for reasons of cost) rejected the earlier, more elaborate styles in favor of a totally stripped-down look: stark beige or white brick or concrete walls, and aluminum-framed windows. The interior offices or apartments usually had smaller rooms and lower ceilings. It took a while for customers to catch on, but today "prewar" is a selling phrase in real estate ads. Many people who live in these older buildings appreciate the extra space, and even the exterior decorations, which are now considered original and elegant—or, by the more sophisticated, ironically charming.

Simple buildings are not always informal, nor are complex ones formal. A small Greek temple or a New England church is simple and formal, like the greeting, "How do you do?" A log cabin or a bus shelter, on the other hand, is simple and informal, the architectural equivalent of "Hi there!" A French chateau, like an official political speech, is complex and formal, while the witch's overdecorated gingerbread house in "Hansel and Gretel" is complex and informal.

LARGE AND SMALL

A very large building, like a loud voice or a hefty physique, is the architectural equivalent of a shout. It takes up space, and has obviously been expensive and time-consuming to erect. Next to it other buildings look small, and so do we. This is even truer if the component parts of the building are also supersized: for instance if it has broad, high doors and windows, and walls built from giant blocks of stone. The imposing effect is increased when we must climb a flight of steps to reach the entrance, as in some churches, museums, and government buildings. Even large, famous, and powerful people are dwarfed by structures like the Houses of Parliament, Notre Dame Cathedral, many famous opera houses, and the Supreme Court of the United States, with its long flight of steps and giant columns.

Inside, oversized proportions emphasize the significance of whatever the building contains or represents. Massive double doors, immense entrance halls and staircases, high ceilings, and long wide corridors suggest that the building's natural or symbolic residents (Gods, Kings, Politicians, Art, Music, Drama, Education, Science, Justice) are important and powerful, while we are relatively small, insignificant, and weak. In the vast entrance hall of the Metropolitan Museum of Art, in New York, for instance, visitors are dwarfed literally and symbolically not only by the oversized, echoing space, but by the tall Corinthian columns and the huge and famous flower arrangements, which resemble wedding bouquets for giants.

Occasionally a building seems to have been deliberately designed to make us feel like small children. The doors and windows of such structures are not only huge, but almost impossible to open: their handles are too high and too large and/or turn with great difficulty. Their staircases break the standard rules of construction, which dictate that the sum of riser and tread should equal about twenty-five inches. Public buildings customarily have wider treads and narrower risers, and their staircases therefore take up more ground space and look more important. Indoor stairs tend to have narrower treads, especially if they lead to an attic, so that in extreme cases we climb the steps with difficulty, as a small child does.

Most successful and ambitious people try to build large, for both practical and psychological reasons. As Stewart Brand points out, "more space in domestic buildings is equated with freedom. In commercial buildings, more space means profit. In institutional buildings, it means power." Or at least, it tries to suggest these things. Banks especially try to look large and impregnable, to reassure depositors that money will be safe in their vaults forever.

Large rooms and high ceilings, whether in public or private

buildings, traditionally both predict and favor formal encounters. When we enter the office of a government official or corporation president, usually after a long journey through waiting rooms and corridors, we must still often walk quite far to reach his or her desk, which tends to be very big and almost empty of papers. The symbolic message is that this person is far from us, and difficult of access, and also that he or she makes only large far-reaching decisions: any necessary shuffling of paper is done by underlings. Political leaders, partly for security reasons, often exaggerate the distance to their desks, a choice memorably parodied in Chaplin's *The Great Dictator*, where you must walk what looks like the length of a football field to reach the Great Leader. In the offices of very important people, the very important person also typically sits in a very important-looking chair. Smaller chairs, or sometimes even none, are provided for visitors, so that they may become aware of their own unimportance.

The same effects of size also appear in everyday life. The loud, penetrating voices of the rich, which have often been commented on, have their parallel in the lobbies of big hotels and the huge living rooms of city mansions and grand country houses. With their outsize carpets, mirrors, pictures, and sofas, they tend to awe and embarrass visitors, though habitués may avail themselves of the intimate groupings of furniture that float like islands of refuge here and there.

The size of a room naturally influences what goes on in it. Small rooms encourage intimacy—large ones favor formal behavior. A huge theatre or concert hall invites, and complements, impressive and elaborate productions; a small one suits chamber music and plays with only a few characters. More than one successful intimate family drama has failed when transferred from a theatre that seats fifty people to one that seats a thousand, and the audience therefore anticipates something serious and of universal significance.

Where land was cheap, buildings tended to spread outward rather than up. Rising land values changed all this. Today, though the country mansions of billionaires still sprawl over the landscape, in many places developers (if zoning allows) will build four or even six ostentatious "homes" on a single acre. As a result, it is sometimes possible to date houses by the relative size of their lots. In my hometown, for instance, a developer has recently put up a group of rather convincing reproduction Colonial mansions, but the way they are crowded together proves that they were not built in Colonial times.

The invention of the elevator also altered the look of towns and cities drastically. Before the late nineteenth century, apartment and office buildings seldom rose beyond four or five stories; today their height is limited only by zoning rules and by costs, since beyond a certain number of floors the amount of space that must be devoted to both elevators and stairways reduces the area that can be sold or rented. The Empire State Building in New York can charge high prices per square foot because it is a famous landmark, but usually anything above thirty or forty stories is unprofitable, especially in commercial buildings, where the increased traffic means that there must be many elevators.

In big cities a building may sit on a fraction of an acre without losing prestige, and even the smallest front garden or row of shrubs and flowers is a sign of affluence. Developers build up rather than out, competing over relative height and often calling their finished project The [My Own Name] Towers. To those in the know, square footage is impressive according to its net worth on the real estate market, but out-of-town visitors do not always appreciate this. It is traditional for country mice to be appalled by the cramped dwellings of city mice, which cost ten times more than their own large, comfortable rural or suburban homes.

In general, a small house suggests a small income; just as a small church suggests a small congregation and a small store a limited number of customers. As a result, ambitious princes, politicians, and profiteers have usually favored large, impressive buildings. But many, perhaps most of these large structures also contain small, enclosed rooms where privacy and secrecy are possible. Government buildings are full of little offices; mansions include dressing rooms

and studies; churches contain vestries and confessionals. An important politician or the executive of a corporation is likely to have a
den with a bar and comfortable chairs just off his or her impressive,
formal office; and almost every store or school has a break room or
lounge for its employees. These spaces tend to be concealed from
the public, but they are necessary if the organization is to function
smoothly. A building that lacks them is like someone who can only
speak in a loud, booming voice, and as a result tends to drive us away.

At times, those who can afford to build on a grand scale may
prefer to keep things small. If you already own a big house, an extra
little one may seem charming, especially if it is elegantly constructed
and furnished. In the eighteenth century, cottages and pavilions and
playhouses and summerhouses began to appear in the gardens of
the rich, to serve as a temporary refuge from the formal life of the
palace or mansion: Marie Antoinette's Le Hameau de la Reine at
Versailles, where the queen played at being a dairymaid, is the classic example. The custom has never died out, and similar structures
can be seen today on many modern estates. When their famous or
powerful owners want to relax and act like adolescents or children,
they use these pool houses and playhouses and lodges, which are the
three-dimensional equivalent of teenage slang or even baby talk.

NESTING AND PERCHING

One way of looking at small homes is to see them as the domiciles
of different types of animal and bird. Someone who is essentially a
bear will establish a den: a cozy retreat from which most others are
excluded. A bowerbird will create an elaborate, decorative nest to
attract and impress potential mates, while a cuckoo will move into
someone else's nest and gradually take it over, in the process pushing
out items of furniture (and possibly even people) that belong to the
original owner.

A small house or a small room can feel cramped and insignificant,
but it may also seem cozy or snug. As Jerry Griswold remarks in

Feeling Like a Kid, children's literature is full of enclosed, safe places, where one is sheltered from the dangerous outside world and "can sleep or nap undisturbed." If they do not have a playhouse or tree house, many children will create such snug places under tables, in closets, in discarded appliance cartons, in nests of pillows or outside among the shrubbery. Ideally, such a location, according to Griswold, has nine qualities: it is small, enclosed, tight, well designed, remote, safe, self-sufficient, owned (that is, private), and hidden.

In adult life, too, we see dwellings and rooms that appear to have been constructed or furnished according to these principles. Often they seem intended to suggest the closeness and safety of the womb, or perhaps of ancient cave dwellings. Whether we feel comfortable in these places or not appears to depend on our personality and history. As Griswold puts it, "A child's sense of security determines whether enclosed space is perceived as reassuring and desirable or confining and abhorrent."

Psychologists have suggested that all of us are either slightly claustrophobic or slightly agoraphobic, depending on whether, as children, we were more afraid of being abandoned, or afraid of being confined and dominated. The story of Hansel and Gretel may be popular partly because it expresses both these fears: Hansel and Gretel are first deserted in the forest, and then imprisoned by the witch. Childhood anxieties often survive in a diminished form into adulthood, and as a result some of us will be at ease in a tiny cottage with little, low-ceilinged rooms, while others will be happier out-doors or in a loft with a terrace and a view. If you feel cramped and claustrophobic in a small office with a single small window and only one door, you may once have felt restricted and imprisoned; if you are uncomfortable in a large, high-ceilinged office with too many doors and windows, you may once have felt abandoned or exposed.

Some people, perhaps the majority, may prefer to avoid the draw-backs of both overenclosed and overexposed dwellings. According to Winifred Gallagher, the author of *House Thinking*, what most of us really want in a home is some combination of what Frank Lloyd

Wright called "perching and nesting." Grant Hildebrand, a professor of architecture at the University of Washington in Seattle, prefers the terms Prospect and Refuge. Hildebrand noticed that among his students, houses designed by men contained more Prospect, while women's contained more Refuge. Today most architects are still men, and many great rooms, as Winifred Gallagher points out, are almost all Prospect. Large public spaces, such as plazas and town squares, may be seen as unpleasant unless they combine both Prospect and Refuge (the latter in the form, most often, of outdoor restaurants and shops around the periphery and benches backed by low walls or hedges).

We expect a large building to contain many large, high-ceilinged rooms, at least on its main floor. If it does not, even people who like cozy cottages may feel oppressed. This might be one reason why many prisons and hospitals and office buildings make us uneasy. A house or studio apartment that essentially consists of only one big room, possibly divided into sitting, cooking, and sleeping areas, can seem uncomfortable because it offers no privacy except in the bathroom. We are less disturbed when there is essentially only one large room inside a small public building, since we are used to this layout in stores and churches.

PROPORTION

In both public and private buildings, rooms come in very different shapes. In general, an unusually long and narrow room suggests a hierarchical situation, in which the most important people are set apart far from the entrance. In some cases there may be a raised platform at the far end, as in a throne room, a church, or the high table of a traditional university dining hall. A recent example of the latter can be seen in the film versions of the Harry Potter books, where the masters sit at a traditional "high table" on a dais at one end of a huge room, while the students are ranged at long parallel tables on a lower level. A room that is more or less square, by contrast, tends to make its inhabitants feel equal. Another possibility, often seen in official buildings, is a large public space enclosing a semiprivate area that may be partly or almost wholly separated from it by a partition or glass-walled counter. This configuration allows those in authority to see what is going on and retreat as desired, an arrangement that is often observed and resented in places like the motor vehicle office, where many clerks seem to be present but none are available to answer questions.

Round or oval rooms, though rare, are often considered beautiful. They are expensive to build and difficult to furnish, but this may add to their prestige, as with the Oval Office in the White House. Rooms of irregular shape, even after a century of modernism, tend to cause discomfort. Many of them have a kind of trapezoidal floor plan, making placement of furniture awkward and creating empty angled corners into which nothing fits very well. Small interruptions to a box-shaped room, however, like a bay window or a protruding fireplace, may add charm to any space, either public or private.

We expect most large rooms to have high ceilings, and most small ones to have low ceilings. When these unconscious rules are overturned, we may feel uncomfortable. A large room with a low ceiling suggests either poverty or antiquity, often both. We associate such a room with down-market bars and restaurants and shops, especially those that were built many years ago: the classic beer cellar is a prominent example. In the past people were generally shorter than they are today, and a six-and-a-half or seven-foot ceiling was no problem, especially for the ill-nourished working classes. Today a charming eighteenth-century country cottage may force its owner to duck his head constantly as he passes from one room to another. Contemporary designers of apartment houses sometimes save money by shrinking the height of each floor, allowing them to cram in more units and achieve a greater square footage for the building as a whole. Once the inhabitants have moved in they may experience an unexplained but definite sense of claustrophobia.

A small room with a very high ceiling can also create unease. Usually our first experience of this configuration takes place in buildings where large spaces have been partitioned, as in old hospitals where big public wards have been subdivided into single- or two-patient rooms. In general we expect rooms to be wider or longer than they are high, and the opposite configuration has a tendency to make us feel uneasy and confined. It also possibly reminds us of being very young children, when the ceiling was relatively far away.

OPEN AND SHUT

One of the first things we notice about any communication is whether it is clear, friendly, and informative, or the reverse. In the same way, we notice whether a building is accessible or inaccessible. Some houses seem naturally welcoming, others inhospitable or even actively intimidating. If you want to keep people away, there are two basic architectural methods: distance and enclosure. A house that is miles from anywhere, reached only by a narrow road in bad repair, will have few visitors; move it to the intersection of two city streets, and it will have many more. The same thing is true of public buildings, including shops, churches, libraries, museums, and schools. High walls and hedges, especially those that cannot be seen through, are a further discouragement.

Simple, easily understood speech is associated with ordinary people; elaborate, incomprehensible diction suggests academic or governmental authorities. In the same way, the easier it is to get into any building, the more friendly it feels, but the lower its prestige. The front doors of many working-class houses and apartments open directly into the main living space, and those of modest shops into a single room. In many small towns people do not lock their doors while they are at home during the day, or even shut them; and in warm weather stores are often open to the street. Some city apartments, by contrast, may have as many as six locks on the front door, and some expensive shops only admit customers through a locked door after a salesperson has looked them over.

To reach the office of a very important person we will usually have to pass through many gates, doors, corridors, and anterooms, and be inspected by soldiers, guards, secretaries, and/or machines. A very expensive house may have an outer wall with a gate, a long drive, heavy front doors, a vestibule, an inner door, and finally a big hall that we must negotiate before we can meet the owner.

There are several ways of making a building seriously unapproachable: high walls topped with razor wire or broken glass; locked gates; long, steep driveways; heavy doors; armed guards; and hungry, angry watchdogs. At one time, the homes of the rich and powerful were often in real danger of invasion. Medieval castles were designed to keep out enemies: thick stone walls pierced with narrow windows, moats, drawbridges, heavy ironclad oak doors, and towers with crenellated walls suitable for shooting at attackers. Many of these historical solutions to actual dangers have survived as symbolic details of public buildings, especially churches and universities, which may of course still be unconsciously thought of as under siege from the heathen and philistine public.

Another method of making a building inaccessible is to complicate its design, just as much legal and political speech is complicated. If you live in a castle surrounded by potential enemies and filled with possibly treacherous courtiers and servants, concealed doors, secret staircases and tunnels, sliding panels, and hidden rooms are useful and even essential. They are still handy today if you are engaged in an illegal or risky occupation, or want to make a quick getaway from unwelcome visitors. During Prohibition, many speakeasies had concealed trapdoors to cellars that could conceal bootleg liquor and occasionally individuals wanted by the cops.

Even law-abiding enterprises may engage in intentional or unintentional architectural obfuscation. As public buildings grow larger, they tend to become more complex; but as long as they have a fairly basic rectangular ground plan and good signage, it is possible to find your way around. In some cases, however, these buildings, like Kafka's Castle, appear to have been deliberately complicated, either for aesthetic reasons or to confuse or awe strangers. Long, ill-lit, seemingly identical corridors that appear to lead nowhere, doors that give no indication of what is behind them, and staircases and elevators that cannot be easily located are common ploys. Many visitors to large hospitals and government offices have complained bitterly of becoming lost in such places, and made to feel stupid or unwanted.

There are, of course, ways of excluding some people from certain buildings, or parts of them. Signs like "Men" and "Women" discourage members of the opposite sex from entering washrooms; and when I was a child you could still see, in the South, places designated as "Colored Waiting Room" and "Colored Entrance." In the nineteenth century, patrons of the opera and theatre might use different entrances and lobbies according to how much they had paid for their seats, so that the upper classes would not have to associate too closely with the middle classes or the poor. As Marvin Carlson puts it in *Places of Performance*, to go to a play or opera was to know where you fit in the class system and continually be reminded of it. Even today, some opera houses include a set of narrow back stairs for those who can only afford the top balcony.

Ways of making a building seem friendly and welcoming also have a long history. Removal of walls, gates, and hedges is an obvious first step, and a well-mown lawn with bright flower beds is always encouraging. Window boxes full of geraniums and pansies are even better. Open porches and verandas, especially when furnished with casual, comfortable-looking furniture, provide an easy and reassuring transition area. It also helps if the interior of the building is partly visible from outside: its windows mostly unblocked by curtains or blinds, and its doors propped open, or with glass inserts that allow a visitor to see that there is nothing strange or dangerous inside.

Modernist architecture has always favored large windows and even occasionally walls that are mainly glass. Philip Johnson's famous Glass House in New Canaan, Connecticut, is essentially a transparent rectangular box in which only the bathroom is enclosed by a permanent inner wall. Of course such transparency has its disadvantages, the most obvious of which is loss of privacy, but there are solutions to this problem: Johnson's Glass House, for instance, is isolated in the middle of a forty-seven-acre estate and has heavy curtains. Many urban International Style dwellings turn their picture windows toward a courtyard or walled garden, or raise them far above the street. American cities today are full of tall buildings with giant windows. The apartments or offices they contain have striking views, and what goes on inside them can apparently be seen only by birds—though it may also be visible to neighbors with high-powered binoculars.

Many large retail enterprises today have glass doors, and large windows for the display of merchandise. Smaller shops tend to have windows that both present goods and show some of the interior. This is often deliberate, because a store that customers cannot see into always has a slightly unwelcoming air. Occasionally, of course, a closed-in appearance is designed to exclude customers who lack cash or confidence. Most bars and nightclubs, regardless of the economic or social level of their patrons, are difficult to see into—indeed, the more notorious or dubious the activities that take place within them, the more closed off and inscrutable they tend to be.

DARK AND LIGHT

A statement may seem threatening not only because of what it says, but also because of the tone in which it is uttered. In the same way, a building may look sinister if it is constructed of naturally dark materials or painted a gloomy hue. It may also be cut off from light by nearby buildings or heavy trees. In literature, houses in which difficult characters live or tragic events take place tend to be both dark colored and overshadowed. A classic case is Nathaniel Hawthorne's eponymous *The House of the Seven Gables*, "with its black shingles, and the green moss that shows how damp they are . . . its dark, low-studded rooms. . . ." In the hero's view, it "is expressive of that odious and abominable Past, with all its bad influences." The convention that dark deeds take place in dark places is even stronger in movies and television: the house in the classic film *Psycho* is almost black and surrounded by creepy black trees. A light-colored building that is easily visible from outside always has a more innocent air, even when we know that crimes have taken place inside it; the White House in Washington, D.C., is one prominent example.

The interior rooms of a building may be dim because they have dark walls and furniture or because very little light reaches them from outside, or both. Such rooms may be seen as warm and sheltering, or as imprisoning and ominous. In the eighteenth and early nineteenth century, pale colors and uncurtained windows were admired. Victorian architects and decorators, on the other hand, preferred dim, cavelike interiors. The classical Victorian parlor had heavy mahogany or oak furniture and wainscoting, dark patterned wall coverings, and windows shrouded in two or more sets of curtains and drapes. The implication was that life was complex, heavy, and serious, and that families had secrets that needed to be concealed. Historians of architecture have pointed out that after the death of Queen Victoria's husband, Prince Albert, in 1861, British interior decoration became heavier and darker, as if the sitting rooms of the nation were also in deep mourning.

In the early twentieth century a younger generation reacted strongly against this kind of interior and the manners and morals it implied, which were seen as confining and oppressive. Decorators pulled down the curtains, painted the walls in light colors, and replaced the bulky dark furniture with the light woods and simpler designs of Art Nouveau and Art Deco. In these rooms people felt able to speak and act more freely—even wildly by the old standards. Most contemporary designers still tend to prefer pale walls and unblocked windows, though they may choose darker colors for bedrooms, suggesting that a kind of warm, sheltering gloom is appropriate for sleeping. Since computer use and the viewing of television are difficult when direct light shines on the screen, many offices and private homes now include rooms with few or no windows and artificial lighting that can be dimmed.

Electricity also revolutionized the experience of going to the theatre. When plays were presented outdoors in daylight the spectators were just as visible as the actors. Often, as in Shakespeare's Globe Theatre, the orchestra area was flat and open, without any seats. All this encouraged playgoers to move about during a performance, and turn their attention from the stage to each other. The same thing still tends to happen in outdoor theatres during daylight performances.

Today, in a big theatre or concert hall with fixed rows of seats, the dimming of the lights before a performance—like the whispered shushing that may accompany it—encourages us to fall into a kind of trance state. It also tells us that we are important only en masse. We should not expect to be seen by those onstage, and usually must not be heard, though we may applaud (or even hiss or boo) at certain moments. A large formal church with lighting focused on a preacher or soloist radiates a similar message. We may be invited and even encouraged to sing or pray aloud, but not in our own words, and we will usually act as a group rather than as individuals.

CHAPTER 2

Architectural Languages

DORIC ⟶ IONIC ⟶ CORINTHIAN

Just as there are many spoken and written tongues, the language of architecture is not universal. In our hometowns we usually understand most of the buildings we see, but the farther we travel the less we comprehend. For a little-traveled New Englander, Southern cities may be as hard to understand as a Deep South dialect, and Los Angeles may seem a confusion of both unfamiliar building types and entertainment industry jargon.

FOREIGN LANGUAGES AND FOREIGN ACCENTS

For most Americans, the architecture of European cities is like a half-learned foreign language. When we are hungry and thirsty we can probably find a restaurant or a café, but we often can't tell from outside what sort of drink and food will be served inside or whether we will be welcome there. In Africa or Asia architectural signs that are obvious to locals can be completely unintelligible to us. We may not even recognize places where food and drink are for sale; we may mistake a palace for a temple, and a private house for a government office, or vice versa. We may shock or anger local citizens when we enter spaces that to them are obviously out of bounds for us, as I once did when I followed my husband into a mosque and was met with what sounded like an operatic curse.

Of course, just as sophisticated speakers and writers sometimes drop foreign words or phrases into their native discourse, so builders may deliberately copy foreign styles. Dark wooden beams and plaster will imitate the construction of an English Tudor shop or house; a mansard roof and elaborate trim will suggest a French hotel or chateau. The result may reveal or encourage a fantasy life in which you are an English millionaire or a French aristocrat, but in most cases they only imply admiration of or familiarity with the cultures they represent. In the absence of other clues it is difficult to tell whether the owner of a miniature hacienda has spent years in Mexico, or simply wishes he had done so. Occasionally financial limitations or a less intense commitment will limit exotic architecture to outbuildings; then a small Japanese "tea pavilion" or a pool house in the form of a Greek temple may appear in the backyard of a conventional American home.

Commercial buildings often speak in what is not so much a foreign tongue as a foreign accent. Restaurants, for instance, are often designed to persuade us that the food served inside them will be authentically Japanese, Indian, Italian, or Mexican. A hotel may be decorated to look like a Venetian palace; a ski lodge may have the heavy overhanging roofs and beams of a Swiss chalet. Inside, the décor will usually keep up the act, at least in the lobby, bar, and dining room, and even the bedrooms may have gilded Baroque mirrors or Swiss cuckoo clocks.

REGIONAL AND DIALECT ARCHITECTURE

In the United States regional styles of speech have always been associated with regional styles of building: the Cape Cod cottage, the Midwestern farmhouse, and the Southern plantation mansion all have their equivalent in spoken dialect. These buildings may be old and genuine, or they may be recent reproductions, the equivalent of an assumed rather than a native accent. As James Howard Kunstler says, "half-baked versions of Scarlett O'Hara's Tara now stand replicated in countless suburban subdivisions around the United States." In some cities and towns, especially where tourism is an important part of the economy, zoning codes may make a sort of artificial authenticity compulsory. Houses in the historic district of Key West, Florida, for example, whether new or remodeled, must be built of wood in a traditional style, and there are only a few permissible colors of paint, white being preferred. From the street these houses may look like the simple cigar makers' cottages and sea captains' mansions they imitate. Inside, however, where zoning does not reach, they often contain recessed lighting and state-of-the art kitchens and bathrooms. Their back walls, which cannot be seen from the street, may be mostly glass, offering a view of barbecue equipment and swimming pools.

Local architecture always tells us a lot about local weather conditions. Most buildings in Southern California and the Southwest, for example, suggest a dry semidesert climate of hot days and cool nights. They have high ceilings that allow the circulation of air and thick walls that absorb heat during the day and release it at night. Central courtyards block desert winds and blowing dust and sand. Since there is little rain and almost no snow, the roofs of these houses are usually flat or low-pitched, and extend well beyond the walls to provide shade. There are wide porches and verandas to catch the breeze, and often a system of gutters and pipes to funnel the infrequent rainstorm water into cisterns and tanks.

In hot, damp climates, like much of the Deep South, big trees can supply shade, but air circulation is still important. Here you will see deep, high porches, wide-open hallways that run from the front to the back of the building, and floor-to-ceiling windows. Roofs are steeply pitched to allow for the rapid runoff of rainstorms, and have big gutters and downspouts. Awnings shield the windows from both sun and rain; huge ceiling fans (once moved by slaves and later by electricity) circulate the air, and netting veils the beds against a vast population of bugs.

In regions with cold damp climates, such as New England, traditional buildings tend to be compact, to reduce the exterior wall surface and limit the escape of heat. They may have small windows, heavy shutters that can be closed against storms, and big chimneys with fireplaces on each floor. Their steeply sloping roofs are designed to shed not only rain but also snow, and may have baffles to prevent the buildup of icicles.

In cold dry climates, as in much of North Dakota, Manitoba, and Saskatchewan, effort is concentrated on preserving heat and saving water. Early pioneer sod dwellings were built partly or mostly underground, and the rain barrel was an essential accessory for many farmhouses. If the air is dry, the temperature differential between the shady and sunny sides of a hill is often considerable. When possible, therefore, buildings were located on a south-facing slope. Even today this custom continues, especially among ecologically concerned architects whose roofs are designed to support solar panels.

As time passed, the installation of sewer and water systems and the invention of central heating and air-conditioning made these early solutions to climatic problems less necessary. Regional styles endured, however, partly because they were effective and partly because they had become symbolic. Today New England is full of brand-new white Colonial-style homes and shopping centers with (usually inoperable) green shutters, and steep roofs decorated with weather vanes. In the Southwest and Southern California, both houses and commercial buildings imitate traditional architecture, or what is believed to be traditional architecture. Ross Macdonald, the classic mystery writer, describes this effect in his story "Gone Girl."

> [It was a] middle-class motel room touched with the California-Spanish mania. Artificially roughened plaster painted adobe color, poinsettia-red curtains, imitation parchment lampshade on a twisted black iron stand. A Rivera reproduction of a sleeping Mexican hung on the wall over the bed.

Though this was written in 1953, such motel rooms are still visible today in the Southwest, though now they are apt to be more low-end.

We usually pay little attention to typical buildings in their native habitat. What we notice are structures that do not match their surroundings. If we see a terra-cotta pink stucco building in New England, we suspect eccentricity—or, of course, a Mexican restaurant. A Northern-style house in a hot climate is almost equally conspicuous. In South Florida, you can sometimes see a classic white New England Colonial house with a fanlight over the front door, an eagle weathervane, and an expensively watered carpet of grass instead of local plants. The effect is to suggest nostalgia for the North and possibly old-fashioned values.

Another use of antique or regional styles occurs when developers try to make identical buildings look different from one another. This trick is especially popular in large-scale housing developments, where a potential buyer can choose from a Colonial, Plantation, Texas, Southwestern, or New England model. Usually the details are superficial: the Colonial "home" has pilasters beside the front door and a shallow bay window; the Plantation has floor-to-ceiling windows on the ground floor and two-story columns that pretend to hold up its roof. Even this sort of false regionalism suggests that though we may value diversity, we tend to feel happier and safer in an environment that reminds us of places we have known and loved.

The ambiguity of many stores and hotels, on the other hand, denies regionalism. As Robert Sommer has remarked, "If one were to kidnap, blindfold, and confine people inside supermarkets in cities around the United States, it is doubtful that many could determine their location from . . . the store's interior." For some people, this repetitive anonymity may be disorienting or depressing; for others it can be comforting.

HISTORICAL ARCHITECTURE

The equivalent of archaic words and phrases often appears in architecture. From the eighteenth to the twentieth centuries, and even sometimes today, civic buildings have been deliberately designed to remind the viewer of classical Greek and Roman temples and suggest ideas of tradition, wisdom, and justice. American political conventions, both Democratic and Republican, tend to pose their candidates against a classical backdrop, making dramatic use of artificial columns or pilasters.

Architects have always been familiar with the traditional meaning of the three different classical orders—Doric, Ionic, and Corinthian—and many know of their connection to the classical gods. The simple, austerely fluted Doric column was associated with the sturdy adult male body, and with temples to Mars and Hercules. The more elegant Ionic column, with its curled top, was thought to suggest a mature female body, and to be appropriate for temples dedicated to Juno or Diana, and sometimes to Bacchus, who was noted for his curling locks. The elaborate Corinthian column, with its effects of sprouting foliage, was associated with graceful youths and girls, and assigned to Venus, Proserpine, and the Nymphs. In the nineteenth century, art museums, theatres, and opera houses preferred Corinthian columns, while banks and law courts and memorials to the honored dead tended to go for the Doric order: the Lincoln Memorial in Washington, for instance, is surrounded by thirty-six Doric columns. The United States Capitol dome, on the other hand, perhaps in a kind of unconscious attempt to neutralize the often heavy and acrimonious goings-on beneath it, features light, elegantly leafy Corinthian columns.

The dwellings of the rich in eighteenth- and early-nineteenth-century America tended to draw upon classical models, perhaps to suggest that their owners' lives embodied the classical virtues of honesty, authority, and justice. Later, in the mid-nineteenth and early twentieth centuries, multimillionaires seemed to prefer to identify with medieval dukes or Renaissance merchants and princes instead of with classical philosophers and statesmen. Their newly built mansions tended to resemble late-medieval castles or Venetian palaces rather than Greek temples.

The tastes of the post–Civil War rich in America were eclectic, and so was their greed for possession. The millionaires of the period looked to Europe and Asia not only for models, but also for actual historical buildings. If they could afford it they sometimes imported entire small Greek and Roman temples, medieval castles, French chateaux, or Oriental palaces. When complete buildings or sufficient cash were not available, they employed architects to construct new mansions in favorite historical styles, incorporating architectural elements or sometimes entire rooms that had been purchased abroad and shipped home. The Isabella Stewart Gardner Museum in Boston, which was once a grand private house, features a more or less authentic Renaissance Venetian courtyard that includes bits and pieces of genuine imported Italian architecture. Frederic Church's Olana in Greenport, New York, on the other hand, with its wonderful mishmash of Victorian, Moorish, and Persian styles, was built from scratch.

Like the use of Latin or Greek in prose, the use of historical detail in a house suggests learning and adds prestige. Even today eclectic architects may include bits and pieces of earlier buildings in their creations, so that an expensive house finished yesterday will have siding or beams from a Colonial barn, an eighteenth-century terrace with antique stone lions or nymphs, or a Victorian stained-glass window (Tiffany, if possible) in the grand entrance hall. If genuine fragments are unavailable or too pricey, reproductions may be substituted.

BEAUTIFUL AND UGLY BUILDINGS

Like language, architecture can be beautiful or ugly. There are buildings that are the equivalent of a great poem or speech: we are moved and even transported when we look at them. But just as we may like one famous writer more than another, many great buildings do not appeal to everyone. Some may admire the Parthenon or Jefferson's Monticello; others will prefer the Cathedral of St. John the Divine in New York or Gaudí's Sagrada Família in Barcelona. Most of us also have favorite historical periods. We may like to imagine ourselves as inhabitants of a French eighteenth-century villa or an English country village. There are also those who praise currently despised styles, sometimes so eloquently that others are convinced, as when John Betjeman commended the imitation-Gothic buildings of late Victorian England, or when Robert Venturi and Denise Scott Brown extolled the extravagant architecture of Las Vegas.

Our taste in private homes also varies widely. We may value Frank Lloyd Wright's Fallingwater or Le Corbusier's Villa Savoye as aesthetic objects, but not want to live in them. Instead, we apparently prefer more modest and conventional structures that seem to us the best of their kind: the perfect Victorian Italianate house, Arts & Crafts cottage, or contemporary split level. Such modest but attractive vernacular architecture may be compared to light verse or popular song, especially when the building has strong personal associations—if we have grown up or been happy there. As a result, a run-down old farmhouse may seem more beautiful to us than a great mansion.

According to Alain de Botton, we call a building beautiful if it reflects our values. "The buildings we admire are ultimately those which . . . refer, whether through their materials, shapes or colors, to such legendarily positive qualities as friendliness, kindness, subtlety, strength and intelligence." But ideas about what buildings have these qualities change over time. In Europe, from the Renaissance on, an ideal structure was often classical Greek or Roman in inspiration: usually adapted to the local landscape and climate, but featuring classical columns, pediments, arches, and statuary. In the late eighteenth century, Gothic revival architecture gradually became a fashionable alternative, and by the mid-1800s you could order up a house in many exotic international and historical styles: Swiss, Indian, Chinese, Egyptian, Jacobean, etc.

For several hundred years, elaboration, variety, and decoration in architecture were almost universally admired. Eventually, however, there was a reaction, led at first by scientists and engineers. Iron framing and poured concrete gradually revolutionized construction and design. Architects abandoned older forms in favor of newer and less complex ones that also reduced construction costs. Eventually, for committed early-twentieth-century modernists, only unadorned simplicity was beautiful; all decoration was ugly and superfluous.

One of de Botton's most interesting assertions is that people have always found buildings beautiful not so much when they embody current values, as when they embody values that society lacks. Today, in a world of material abundance and elaborate rules, we may long for a more simple, natural, and casual life. This might account for the popularity, in cities like New York and London, of apartments with minimal (but obviously expensive) furniture, and walls stripped down to raw brick or rough weathered planking.

Architecture can make us happy, but like a vulgar, dishonest speech, it can also make us miserable. Ugly, badly constructed buildings are unpleasant to live or work in, and dirt, disorder, and failures of décor can also be deeply depressing. As de Botton puts it, "What will we experience in a house with prison-like windows, stained carpet tiles and plastic curtains?" Clearly, we (or at least anyone as sensitive and perceptive as de Botton) will experience horror and dismay.

Perfection in architecture is rare; most people cannot afford to live in really beautiful buildings, and the average house usually has something wrong with it: the stairs creak, the closets are too small, the cellar is damp when it rains, and there is a crack in the bathroom ceiling. For most of us, a certain amount of self-protective blindness to our aesthetic environment is necessary, especially if we have small children or a spouse who is relatively indifferent to décor. Indeed, anyone who reads architectural magazines or the House and Garden section of a major newspaper will have seen many photos of interiors that strongly suggest their owners prefer kidskin sofas to kids.

GOOD AND EVIL ARCHITECTURE

Just as a remark, an article, or an entire book can strike us as generous and encouraging, or mean and destructive, so architecture can appear to send out positive or negative vibrations, and even to be conscious of doing so. For young children, of course, everything may seem alive—not only their own toys, but also trucks, tables, and TVs. The half-conscious belief that objects have intention and agency often persists into adulthood; even today you will often hear someone say that his new Honda is a real sweetie and never lets him down, or that her mean old computer is acting up again.

To a child, buildings may seem to have faces, with the windows as eyes and the door as a mouth, and even today a house with symmetrical windows on either side of the front door sometimes looks to me—and, I have discovered, to others—like a mask, if not a face. As kids, my friends and I also often saw buildings as friendly or unfriendly, comforting or threatening. Almost every suburban neighborhood had a "haunted house" that we dared each other to approach on Halloween. Usually it was badly maintained, set far back from the street, and surrounded by overgrown bushes; no children lived there and the curtains or blinds were often drawn.

Many different types of buildings may have the reputation of being haunted. According to Wikipedia, in the United States alone there are at least six haunted hospitals and insane asylums, and five haunted hotels, including, notoriously, the Chelsea in Manhattan, where Dylan Thomas, Eugene O'Neill, and Thomas Wolfe have been seen after their deaths. There are also ghostly theatres, cinemas, schools, colleges, and prisons. Mental hospitals are notoriously haunted by former patients and attendants; factories are haunted by the spirits of workers who died there, lighthouses by their keepers, and in Sunnyvale, California, there is a haunted Toys 'R' Us. Occasionally, rather than housing the spirits of former occupants, such structures have a malevolent (or rarely, benevolent) spirit of their own. For me and my childhood friends, it was sometimes not only the witch but also the house itself that was out to get us.

Another version of belief in the positive or negative effects of buildings is the Oriental science of architectural design, feng shui. According to some feng shui experts, a wrongly placed door or window can make you poor, miserable, or neurotic, while a well-situated mirror or screen can at least partly correct the problem. Today many people of Asian origin will not move into a house or an office until it has been inspected and rearranged by experts in this system.

ARCHITECTURE AS A MORAL FORCE

For centuries both architects and philosophers have claimed that beautiful buildings could make people virtuous as well as happy. In early Christian and Islamic theology, Alain de Botton writes, "Attractive architecture was held to be a version of goodness . . . and its ugly counterpart, a material version of evil. . . . The moral equation between beauty and goodness lent to all architecture a new seriousness and importance." Many writers have reported feeling calmed and uplifted in churches and temples, or even the remains of one, as Robert Browning was by an ancient vine-covered tower in his "Love Among the Ruins."

For early International Style architects, as Alain De Botton remarks, "a structure was correct and honest in so far as it performed its mechanical functions efficiently, and false and immoral in so far as it was burdened with non-supporting pillars, decorative statues, frescos or carvings." They wanted houses to look toward a better future and the triumph of simplicity and truth; many of them believed that they could design buildings—and sometimes whole cities—to make their inhabitants morally healthier. High-rise public housing projects would not only bring light and air into dark, crowded slum neighborhoods; they would reduce crime and promote community. This turned out not to be the case; instead, most such projects became crumbling centers of violence and fear and despair. They were often situated in undesirable areas far from shops, schools, and churches, and made no provision for neighborly contact. In many cases not only were they designed to be as cheap as possible, but political corruption made them even cheaper. Both materials and construction were third-rate, and it was not long before elevators broke down, paint peeled, and roofs and windows leaked. Their inhabitants became anxious and depressed and apt to become involved in drugs and crime. Within the next few decades many of these projects were deliberately demolished, both in America and in Europe.

GOOD AND BAD DESIGN

The architects of the early and mid-twentieth century wanted to solve social problems and change the world. Many of their successors, however, had less interest in these goals. Instead, they wanted to surprise and show off, and their employers were not local governments but the rich and their favorite institutions. As a result, Nathan Glazer claims, "Present-day modernism expresses itself in advanced and experimental architecture that has become reserved most typically for museums or cultural centers or concert halls where the architect can count on a sophisticated, elite client." Such architects "design walls that cant and lean, roofs that bubble and heave, buildings that look as if they are instantly ready to take off into space or collapse in a heap of tin. They are not models for a city, only models for what the architect hopes will be truly astonishing, something to hit a nerve of contemporary excitement that he can exploit." Glazer does not hesitate to name names, among them Frank Gehry, Daniel Libeskind, Zaha Hadid, and Peter Eisenman.

We may admire these structures as art, but it can be hard to live or work in them. The swooping free-form counters and islands and ramps once fashionable in expensive department stores were confusing and annoying to customers, who often could not find what they were looking for, and left without buying anything as soon as they located an exit. As Stewart Brand points out, triangular buildings like the East Wing of the National Gallery in Washington (by I. M. Pei) also cause problems. "Every space in the building is a pain to work with . . . the shelves in the library end in acute or obtuse angles that won't hold books."

The same thing is true of domestic architecture. The famous octagon houses of mid-nineteenth-century America, popularized by the phrenologist Orson Squire Fowler, saved on heating and looked charming from the outside, but they created problems within. Rooms were oddly shaped, and the central circular staircase of the original plan made it impossible to reach some bedrooms without going through others. Today, though a few families (often those of architects) seem to do well in oddly shaped modernist dwellings, most people do not want to live in a house in which the floors and walls slope, or the rooms are triangular, trapezoidal, or oval. The necessity of making a floor plan intelligible is generally recognized, so that within even such an extremely innovative building as Frank Gehry's Guggenheim Museum Bilbao there are level floors, vertical walls, and even some rectangular rooms.

The flip side of the good effect of good design, of course, is the pernicious effect of bad design. But though unattractive, cheap, badly designed buildings appear to have a negative effect on both mood and morals, beautiful buildings do not always make people happy or good. John Ruskin admitted that in fact few Venetians seemed morally elevated by their city, and some of the most disagreeable tyrants of all times have dwelt in handsome palaces. For the average man or woman, however, the psychological influence of architecture appears to be significant.

If we have the money and good luck to live in a beautiful build-ing, we may become happier and perhaps even nicer. But the attach-ment to our home that we then develop, like all human attachments, is threatened by change and loss. In E. M. Forster's *Howards End*, Mrs. Wilcox cares more deeply for her family house than for her family, who do not value or deserve it. On her deathbed she tries to leave Howards End to her friend Margaret; and though at first she seems to have failed, she is eventually, almost supernaturally, trium-phant. Love of a domestic dwelling can also involve constant grief at its need for upkeep and repair—a grief familiar to anyone who has returned to a beloved house after even a few months away. We may also fear to commit our affections to a beautiful church or school or office, just as we may fear to commit to a human being, knowing that buildings, like people, may be destroyed by acts of God or man, and that they eventually fall apart.

TRUTH AND FALSITY

It is possible to lie in the language of buildings, though not as easily as in speech or writing. There are many reasons for a verbal lie, including most of the seven deadly sins, as well as common unpleasant emotions like fear and embarrassment. Architectural falsity, however, usually has one of two motives: ambition or greed.

Many striving and successful people try to build large, and if time or resources are limited, indulge in the architectural equivalent of empty boasting, by, for example, affixing second-story façades to what were essentially one-room shacks in nineteenth-century American frontier towns. These flat two-dimensional constructions were a Wild West version of the so-called Potemkin villages, said to have been erected at the direction of the Russian minister Grigori Alexandrovich Potemkin to fool Catherine the Great during her visit to Crimea in 1787.

Nineteenth- and early-twentieth-century builders trying to cut corners and still make a house look impressive sometimes skimped on the basic structure, while slapping on porches and bay windows and wooden gingerbread and inaccessible nonfunctional turrets. All of these additions were cheaper, and faster to put up, than additional indoor rooms—and they did not have to be insulated or heated. Similar tricks were used in cities. An office block or apartment building that was essentially constructed of or faced with brick would often have a ground floor and possibly also the one above it clad in stone blocks. To the casual observer at street level, these structures would look like impressive granite or limestone buildings. In some cases a building would be completely faced with stone but have side and back walls of brick, clearly visible from the side or the rear.

In the suburbs today what are essentially traditional three-bedroom boxes are often glorified by a two-story entrance hall known as the "foyer," and the conversion of nearly all the downstairs space into a so-called "great room" with a "cathedral ceiling"—at a considerable saving on interior wall and floor construction. The result, depending on your taste, will be either impressive or pretentious. Because the high ceilings of the foyer and great room have preempted much of the second-floor area, these houses tend to be short on closet space and have only one decent-sized bedroom.

There is, of course, the reverse type of deceptive construction, which might be described as the architectural equivalent of false modesty in speech or writing: the house that looks small, low, and unimpressive from the front but opens out strikingly in the rear, sometimes in the form of descending levels down a hillside. The Pacific Coast Highway north of Los Angeles, for instance, is lined with such houses, which appear from the road to be inexpensive shacks. Houses like these are often favored by well-known people for whom privacy is valuable and hard to come by, and also sometimes by those whose occupations are less than respectable.

Lying in architecture may be more or less easy to detect. We can usually tell whether a Palladian villa or a Gothic cathedral is original or a modern reproduction, but repairs or additions to ordinary domestic buildings may blend in so well that only an expert can spot them. Plastic siding can imitate wood very skillfully, and vinyl can mimic marble. Furniture is even easier to fake: an expensive copy of a Chippendale chair may fool even some antique dealers. In the past (and still occasionally today) the mounted heads of antlered deer and moose, and the stuffed skins of giant fish, silently and often falsely declared that their owner was a successful big-game hunter or deep-sea fisherman. And if a homeowner or business executive wishes to deceive us as to his background, he or she may purchase genuine eighteenth- and nineteenth-century portraits and pass them off as pictures of his ancestors.

Some forms of architectural deception are so familiar by now that we hardly consider them lies. Most public buildings today are held up by steel and concrete, not by the massive columns that adorn their entrances. Houses in traditional styles are often trimmed with window shutters that are never shut (and often cannot be shut). New Tudor mansions may appear to be built as houses were in Shakespeare's time, of huge oak beams and stone fill covered with white-washed plaster, but this is usually only a skin an inch or two thick over standard frame construction. If we stop to think about it, we will realize that such effects are probably phony, but mostly we don't really care. Such buildings are the architectural equivalent of the white lie, accepted even by those who know them to be false because they are impressive, charming, or even beautiful.

Today a building of important regional or historical value may be completely gutted and filled with modern architecture. Often, only the façade of a beautiful historic house or hotel or college lecture hall will remain: inside, all is steel and glass and vinyl. The resulting structure is the material equivalent of a well-known science fiction theme: the apparently normal good guy whose brain and nervous system have been taken over by a cold, evil, avaricious alien.

Postmodern architecture, on the other hand, is neither deliberately nostalgic nor deliberately misleading. Rather, it is the three-dimensional equivalent of archaic or dialect words or phrases dropped into standard speech. It is not meant to deceive, but to amuse or impress. Architects who add a classical pediment to a seaside cottage, or a neon sign to an office block, or paste pilasters on the addition to a museum, as in the case of the Sainsbury Wing of London's National Gallery, are not trying to fool anyone. They are merely advertising their expert knowledge of traditional styles and their sophisticated, ironic sense of humor.

CHAPTER 3

Materials and Styles

Once upon a time there were three little pigs, and each of them set out to build a house. Their plans were identical except for the choice of materials, but the results were momentous. This is also sometimes true in real life. When a hurricane or flood hits, wooden structures can be reduced to piles of kindling, while brick and stone are often almost untouched. In aerial photographs of towns after a disaster, a stone or brick church or town hall often stands up among the rubble. Today it is mainly such buildings that survive from the distant past, since they were much less vulnerable to the wolves of fire, flood, wind, and war.

The stuff of which buildings are made not only affects the survival of pigs and men, but also the meanings they project, which can roughly be compared to tones of voice in speech. A statement alters its significance if it is spoken loudly or softly, sincerely or sarcastically, affectionately or harshly. In the same way, two houses of identical design will give a very different impression if one is made of smooth, polished stone and the other faced with cheap asbestos shingle. In general, the more difficult to work with and expensive a material is, the greater both its strength and its perceived status.

• • •

STONE

Stone slows construction and increases cost, but it also confers toughness and endurance and implies strength and wealth. For centuries it was the first choice for any important public building, from a pyramid to a town hall. In the Middle Ages churches and castles were built of stone. Peasants' huts, like the dwellings of the two foolish pigs, were usually made of rough wood or of wattle and daub (a lattice of sticks filled in with some combination of earth, clay, sand, dung, and straw). The houses and shops of the middle and upper classes were often of brick, or of heavy wooden frames filled with rubble and plastered over.

Among types of stone, marble has often been preferred. For centuries it was felt to be almost essential for buildings and monuments of classical design. Polished white marble is the equivalent of, and somewhat resembles, a shiny gift box; it announces to the world that what is inside is expensive and valuable. The Morgan Library & Museum in New York and the Beinecke Rare Book & Manuscript Library at Yale University are classic examples—the latter is actually known familiarly on campus as the Wedding Present. Granite is almost as impressive as marble, and limestone or even sandstone will do, though they are less durable.

Smoothly polished stone blocks closely fitted together outrank rough-cut ones held together with visible lines of masonry, and buildings made of them are also stronger. Rough-cut stone, because it is cheaper and looks less formal, has often been used for houses, country churches, libraries, and schools. Uncut lumps of stone in a thick bedding of plaster were for many years favored for the construction of rustic buildings such as boathouses, hunting lodges, and park pavilions. These buildings are the architectural equivalent of L.L.Bean hunting and fishing and camping outfits, and like them tend to suggest both virility and expensive recreation. Inside them or on their porches we are apt to find furniture shaped from branches with the bark still on, or sometimes from the horns of deer and moose. The suggestion, though seldom the truth, is that their owners have chopped down trees and shot large animals in order to create these peculiar, often rather uncomfortable chairs and spiky coatracks. When I was a small child, friends of my parents had a deer-horn chair on the porch of their rustic summer house in the Catskills. I was always afraid to sit in it, fearing that it would come to life and scratch me.

The choice of stone depends on what is locally available. In Italy for many years marble was relatively cheap, and was once common in both homes and public buildings. In early New England, where the cleared farmland was as full of rocks as a fruitcake of raisins, uncut stone was used for both walls and simple houses. Marble and granite were available under a thin layer of topsoil, and soon northern New England quarries were supplying most of the materials for New England public buildings.

The familiar "brownstone" row houses of nineteenth- and early-twentieth-century America were constructed of a variety of sandstone mixed with red iron oxide that was once abundant in the Connecticut River valley and New Jersey. A hundred years ago these houses indicated middle-class security and comfort. Blocks of classic family brownstones still survive in many cities, though now, if not subdivided into shops, restaurants, offices, and apartments, they are often the homes of prosperous institutions.

All types of stone give a building prestige as well as greater strength. Stone pillars in front of a brick church or library, a stone porch on a stucco bungalow, or pebble-dash walls for the first story of a cottage are attempts both to reinforce the structure and to make it look grander. When there are three otherwise almost identical houses for sale, one of stone, one of brick, and one of wood, the stone house will usually sell for the highest price.

BRICK

Brick is less expensive than stone, but it is essentially solid and respectable. In the coastal mid-Atlantic states and many parts of the

South the land was often swampy or sandy rather than rocky, and the cost of importing stone was high. Clay, on the other hand, was readily available. Partly as a result, mansions, statehouses, churches, libraries, and college buildings were often made of brick. While some exceptionally well-endowed universities, such as Princeton and Duke, imitated Oxford and Cambridge by building in stone, many others followed the lead of two famous Colonial colleges, William and Mary and the University of Virginia, and erected classrooms, libraries, and dormitories of red brick with elegant white wood trim.

Once steel framing was introduced, brick walls could rise beyond a second or third story, and the height of apartment or office buildings was limited only by local ordinances or by how many flights tenants could be expected to climb (more for the poor—fewer for the wealthy). Before the invention of the elevator, five or six stories were usually the limit even in tenements. But only the largest and most impressive buildings spread outward rather than upward. Today the country mansions of billionaires still tend to sprawl over the landscape, but in cities developers still build up rather than out, competing in height and tending to name the finished structure after themselves.

Brick has remained popular for private homes, and is still considered prestigious. A brick house in a town where most houses are of wood suggests strength and permanence. Even people who know nothing about architecture can usually tell the difference between a genuine solid brick building and one that was slapped up over a lumber or metal frame and faced with a thin layer of real bricks or with embossed vinyl siding.

WOOD

When North America was settled, its eastern half was largely covered with forests; wood was not only readily available and cheap, but easier to work with than brick or stone. The classic log (or rough-cut board) cabin still survives here and there, especially in southern Appalachia and the rural Midwest, where it has always been a sign of honest poverty and simple pioneer virtue. Country music stars, even if they did not grow up in such a cabin, will sometimes own an over-weight modern version of one. Relatively new log cabins are also common in mountainous resort areas, where they are popular as ho-tels and second homes. They announce to the world that the owner probably wears flannel shirts and hiking boots, carries bird-watching binoculars, and is environmentally aware—but not necessarily a lib-eral or even a Democrat. Inside the expanded log cabin there may be heads of deer, and, hanging over the fieldstone fireplace, the Ten Commandments, etched into a slab of oak.

Today, in most of the United States, wood remains the most com-mon domestic building material, so common that we almost do not notice it. The typical house has wood-frame construction and a ga-bled roof, and its exterior walls are covered with horizontal siding or shingles. Versions can be seen almost everywhere in most Eastern, Southern, and Midwestern American small towns and suburbs, from a tiny cottage to a three-story mansion. But whatever its size, the standard American wood-frame house, if it is in reasonably good shape, suggests comfort, respectability, and financial security.

A public building made of wood, however, is slightly suspect un-less it is a church. We expect government offices, libraries, schools, banks, and hospitals to be constructed of stone, brick, or concrete. The same is true of most commercial buildings. A wooden antique shop or ice-cream parlor may seem quaint and attractive—but ex-cept in a small town, a wooden insurance or doctor's office looks flimsy and temporary. In rural areas that attract tourists, well-pre-served or newly built old-fashioned country stores are often made of wood. They will be equipped with wooden porches, benches, and in an extreme case, hitching posts. Usually this is a sign that the store will sell old-fashioned candy, gingham aprons, maple syrup, and hand-made soap, often at amazingly high prices.

In cool climates wood has a special advantage over most other building material because it feels warm to the touch. As Edward Allen explains in *How Buildings Work*, things that feel warm "are low in thermal capacity and high in thermal resistance . . . [so that] the body quickly warms a thin surface layer of the material to a temperature approaching the temperature of the skin." Materials that feel cold have high thermal capacity and low thermal resistance. "When one touches a room-temperature surface of metal, stone, plaster, concrete, or brick, heat is drawn quickly from the body for an extended period of time." In hot climates, of course, this may be an advantage.

PLASTER AND CONCRETE

Wood is relatively easy to cut and shape, and once it has been painted or sealed, it does well in a cold, damp climate; in a hot, dry one it is vulnerable to termites and fires. Sand and clay and earth, on the other hand, are hard to work with when it is cold or wet, and apt to become soggy and moldy; but they stand up well in a dry environment. For centuries, in many parts of the world, people dug their building materials right out of the ground. Where the climate was both hot and dry, especially if trees and stones were scarce, buildings were constructed of mud, concrete, cement, or cinder block.

In many parts of the world these materials remain standard. At one time both public and private buildings in the Southwest were constructed of adobe, a mixture of sand, clay, and straw that has been shaped into bricks and dried in the sun on wooden frames. Because adobe stores and releases heat very slowly, it was perfect for a desert climate with its hot days and cool nights. But though it seldom rained, when thunderstorms came they could be violent, and sun-baked adobe bricks would become soggy and moldy. To prevent this they had to be frequently painted.

Concrete block, which is made of cement and aggregate (usually sand or gravel), has become the preferred material for small commercial buildings. Today in many parts of the world, offices, churches, museums, and shopping malls are made of concrete block reinforced with metal rods, smoothly finished with plaster or cement and then painted. Most private houses in a modernist style are of similar construction, on a less expansive (but sometimes equally expensive) scale. In the South and Southwest such buildings may be designed to look Spanish or Latin American, with wide porches and verandas designed to catch the breeze and shade the interior; for those who can afford them, huge fans and central air-conditioning also cool the rooms.

While wood, brick, and cut stone naturally create rectangular shapes, concrete allows for, even encourages, rounded shapes and curves. The result is a building that suggests ease and relaxation. If its walls are painted in the natural colors of sand and clay, it may seem to have grown spontaneously out of the earth. The more a house in the Southwest looks like an Indian pueblo, the more likely it is to be full of Native American rugs and pottery and belong to people who are interested in Indian art and traditions, organic gardening, and solar power.

METAL AND GLASS

The invention of steel-framed construction in the mid-nineteenth century revolutionized architecture. The Crystal Palace, the center of the Great Exhibition of 1851 in London, resembled a huge greenhouse, with a cast-iron armature supporting large glass panels. It became the inspiration for thousands of stores and office buildings all over the world. Most had very large plate-glass windows, though only a few were almost totally transparent like the Crystal Palace itself.

In the early years of the twentieth century what is now known as the International Style extended the new building methods to private homes. At first, not all twentieth-century architects took advantage of the possibilities of metal and glass and concrete, because of the costs involved, but some developed them brilliantly. The soaring fans of the Sydney Opera House and the elegant snail shape of the

Guggenheim Museum in New York both depend on the flexibility of steel and concrete.

Steel-framed construction was also relatively light. If a stone building is to have more than two stories its lower walls must be extremely thick to bear the weight of the upper ones, as in a medieval castle. With a steel-beam frame filled in with thin panels of wood or metal or plastic, and panes of glass, there was almost no limit to how high an architect could go. Today buildings largely made of metal and glass are either very high status, like steel-framed and metal and glass-clad skyscrapers, or very low status, as with the beetlelike forms of the trailer park.

Glass was once very expensive and therefore a sign of wealth. Before the nineteenth century most windows were made of many small panes of blown glass that had been cut open while hot and spun on a table so that they became flat and could be trimmed to fit into a small wooden or metal frame. Often the glass in these windows was marked by changes in color, bubbles, or central lumps. At the time, these were seen as flaws; today, authentic or imitation Colonial houses sometimes preserve the old-fashioned look on purpose.

In England between 1698 and 1851, glass windows were taxed and there was a sliding scale, depending on how many inhabitants a dwelling had. As a result, some people chose to brick or board up many of their windows, thus proclaiming themselves to the world as penurious or miserly: the resulting scars can still be seen on the façades of some old houses. The invention of cheap plate glass in the mid-nineteenth century changed all this, but glass still has some prestige value, since it remains more expensive and fragile than a sheet of wood or metal the same size. As a result, the more glass there is in an office building, an apartment house, or a private home, the more upmarket it looks.

American cities today are full of steel-frame apartment buildings with giant windows. On the ground floor these windows entice the public into shops and restaurants; farther up they provide the tenants with striking views and with extra light, an important factor in a city of deep, man-made canyons that often get sun for only an hour or two a day. Office and apartment towers with floor-to-ceiling windows appear wonderfully elegant in architectural photographs. Unfortunately, once the inhabitants have moved in the place is likely to look rather messy from the outside, especially in the case of office buildings. As Stewart Brand puts it, they often seem "to be advertising the firm's ankles and wastebaskets."

HARD AND SOFT

The sociologist Robert Sommer has distinguished between hard and soft architecture. A hard building "is designed to be strong and resistant to human imprint"; steel, concrete, and electronic equipment will dominate its construction. It will be expensive to construct or change and will emphasize separation between inside and outside: there will be few windows and doors. There will be uniformity in design and layout, and high security, with specialized staff and machines such as video monitors. Such a building, according to Sommer, causes anxiety, irritation, and the (sometimes unconscious) wish to leave. Eventually, those who cannot get out will become either restless and angry, or passive, withdrawn, and numb.

The most obvious example of this kind of building is a prison or a zoo, but similar characteristics all too often appear in public housing, and in some schools, factories, and offices. The underlying implication of this sort of design is that the inhabitants cannot be trusted. For similar reasons, factory floors and office cubicles are brightly lit and open to observation from anyone who walks by. Opponents of public housing also sometimes claim that certain buildings appear to have been designed to be hard, cold, and unpleasant, with the idea that this will encourage those who live there to move, or punish them for their lack of worldly success.

One recent and striking example of a hard building, according to Sommer, is the airport terminal. There are high ceilings, long, bleak corridors, and the waiting areas have rows of hard seats bolted together and interrupted by armrests that make it impossible to lie down, even though canceled flights may make it necessary for travelers to spend many hours and sometimes whole days and nights in the airport. A possible motive for this unpleasant design is to drive us into the nearby bars, restaurants, and shops. Another might be to persuade us to pay to join an airline club, where we can find free coffee and juice and newspapers, big, soft chairs, and even sometimes a sofa on which to nap.

COLOR

Stone buildings come in many but usually subdued colors. They are seldom painted, both because it is unnecessary for preservation and because paint does not adhere well to stone. When most buildings in a region are made of the locally available stone, they often become a recognized and beloved characteristic of the landscape. The yellow-brown sandstone country houses and cottages and churches of the British Cotswolds, the dark gray granite townscapes of northern Scotland and Canada, and the brownstone row houses of Northeastern American cities are famous, and anyone who paints them may be seen as offending local tradition.

Because brick is porous, painting it is costly, and in Europe and much of the United States it is usually left as is. In parts of the American South and the Pacific Northwest, however, where the climate is damp, bricks are apt to disintegrate gradually, and they are often painted, usually in light colors. Many brick houses and apartment buildings in Europe and the United States have instead been covered in a layer of plaster and then painted.

Most wooden buildings must be painted regularly in order to protect them from damp and rot. Early Colonial houses and farmhouses were most often white, partly because white paint is easier to match and usually cheaper. This choice also echoed the simplicity and purity of the lives these houses sheltered, the drab hues of their inhabitants' clothes, and the unadorned rhetoric of most public utterances. Barns, though occasionally white like the standard farm-house, were more often red. Originally, they were coated with white paint to which rust (ferrous oxide) had been added, in order to kill the molds and mosses that tend to grow on the damp wood often found in unheated barns. Today, a barn in good condition that is not red or white may have artistic or eccentric owners, while an unpainted barn suggests poverty.

In the mid-nineteenth century, and especially in the so-called Gilded Age after the Civil War, literary style, dress, and architecture all became more elaborate and colorful. Some houses were not only lavishly decorated with wooden cut-work "gingerbread" trim, but appeared in color combinations that recall the women's fashions of the era: pink and white, gray and burgundy, mauve and maroon, umber and dark green. Keeping up such paint jobs is expensive, and suggests not only a substantial income, but artistic tastes and occupations and/or a love of tradition.

In theory buildings may be painted in a wide range of hues, allowing their owners to make the same sort of statement that we make when choosing what color shirt or sweater to wear, though one with a far more lasting message. Public buildings today are almost always neutral in color, like business clothes: gray and tan are dominant. White is another conventional choice, perhaps because of the unconscious influence of architectural education: I have never yet seen an architect's model that was not white or light gray. But in real life other colors are often used, especially in dry climates. Tones that match that landscape—beige, tan, light brown, sand, and dark green—are popular in some parts of the country. Orange, bright green, sky blue, or lavender, however, suggest an inexpensive restaurant or gift shop.

Where choices are not limited by zoning restrictions or local tradition, color in architecture can suggest personality traits: the unobtrusive gray of a modest and retiring homeowner, the sunny yellow of a fun-loving extrovert, the brown of a solid, conservative citizen, or the barn red of a devoted gardener or horse lover. Just as a scarlet outfit calls attention to itself and a gray one tends to fade into the background, color can make a building stand out or almost disappear. A structure of dark or unpainted lumber, closely surrounded by foliage or covered with vines, on a heavily wooded lot, may look as if it had been deliberately camouflaged so as to blend into the landscape. Its owners may hope to discourage visitors, or want to announce that they are deeply in sync with nature. The hand-built log cabins and cottages of former or current countercultural types are often most admired when they are painted or stained in mushroom colors and appear to have grown out of the ground like mushrooms.

In conventional settings there seems to be a preference for conventional colors in domestic architecture. A crimson or Kelly green or royal blue or purple house, especially if it is made of painted plaster, seems either down-market or freaky, suggesting a household of lowbrows or eccentrics. Even when unusual colors are more subdued, they are generally rejected. In an informal survey, twenty-six students and faculty members at Cornell University were shown photographs of a suburban reproduction-Colonial house painted different colors by a computer program. Analysis revealed a preference for white, yellow, and tan and a dislike, rising sometimes to disgust, for pink, lavender, and turquoise.

Of course, a survey undertaken in another part of the country might produce different results, since color in architecture can be considered as the equivalent of a regional dialect. The popular hues for buildings everywhere are often those of the local landscape— and, like regional speech, they may suggest long-term residence or a loyal identification with the area, or both. Beach communities, including seaside resorts and motels, favor sandy building colors. They also go for what might be called sherbet hues—lemon, orange, peach, strawberry, pistachio, and occasionally the aquamarine of a swimming pool on a fine day. Mountainous, thickly wooded resort areas in relatively warm climates favor warm browns and grays and the medium greens of deciduous trees.

In the desert landscapes of the far West and Southwest, tan, umber, dusty gold, and terra-cotta are popular; in northern New

England there is a preference for the whites and grays of a snowy or rainy day, and the dark greens of pine and fir and hemlock. Along the seacoast everywhere, unpainted buildings are often allowed to weather in the salty air (which preserves raw wood) to the silver grays of fog and mist; they may also recall the colors of the nearby ocean with white, sea-blue, or sea-green shutters and trim. In contrast to the New England monochrome is the French Canadian love of brightly hued houses. When you drive across the border between Vermont and Quebec, the difference is immediately apparent.

In big cities many buildings are off-white or light gray, and project a low-key, neutral image, just as the conversation of many businesspeople and government officials does, or at least attempts to do. But just as some city dwellers choose to speak loudly, or use more colorful language, in order to attract attention and gain dominance in a noisy, busy environment, so very bright colors may appear in urban buildings, usually in connection with commerce and the arts. Theatres everywhere have often featured flashing rows of lightbulbs and brightly painted signs, later supplemented by neon and electronic displays. For well over a century such signs have glared from the sides and tops of buildings on Broadway—see *Times Square* by Darcy Tell, for many examples and a fascinating history of the genre. Shop fronts all over America may be painted a glaring red or orange in order to attract attention, though the larger or more upmarket the business is, the more likely it is to choose near-neutrality. Most big-box stores and malls and supermarkets are usually off-white, tan, or a very subdued yellow or peach or pink—comfy baby-blanket colors, as one friend of mine put it.

PRESTIGE AND PRESERVATION

For many years, the most important structures in American and European towns and cities, those that were meant to last, were built of stone, and slightly less important ones of brick, and everything else of wood. Today the results of this rule can still be seen: stone government buildings and churches and libraries, brick town halls and offices and expensive houses. Modern concrete and metal construction, however, appears at all levels of cost and status, from the billion-dollar arts complex to the one-room shed. Often it is impossible to estimate how long these structures will endure.

Of course, over time, all languages change, and many deteriorate, falling into sloppy grammar and pronunciation and word use. In extreme cases speakers and writers may become almost inarticulate, unable to finish a sentence or blurring their communications with phrases such as "it's uh, like, you know."

Buildings, too, are subject to the vagaries of time. The overall impression we get from any structure depends not only on the materials from which it is made, but also on how well it is maintained. Rain, snow, wind, and air pollution will eventually damage even the strongest stone or brick wall, and wood and plaster are even more vulnerable. Wood rots, mortar crumbles, paint peels, plaster cracks. At one time the air-conditioning unit in the window of a building was a sign of modernity and prosperity; today, when many houses and offices and stores enjoy central heating and cooling, a rusted, dripping, humming metal box protruding from a window is a low-status indicator.

Certain building materials, even when well maintained, have little prestige. Obviously fake wood or brick siding and plastic shingles are at the top of the list. Concrete has low status unless it is covered with stucco or paint, when it can in fact be chic or trendy. Uncovered concrete, however, will usually be seen as bringing down the tone of the neighborhood almost anywhere. An unpainted, unplastered cinder-block wall looks rough and drab even when it is only a few feet high and covered with vines and flowers. Glazed concrete block, which is water-repellent, is also seen as aesthetically repellent, except when associated with car washes, pools, locker rooms, and school cafeterias—and sometimes even then.

Metal is also subject to corrosion: one of the saddest architectural sights today is a once-beautiful twentieth-century modern house whose white concrete walls and metal window-frames are streaked with damp and rust.

Something near to contempt is a common reaction to materials that imitate other materials, like obviously fake wood or brick siding and plastic shingles. A down-market trailer is described by Allan D. Wallis as composed of "siding with a wood grain pattern printed on it, interior paneling laminated with the photographic image of decorative wood, ceilings made of a material that looks like stucco but is actually foam padding, [and] hardware finished as if it were antique brass." Yet for many people a well-kept and well-organized mobile home is more pleasant to visit or live in than a dirty, run-down mini-mansion. In the end, except in the case of an historic stone castle, good maintenance probably pleases us more than expensive construction.

Many and perhaps most public buildings in America are well designed and fairly well maintained, but today, according to the architectural critic James Howard Kunstler, financial greed causes others to be "constructed with the fully conscious certainty that they will disintegrate in a few decades." Usually there is no ornamentation on these buildings "except for the sort of cartoon decoration that serves to advertise whatever product is sold on the premises." Private housing today, according to Kunstler, is also in a bad way. Some tract homes, for instance, are designed as inexpensively as possible. "The result is a house that is built like a television set. Only the front matters, and it only matters insofar as it can broadcast some cartoonish image of what we want others to think about it. . . . Often the sides are clad in a cheaper material than the front, and completely incompatible with it. . . . You get harlequin bricks on the front and yellow vinyl 'clapboards' on the side. . . . The rear is a mess of ventilation ducts and weirdly shaped windows."

When we see such homes we tend to distrust their inhabitants, especially if they live in an expensive neighborhood. Possibly they are the kind of people who at first glance seem impressive and likable, but will turn out to be pretentious and dishonest. Alternatively, they may be poor dupes, easily confused by first impressions and conned into purchasing an inferior product. An attractive and well-kept-up housing development, on the other hand, may cast a rosy glow over all its residents—unless, of course, we are repelled by any sort of standardization.

CHAPTER 4

Outside the House

Public buildings, in general, speak to us; our homes, on the other hand, speak for us. But unless we are professional architects or unusually well-to-do, they seldom say exactly what we would like them to say, since their appearance is usually a compromise between necessity and choice. Though we know this, it is difficult in most cases not to assume that people will match their dwellings, as in the old nursery rhyme:

> There was a crooked man, who walked a crooked mile.
> He found a crooked sixpence beside a crooked stile.
> He bought a crooked cat, who caught a crooked mouse,
> And they all lived together in a little crooked house.

BIG HOUSES FOR BIG PEOPLE

The physical appearance of our home is partly the result of deliberate choice. Some people may decide to put a disproportionate share of their resources into a large house; they may even prefer a big, rather ugly dwelling to a small attractive one. If they are short of funds, their home may have an impressive façade and dwindle into insignificance behind it. The standard McMansion, with its two-story columns and bulging windows and towers, often looks like nothing much from the rear. Sometimes, especially if this house is part of a development, it will have been sited with no concern for geography or the local landscape: its porches and decks may face north, so that they never get any sun, and the view from its living room window may be of someone else's garage.

The desire for a large, impressive house, which has caused so much financial havoc over the years and led to so many bankrupt-cies and foreclosures, appears to be widespread even among those who cannot really afford one. In "The Mansion: A Subprime Para-ble," the journalist Michael Lewis tells how he and his wife rented a house in New Orleans with two dining rooms, ten bathrooms, seven bedrooms, and sixteen TV sets. At first it was the source of great pleasure and excitement, but soon it began to destroy their peace of mind and bank account. They began to feel that the house did not like them because they were not rich enough, and then that it was actively hostile: "The mansion was not satisfied with making us un-easy. It wanted us out. It preferred us to leave quietly, without a fuss. But if we didn't, it was prepared to get violent."

The elevator broke down between floors with small children in it; the heating system failed, making some rooms icy cold and others intolerably hot, and when Lewis tried to fix it a shrieking alarm went off. Soon "two squad cars with lights flashing sped into our drive-way. Four police officers leapt out and banged on the front door. The mansion had phoned the cops." His conclusion was that "we are quite obviously, a nation of financial impostors, poised to seize the first opportunity to live in houses we cannot afford."

Not everyone, of course, is subject to these desires. Well-to-do people who prefer to spend on travel, education, and entertainment may deliberately rent, buy, or build small. Or they may, out of modesty or fear of crime, try to conceal their prosperity, like those New En-gland aristocrats whose old-fashioned Colonial or Cape Cod houses look unpretentious from the street but extend a long way back, per-haps throwing out wings that are concealed behind walls and hedges.

It has been suggested that there are connections between the recent increase of obesity in the United States and the increase in the size of our houses. The average new home size in the United States was 2,673 square feet in 2013, up from 1,400 square feet in 1970 and a mere 983 square feet in 1950. Meanwhile, though the average size of the American family has been shrinking, the size of individuals has increased. According to a Gallup poll, in 2012 74 percent of adults were overweight or obese, more than twice the proportion thirty years earlier. Perhaps the ballooning of the American home is not only the result of a wish for self-aggrandizement, but also related to the recent ballooning of the American physique. The larger you are, the more space you may feel you need.

It has also been proposed that modern architectural design has contributed to obesity. In the past, people burned calories by climbing stairs and keeping temperatures below 70 degrees. Even after elevators had been invented, most two- and three-story buildings did not have them. Today elevators and escalators are everywhere, and it is common for thermostats to be set at 72–75 degrees. Visitors from Europe, where people are still less likely to be fat and out of breath, and stay comfortable in winter by wearing warm undergarments and dressing in layers of wool and thermal fabric, are often dismayed by the high temperatures at which Americans keep their homes and businesses.

The trend toward larger and larger homes is not universal, however. In some places, rising house prices have led to what is now called cocooning, in which people who are determined to live in the center of expensive cities huddle in tiny, claustrophobic apartments, sometimes with only a single room.

OPEN HOUSES AND SHUT HOUSES

Every house dramatically regulates contact between its inhabitants and outsiders. One will be separated from the street only by low bushes or flower beds; its door may be part glass, and it will be possible to get a fairly good look into the front rooms through large windows. Its less welcoming neighbor will have a high wall around the whole property, and possibly a locked gate. There will be a heavy, solid door, and the windows will be blocked by blinds or dense bushes.

The more usable entrances a house has, the more permeable it is to the world around it. Open doors and windows encourage us to pass freely back and forth from the natural to the human environment; doors that are always shut and locked, and heavily curtained windows, may function like the exterior defenses of a castle, to slow down or repel invaders. A screened or glassed-in front porch is also off-putting, particularly if it is surrounded by thorny, threatening shrubs. Sometimes, in high-crime environments, there is a justified fear of strangers; in other cases the motive is a psychological dislike and distrust of most other people. But in either case, though the message is silent, it gets across.

The porches, terraces, decks, and patios around a house are what sociologists call "liminal spaces." In these transitional areas, open-ended experiences tend to take place: a negotiation with someone who wants you to sign a petition or buy cookies, a conversation with a neighbor about a noisy dog. Open porches and patios, especially when equipped with casual, comfortable-looking furniture and plants, provide an easy and reassuring transition from outside to inside. A house that has no porch, deck, or patio seems to shut itself and its occupants off from the world. In what used to be known as a trailer park and is now more often called a recreational vehicle court, some people will try to cancel this effect by installing an awning in front of the trailer and setting a couple of plastic or metal chairs, a barbecue grill, and some potted plants under it; others will be as tightly shut up in their trailer as if it were a tin can.

Trees make a home look more attractive, but only up to a point. realtors have said that on a half-acre plot up to twenty trees add value, while thirty or more reduce it—they darken the property and crowd possible inhabitants. Interviewers report that deciduous trees that shed their leaves are usually seen as friendly, especially if they have flowers in the spring or turn beautiful colors in the fall; while tall, dense evergreens such as pines and hemlocks arouse dim feelings of anxiety in anyone who has not grown up surrounded by them.

Plants and flowers around a house are almost always seen as a positive sign, and the more there are, and the more informal their arrangement, the more friendly people judge the inhabitants to be. Some people to whom I and my students spoke saw window boxes full of flowers as especially welcoming. A vegetable garden was also encouraging, and apt to suggest economy and a concern for the environment. In a poor neighborhood, even artificial flowers were seen as more welcoming than none at all.

There are, however, some plants—especially certain prickly varieties of cactus and bromeliads—that seem to wish to repel or injure us. They are the material equivalent of hostile, angry statements, and suggest that if we enter the house to which they belong we will regret it. In a very dry climate, of course, it may be hard to grow anything but cacti: a friendly householder there, however, will tend to plant succulent varieties that have few spikes and many flowers. The general effect is rather like that of a pleasant speech delivered in a harsh voice by someone with a bad cold; we are uneasy until we realize that their intention is friendly.

People who live in large apartment buildings usually have little influence on the way the place looks from outside, though the presence or absence of plants may have affected their decision to rent or buy. Sidewalk trees and flowers may make a strong statement: heavy stone tubs planted with ivy suggest formality; displays of tulips, roses, chrysanthemums, or holly according to the season are cheerful and reassuring. Of course, all these messages, like those of any verbal or written statement, may occasionally be ambiguous. The house with the high walls and locked gate may contain pleasant people who are afraid of intruders, possibly because they possess an inconvenient quantity of wealth or fame. The pretty country cottage surrounded by flowers, like the witch's house in "Hansel and Gretel," on the other hand, may have been chosen to attract potential victims.

LOOKING OUT AND LOOKING IN

In the past, when glass was expensive, even the grandest houses had relatively small, many-paned windows. But by the early twentieth century prices had declined greatly, and quite modest new homes might display what real estate agents describe as a "picture window"—a big flat sheet of glass that fills much of one exterior wall. The problem for the tenants is what sort of picture appears in the window. Views of gardens, woods, fields, and hills are often left almost or wholly uncurtained, while a picture of ugly buildings or a busy city street tends to be covered with semitransparent curtains or blinds, suggesting that the owners do not want to look at their surroundings or perhaps are ashamed of them.

If the view is attractive but public, as often happens in the suburbs or a small town, the curtains may be pulled back so that the interior of the house is partly visible, suggesting that the inhabitants have nothing to hide and are, on the contrary, proud of their domestic interior and of the street they live on. In other cases there may be a compromise: the picture window is mostly blocked by curtains or a large plant, but enough space is left so that it is possible to see neighbors or potential visitors without usually being seen oneself.

Traditionally, a haunted house is dark and surrounded by large, ominously dark trees, suggesting that the rooms inside will be gloomy, and so will the inhabitants. We expect heavy old furniture, shadowy echoing corridors, and creaking stairs. In Jane Austen's *Northanger Abbey* the heroine, who has read far too many Gothic thrillers (the early-nineteenth-century equivalent of today's vampire sagas), is convinced by the name of her suitor's home and by its historic origins that violent deeds must have taken place there. She is wrong, as it turns out, but most of us are susceptible to this sort of mistake. A house may also be a physical manifestation of its tenant. In another nineteenth-century classic, Charlotte Brontë's *Jane Eyre*, the ominous appearance of Thornfield, with its gray stone walls and picturesque battlements, surrounded by "mighty old thorn trees, strong, knotty, and broad as oaks," is the architectural equivalent of Mr. Rochester.

In many American small towns and suburbs, the lawns of adjoining houses traditionally run into each other, or are separated only by low hedges. This not only indicates neighborliness, but also creates it, since you are far more likely to exchange news or ask for the loan of a ladder or a cup of sugar if you can easily see and reach the house next door. On a street in which all the other lawns are contiguous, a house surrounded by tall hedges—or, even worse, a high brick or stone wall—suggests that its inhabitants are secretive and unfriendly. A high fence that one can see through, on the other hand, is more likely to indicate the presence of young children or dogs. Neighborliness, of course, varies from one place to another. In general, the smaller the town, the more likely people are to know their closest neighbors, no matter how far apart the houses are.

ORDER AND DISORDER

The condition and surroundings of our homes speak loudly to everyone. A shabby, worn-looking house will suggest poverty or neglect. This is even more true of apartments: we are apt to be more repelled by a multi-occupancy slum building than by the most run-down farmhouse. Tom Wolfe's description of the former is classic in its expression of revulsion and even fear:

> The hallway is painted with a paint that looks exactly like the color, thickness and lumpiness of real mud. . . . and there are three big cans of garbage by the stairway. . . . At some point they painted the mud color over everything, even over the doorbell-buzzer box. They didn't bother to pull the wiring out. They just cut the wires and painted over the stubs. And there they have it, the color called Landlord's Brown. . . .

Our impression of a private home depends on many clues. When paint is worn and peeling, but the grass is cut and the shrubbery and flower beds cared for, we assume that the people who live there are hard up, but doing the best they can. A house in good repair but surrounded by dead and dying vegetation, and a dried-out lawn, on the other hand, suggests that something has recently gone seriously wrong inside. We suspect marital separation, mental illness, financial scandal, disaster, or death.

Broken windows, sagging shutters, and a lawn that has become choked with weeds imply that a house is deserted, or that its inhabitants may be dangerous or depressed. The presence of abandoned automobiles, lawn mowers, rusted and broken swing sets, or smashed plastic toys suggests additional financial, psychological, and/or moral damage. At the other extreme, a lawn that is scalped into a buzz cut and close-clipped rectangular hedges suggest severity and even rigidity of outlook on the part of the owners, especially if the yard is more or less bare of flowers.

There is, interviews reveal, a golden mean between excess care and serious neglect. The longer the grass is allowed to grow between regular mowings, and the more free-form the shrubbery and flower beds, the more informal and friendly the inhabitants of a house are judged to be.

HOME, BEAUTIFUL HOME

Just as speech or writing may be poetic, moving, and beautiful, so can domestic architecture. We may not agree on what this loveliness looks like, but the concept is widely accepted—there is now in the United States a magazine, a TV show, and a website called Beautiful Homes. According to these authorities, the beautiful home is usually large, relatively expensive, and landscaped to within an inch of its life. It is also in perfect condition and very clean. In real life, however, we may find our own home or someone else's attractive even if it is small and slightly shabby, with untrimmed hedges and untidy flower beds.

There are, at any time and place, certain houses that many people find beautiful. Some of them have been officially designated and promoted as tourist sites, examples of what an ideal home should be. Usually these places are well designed, very large, and at least a hundred years old, and they have been restored to a state of perfection that might surprise the original owners. They also represent a wide variety of styles, not all of which will appeal to everyone, just as not all great poems are admired by every reader. One tourist may prefer (and perhaps imagine him or herself living happily in) Jefferson's Monticello; another may dream of William Morris's Red House or Frank Lloyd Wright's Fallingwater.

About ugliness there is greater consensus. Dirt and dilapidation, like vulgar, clumsy speech, are almost universally rejected. Obvious pretension, on the other hand, like consciously flowery rhetoric, may please some and repel others. The brand-new development houses that have recently sprung up in the suburbs of so many American cities, with their nearly identical big garages and gables and bay windows, may depress some observers; others may dream of owning one.

The reproduction of past architectural styles, of course, is always selective. Nostalgia in the arts (and perhaps also in manners and opinions) is usually for something felt to be lacking in the present. Someone who believes contemporary life to be cold and isolated may be drawn to an old-fashioned house with a big front porch and nearby neighbors; someone who thinks of the world as chaotic and corrupt may prefer a well-fenced neoclassical design that suggests dignity, distance, and restraint.

James Laver once proposed that over time fashions in clothes go through a cycle of shock, acceptance, rejection, and rediscovery. According to him, the same costume will be

Hideous   10 years after its time
Ridiculous 20 years after its time
Amusing   30 years after its time

Quaint   50 years after its time
Charming   70 years after its time
Romantic   100 years after its time
Beautiful   150 years after its time

Styles of architecture also go in and out of fashion, though the process seems to be slower. Today we appreciate the Victorian Gothic houses and railways stations that were considered hopelessly ugly once. The Craftsman-style bungalows and Queen Anne or Dutch Colonial houses of the early twentieth century were thought banal and unattractive in the modernist 1950s and 1960s; today they are admired so much that they are featured in real estate advertisements. The stripped-down ranch houses of the 1950s and 1960s, once so popular that nine out of ten new homes were built in this style, are now thought of as dreary and dated. Though it seems unlikely today, in another few decades a new generation may find them charming.

Postmodernist architecture, which draws on the past in what can be seen either as an admiring or an ironic spirit, can make outmoded styles seem beautiful. It is all a matter of time, and perhaps also of level of sophistication. Many people today find early-twentieth-century advertisements quaintly attractive, but consider contemporary ones vulgar and ugly. Perhaps in another fifty years today's ads will seem delightfully old-fashioned, and so will the split-level tract homes that we now look down on. Even the soup cans and Brillo boxes and cartoon advertisements promoted as cutting-edge, super-modern Pop Art of the 1960s are now, inevitably, beginning to look old-fashioned and even cute. The same thing is happening to the glass-block walls and neon lighting of some 1930s modern homes.

PUBLIC AND PRIVATE

Longtime inhabitants of a city know what almost any street address means in economic terms, and also often in social ones. But even if we have never been there before we can recognize districts that are popular with artists and writers by the prevalence of bookshops, art supply shops, and vegetarian restaurants. A predominance of sports bars, gyms, and steak houses indicates another kind of culture, while expensive hairdressers, day spas, designer dress shops, and French bistros suggest that those who live nearby are interested in being seen as fashionable, sophisticated, and, if possible, financially successful.

In many large cities members of different racial or ethnic groups tend to live in separate areas, identifiable to visitors by stores and restaurants with signs in Chinese, Japanese, Spanish, Russian, or other foreign languages. The presence of several Catholic or Greek Orthodox churches, Muslim mosques, or Jewish temples and synagogues, of course, suggests that many of their congregants dwell nearby. If we live in an apartment building, co-op, or condo, all that anyone can usually deduce from an exterior view is a rough estimate of our income, based on the location of the building and how well it is kept up. Awnings, doormen, and expensive plantings suggest wealth; broken or barred windows and peeling paint indicate poverty.

THE SECOND HOME

Most people have only a single dwelling; others, even if they are not rich, own two or even three homes. Sometimes the style and décor of these different houses will be very similar, but often there are significant differences between, for instance, a formal city apartment and a casual, laid-back country place—or a conventional, tidy suburban tract house and an eccentric, messy city pied-à-terre. When they visit these diverse dwellings, guests may be silently informed of things about their friends' or relatives' lives and character that they did not suspect before. I once knew a couple who in their elegant town house were always elegantly and completely dressed. In their messy seaside cottage they went about half naked and let dirty dishes pile up in the sink. My suspicion, which turned out to be correct, was that messy or even illegal behavior was apt to occur over the weekend, and that I might be invited or even expected to join in.

According to Winifred Gallagher, the choice of location for a vacation home, even a temporary or rented one, often fills a lack in everyday life. People who go to the mountains, she suggests, are looking for a challenge, an elevation of mood and an increase in energy and activity; those who choose an oceanside or lake house probably want to relax and slow down. Houseguests are well advised to keep this in mind. Sunbathing on a beach, with an occasional dip in the water, legitimizes doing nothing for several hours, whereas anyone who lies in a hammock on the porch of a mountain cabin for a similar length of time will probably be asked if they want to go for a hike or if they feel ill.

STYLES

Any American town or suburb, whether low-rent or expensive, is apt to contain groups of houses that are more or less similar in size, price, floor plan, and appearance. Sometimes these houses are a hundred years old or more, but often they are later imitations of earlier styles: Colonial, Cape Cod, Queen Anne, Victorian, bungalow, ranch, and so on. But as any successful real estate agent knows, and studies have proved, these diverse styles tend to attract different sorts of buyers and give off subtly different messages,

The cut-rate use of foreign or geographical indicators occurs when builders want to make standard-issue houses look less alike. This sort of thing is especially common in large-scale developments, where potential buyers can express their individuality, such as it is, by choosing from among several different version of a standard model home. Usually the variations are superficial: the New England Colonial model has a fanlight over the front door and (often nonfunctional) shutters; the Southern Plantation house has two-story columns that pretend to hold up its roof, etc. The motive behind these decorative touches is wholly commercial, but it plays into the sentimental fantasies of the buyer. Over time, certain styles have become associated with certain occupations or mind-sets: writers speak of "Stockbrokers' Tudor" or "Victorian camp."

In 1989 the environmental psychologist Jack Nasar showed people from different regions and socioeconomic groups a series of drawings of six common types of houses—Mediterranean, Colonial, Tudor, Cape Cod, contemporary, and farmhouse. He asked his subjects which house they would go to if they were away from home and had to ask for help. The farmhouse, with its steeply peaked roof, big porch, central front door, and symmetrical rows of windows, was chosen by a large percentage of viewers. It was seen as friendly and unpretentious, apt to contain people who would be ready and willing to lend a hand in an emergency.

These feelings, apparently, are persistent. Nearly twenty years later my student assistant at Cornell, Hannah Steinberg, showed other students line drawings of seven standard types of houses from Virginia and Lee McAlester's *A Field Guide to American Houses* (traditional Colonial, reproduction Colonial, Victorian, farmhouse, split-level, ranch, and modern contemporary) and asked which one they would most like to live in. Half the students preferred the Midwestern farmhouse with its wraparound porch, and none chose the ranch or split-level style.

Hannah also asked her subjects what sort of people would be likely to live in each type of house. Here, too, they had definite opinions. Their favorite, the farmhouse, was said to belong to a nice, friendly family with many children. The traditional Colonial either housed rich, conservative business or professional people or was a bed-and-breakfast. The modern Colonial revival was the home of ordinary middle-class or upper-middle-class "regular people." The Victorian house belonged to a well-to-do older couple, or possibly a widow or widower, with refined tastes ("boring old people with old money," according to one young expert), or to "elderly artsy types."

The split-level house was the home of a lower-middle-class or work-ing-class family who were possibly in debt—though it might also be the first house of an upwardly mobile young couple. The ranch house belonged to actual ranchers, to poor people, or to low-in-come retirees. The contemporary modern house was the home of a "trendy" couple with no children, or of "high-end singles," who were either described as "cool" or as "pretentious."

According to experts, many buyers want a house that reminds them of their childhood home, or of houses in the town they grew up in, though they may be willing to settle for a convincing repro-duction. More modern structures do not arouse the same affection, and may even be viewed as hostile. The hero of Richard Ford's story "The Shore" owns the kind of contemporary modern house (built in the late 1970s) that the Cornell students disliked. Though it is on the ocean and has many other desirable features, he is trying hard to get rid of it:

> A mostly vertical, isosceles-angled, multi-windowed, skylighted, slant-roofed, copper-guttered, graying redwood board-and-batten with older, stained solar panels which has within it not two, not three, but five or six levels, consistent with the builder's concern for "interior diversity" and cheap spatial mystery.
>
> How the house "presents," and what the prospective buyer sees, is . . . typical of the period—two mute, retractable, segmented brown garage doors opening pretty much onto the road, two skimpy windows, and an unlocatable front door, beyond which you go "right up" to a "great" room where the good life purportedly commences. The house actually broadcasts a bland, styleless domiciliary arrogance, which says that this building has no front either be-cause no one's welcome or else because everything faces the sea, *that's* the front, and since it's not your house why're you interested anyway? Get over it.

What Richard Ford's hero dreams of himself is a kind of Happy Home: "a white farmhouse and willows and a pond that the sky traf-fics over, and where the sun is in its soft morning quadrant and there is peace upon the land."

THE NEIGHBORHOOD

We interpret the words we hear in terms of their context. A lie is more apt to convince us when it is surrounded by obviously true statements, while a truth that appears among what we know to be lies is seldom believed. In the same way, the impression we get of any building depends in part on its surroundings. As Karl Marx put it more than a hundred and fifty years ago, "a house may be large or small; as long as the neighboring houses are likewise small, it satisfies all social requirements for a residence. But let there arise next to the little house a palace, and the little house shrinks to a hut."

The relative size of a building and its lot always convey information. In the small towns of the past, when land was cheap, a modest house might be built on a two-acre plot, allowing for a big lawn, vegetable and flower gardens, and a barn for a horse and buggy, and possibly chickens and a cow. Even today, in the depths of the country—especially where the land is poor and farming and grazing are unprofitable—you may see cottages or mobile homes on lots of an acre or more. In cities, on the other hand, an old house on a double lot is often a sign that the owner is, or once was, better off than the neighbors. The relative size of the house is not always significant: if unusually big it may have been built many years ago when labor was cheaper and families were larger. If it is unusually small its owners may have wanted extra space for a garden or pets.

One clue to the age of a house is its location on the lot. In eighteenth- and nineteenth-century America, when population was low and traffic was minimal, homes were often built near the road for convenience, especially in parts of the country with significant snowfall. As time passed and traffic increased, they were located farther back. In most small towns and suburbs, eighteenth- and nineteenth-century houses will be close to the road. Twentieth-century houses are usually set in the middle of their lots or, if the road is busy, they may be huddled toward the rear, with trees and bushes and perhaps even a wall to shield them from noise and fumes.

Many city and suburban and small town blocks are internally consistent: though the houses may be superficially different in style, they are usually similar in size and condition. When they are not, we may feel the same kind of discomfort we might get from reading a romantic poem interrupted by vulgar jokes in a different type font— or a book of vulgar jokes interrupted by a romantic poem. A standard two-story, three-bedroom suburban ranch house that would pass unnoticed on a street of similar houses will seem almost a mansion among decaying shacks on the wrong side of town, and neighbors who cannot afford such a house may envy or deeply resent it. (An extensive, expensive remodeling job by longtime owners who have suddenly become more prosperous can have the same effect, only more so.) Move the same ranch house to a street of $3 million homes and it will look small, cheap, and pathetic; its owners may be accused of "bringing down the neighborhood."

In many cases, the more your house resembles those nearby, the more friendly the neighbors will be. Realtors know this, and if well disposed will tell you never to buy the biggest and most expensive house on the block. If ill disposed, they will swear that the area is coming up. But no matter how attractive a place is, the presence of smaller and less impressive properties nearby will lower its value. The neighbors may be unfriendly, and think of you as self-important and boastful. It can also be risky to buy the smallest and cheapest house on the block, causing neighbors to look down on you; but in this case you have at least gained a "good address," and there is always the possibility of doing an upgrade, or selling out at a profit to some richer person looking for a teardown.

The mantra of real estate agents, "location, location, location," affects our impressions of any house we see. When showing property, they will go to great lengths to approach it from a favorable direction, avoiding adjoining run-down areas. In Lee Smith's story "Dear Phil Donahue," the narrator lives in a big, fancy house on Country Club Circle. But, as she discovers, this circle is surrounded by lowlife. By houses that change hands, . . . houses with flamingos and hubcaps in the front yards, houses where men sit outside on the steps bare-chested in summer drinking beer and in the windows behind them you can see women through the slats of venetian blinds, ironing in their slips, . . . with cigarettes hanging out of their mouths.

We judge people not only by their homes, but also by their neighborhoods, and if there is an incongruity between the two we assume that something is wrong. At times it is: the run-down old house on a well-kept block suggests eccentricity or recent disaster; a high-walled mansion on a street of ordinary unfenced small houses makes some people suspect drug dealers or an expensive bordello.

When houses are in a planned or gated community a managing board will probably have dictated what they look like from outside. In some developments, for instance, only certain colors of exterior paint are approved. Vegetable gardens or tool sheds or swing sets may be banned, as well as certain types of lawn furniture. It is clear to any observer that those who live there either approve of such restrictions or at least accept them, though possibly with some reluctance.

CHAPTER 5

Inside the House

Something about the inhabitants can be deduced from the exterior view of a house or an apartment, but there is usually far more information indoors. There, choices of furniture and decoration are a complex language that most of us can read, though perhaps unconsciously or incompletely.

Any home, especially one that has been lived in for quite a while, is a three-dimensional text. Sometimes what it has to tell us is not intentional, but in other cases things have been deliberately arranged to inform us about the inhabitants' tastes, interests, history, and political and religious opinions and beliefs. If they have children, the kids' artworks and craft projects may be abundantly displayed, often in the kitchen. Souvenirs and trophies will call our attention to trips or residencies abroad, regional origin or allegiance, or to the countries ancestors came from.

For many people, the home is a kind of sacred site, one that is chosen carefully and honored in memory; sometimes it may be revisited long after they have moved away. When all is well, ritual occasions such as births and marriages and deaths will be celebrated there. In many cases the home will contain one or more altars upon which family photographs are displayed, with prominence given to the most prominent members of the family, and to important events like graduations and weddings. There may also be framed diplomas and awards, and photos of ancestors, sports teams, and professional gatherings. Family members may appear with friends and school-mates or in the company of local or national celebrities. In almost all the photos everyone will be smiling, suggesting that they are happy and successful and enjoy their lives.

Over the years, the altar will undergo gradual changes as family members are born, grow up, marry, give birth, age, and die. Visitors may be encouraged to observe and admire new pictures and ask questions about them. As time passes, more and more photographs will be added. A divorce or serious family scandal, however, may result in the temporary diminution or destruction of the display; later it may be reestablished in a new form in which some gods have been dethroned, and others elevated.

A tendency to personify the home also appears in the custom of giving it a name: from dignified ones for a large, solid structure, to cute nicknames for vacation cottages. The more identification and personification there is, the more likely it is that any harm to the structure will be felt as a personal injury. Storm damage is like a wound to one's own body, and the emotional effects of burglary resemble those of a rape. When a beloved house is totally destroyed by fire, flood, or tornado, its inhabitants may feel as if a close friend or relative—or in extreme cases, they themselves—has died.

ROOM INSIDE

One of the first things a visitor to any dwelling notices is size: the loud, penetrating voices of expensive people, which have often been commented on, have their parallel in the huge public rooms of some expensive homes. With their enormous carpets, mirrors, pictures, and multiple sofas, these rooms tend to awe, embarrass, or enrage strangers, and silently inform them that they are small and unimportant. A medium-sized room may make a similar point with a massive designer sofa or elaborate restaurant-type kitchen equipment.

In both apartments and private homes, large, high-ceilinged rooms and expansive halls and staircases are impressive partly because they suggest that the inhabitants can afford to waste space and heat huge blocks of empty air. They are a good example of what Thorstein Veblen called conspicuous consumption: the display of excess purchasing power. The existence of rooms that are seldom used, or used only for a couple of hours a day, or a few days a year, is another form of conspicuous consumption. A classic example is the nineteenth- and early twentieth-century parlor, with its piano or organ and its central lace-covered table on which the family Bible reposed, a room often opened only for important guests, or for weddings and funerals. Today some American houses still contain dining rooms that are inhabited for only one hour a day—or sometimes only once a week, for Sunday lunch or dinner.

Small rooms may be perceived as friendly and cozy, or as cramped and oppressive; depending on the ambiance, they may be compared either to wombs or to jail cells. A lot depends on the furniture: thick rugs, soft sofas and chairs, heaps of cushions, and bright but not glaring colors make us feel comfortable. Hard surfaces and dark hues are unsettling, especially when the walls are bare of curtains or pictures. There is also the possibility of a small, cozy space within a larger room; in the late nineteenth and early twentieth centuries many sitting rooms featured an "Oriental corner" or alcove where a soft "divan" was hung with shawls and piled with embroidered and tasseled cushions.

OPEN AND SHUT HOUSES

Temple Grandin, the animal behavior expert, has written extensively on the differences between the living choices of predators and prey. As she puts it, "small prey animals are happiest in small dark places where larger predators can't get to them," while "big prey animals like cows and horses, on the other hand, are fine with wide-open spaces." Medium-sized predator animals like wolves "seem to be perfectly happy out in the open, but even they like to nap and sleep together inside a small den." The same thing appears to be true of most members of the current dominant predator species, man, though possibly those of us who identify with rabbits, those who love horses, and those who run with the wolves will choose very different sorts of dwellings.

LOOKING OUT AND LOOKING IN

No matter how many rooms a house or apartment contains, important meanings are conveyed by its windows and doors. When you enter any room you will note immediately, though perhaps unconsciously, what you can see through its windows. Large windows that frame an agreeable view tend to put visitors at ease, and a glimpse of a garden is encouraging, even when it is partly blocked by curtains or blinds. But if, having entered a room for the first time, you cannot see out at all, you are apt to feel uneasy; you may have a sense of enclosure, perhaps even of imprisonment. Unless the potential view is truly ugly—a power station, a strip mall, or a rubbish dump, for instance—you may also suspect that the inhabitants either want to shut out the world or are afraid that someone out there will see in. Or possibly both.

There are also houses in which the windows are blocked in such a way that it is easy to peer out, but impossible to look in. A tiny slice of the outdoors may be visible between heavy drapes, or a thin curtain may make it possible to glimpse passersby without being seen. The inhabitants of these rooms, we may assume, are curious about the world but also perhaps somewhat frightened by it, or very jealous of their privacy.

Often some windows in a house are blocked or partly blocked part of the time. You can usually see out of a kitchen, but seldom out of a bathroom, since most people don't want to be observed when naked or using the toilet. People who leave their bedroom or bathroom windows open when undressing, however, may be unconsciously hoping for spectators.

In cities, many people who live in tall buildings seem to believe that they are invisible from outside, especially when their home is above the second floor. Their blinds are seldom drawn, and in some of the rooms may not even exist. At the same time, many of these apartments seem to have a pair of high-powered field glasses on a window ledge, which their owners use to spy on neighbors in an almost ornithological manner. (If their sitting room overlooks a park, of course, some of these people may be genuine bird-watchers.)

COMING AND GOING

The interior of any house or apartment regulates contact between both family members and outsiders. Doors that are left open invite us in; when they are shut, they tell us to stay out. The reasons for this are various: the room may be messy, or something may be going on inside that we prefer others not to see. A half-open door is ambiguous, both inviting us to enter and warning us away, with subtle meanings sometimes conveyed by the angle of the opening. People who shut themselves in a communal bathroom for too long may be asked if they are all right or what the hell they are doing in there. Young children may refuse to go to sleep if their bedroom door is shut, or begin to wail and sob if they wake at night and cannot get into their parents' room. Later, these same parents may demand that when teenagers have visitors the door must be left open.

In all these cases the conflict is between communication and privacy. The size of the space does not always matter; in fact, relative privacy is sometimes easier to achieve in a very large room. In a ballroom or large drawing room there will usually be small groupings of furniture, sometimes sheltered by screens or plants, for those who want a private conversation. People who live in so-called "space-saving" houses or apartments, on the other hand, where anything you say is audible almost everywhere, may have to retreat to the bathroom or go outdoors when they want to be alone or speak confidentially. In a studio apartment the problem is magnified.

LIGHT AND DARK

A room that has many large windows can admit more light, and unless these windows are blocked by curtains and blinds we are apt to see the inhabitants as open-minded and cheerful. The effect is increased when the interior walls and furnishings are pale-hued. As evening falls, such rooms will seem to hold light for a long time, and it may be well after sunset before someone gets up to turn on a lamp.

When a room has few or small windows, on the other hand, and the walls and furnishings are dark, we may feel depressed or imprisoned without knowing why. Gloomy, shadowy interiors are traditionally disturbing, and suggest that their inhabitants are sad, guilty, and/or troubled—or perhaps only hoping to cause these emotions in others. This latter attitude is exemplified in the classic lightbulb joke:

"How does a Jewish mother change a light bulb?"

"No thanks, I'll just sit here in the dark."

Any interior, of course, looks quite different at night, after the lights are turned on, but the effect of dark walls and furniture is hard to reverse totally. Ghosts and the grieving traditionally prefer almost totally dark rooms, while a single shaded lamp or a glowing fire on the hearth in a room with a strategically placed sofa or bed is the traditional setting for romance and seduction. In everyday life a few well-placed lamps with warm-toned bulbs can raise the emotional temperature of an oak-paneled parlor or library by several degrees, but the effect is usually one of coziness and affection rather than passion.

Low, shaded table lamps cast a flattering light, and make rooms and occasions seem informal and friendly. Ceiling fixtures, especially fluorescent ones, tend to make any space appear public and formal, like an office or a store. Hanging lamps occupy a middle ground. A modest-sized one over a family dining table can turn dinner into a family ceremony; a big, sparkling chandelier can brighten the darkest ballroom, but there will still be shadowy corners where dancers and spectators can gossip and flirt, and a sense of possible secrets and surprises. During the planning of any high school prom there are apt to be conflicts between the student decorators and the administrators on the issue of lighting, with the students trying to produce a more shadowy and mysterious transformation of the school gymnasium.

Whether it is achieved through painting the walls white or putting high-watt bulbs in the electrical fixtures, the room that is full of light after the sun goes down, or on a cloudy day, encourages a positive attitude. It also makes reading and writing easier, and allows us to see and interpret the expressions and gestures of others. An ill-lit room has the opposite effect. Unless the people there are well known to each other, and naturally friendly, it can produce suspicion, uncertainty, and feelings of being alone in a crowd.

Extremes of light and dark can have drastic and usually unpleasant effects. A room full of brilliant, glaring lights suggests a medical or police investigation, and makes most people uneasy. A very dark room, lit perhaps only by one 40-watt bulb, makes visitors wonder what is lurking in the shadows, and whether something unpleasant is hidden from them. Total darkness is even more disturbing, and most of us will avoid it—unless, of course, we are about to go to sleep.

ORDER AND DISORDER

Extremes of order and disorder make most people uncomfortable. An immaculately clean and orderly house, for instance, can make visitors feel unwelcome. If they lack self-confidence, they may be afraid to walk on the soft pale rugs or sit on the ballooning sofa cushions. Excessively formal furniture arrangements can have a similar effect, transforming the family living room into a kind of luxurious reception area. The implication, even for family members, is that only restrained, conventional intercourse can and should take place here.

We are also made uneasy, though in a different way, by confusion and chaos: stained furniture and crumpled rugs, jumbled clothes and toys, sinks piled with dirty dishes. Such extreme disorder suggests to most of us a temporarily or permanently disordered mind. Allowances are usually made, however, for rooms belonging to high school or college students, where a certain amount of chaos is often to be expected.

EMPTY AND FULL

Rooms that are almost empty of objects and furniture make us uncomfortable. Unless we know that their owners are devotees of simple living or followers of a creed like Zen Buddhism, we may hesitate to commit ourselves to a friendship or romantic relationship. We may even suspect that though someone claims to live in these rooms, he or she may not actually do so, or may suddenly move out, leaving no forwarding address. This is especially true, of course, when the place resembles or actually turns out to be a hotel room.

We are also made uneasy by homes that are overcrowded with furniture and objects, suggesting that there is no room for us in their owners' lives. Collections of things, however—stamps, books, animal figurines, quilts, old toys, beer mugs, and so on—are interesting and give the collector prestige until they take up so much space that they make daily living difficult; then we suspect greed or obsession. We may also wonder if all these objects are a compensation for someone's lack of friends and family or their sense of internal emptiness.

BEAUTY AND UGLINESS

Commercial photographs of and advertisements for beautiful houses and apartments are everywhere. We may not find these interiors as attractive as we are supposed to, but we recognize that a lot of care—and probably a lot of money—has gone into making them look as they do. Most of us are also well aware that magazine articles that claim to be telling us how to redecorate and save are really telling us to spend. Sometimes these articles will show Before and After photos; Before tends to be smaller and is often printed in black-and-white—or rather in shades of gray—while After is larger and glows with color. The implication is that our current interior is ugly, and we need to go out immediately and buy paint, furniture, and drapery materials, or perhaps employ a decorator.

We may also come across pictures or descriptions of what is presented as an ugly house or room. The loft apartment described in Tom Wolfe's *The Kandy-Kolored Tangerine-Flake Streamline Baby* (1965), for instance, is a conservative's nightmare vision of what, to its inhabitants, might have seemed a normal and even appealing hippie pad of the time:

> We walk into a sort of kitchen. There is a stove with all four gas burners turned up, apparently for heat. The apartment is all one room, of the sort that might be termed extremely crummy. The walls actually have big slags of plaster missing and the lathing showing, . . . the floor is impacted with dirt and looks as it if has been chewed up by something.

Tastes differ, and a room that looks ugly to you may seem beautiful to me. As a result, I may seek to know the owners better, sensing that their tastes coincide with mine, while you decide to avoid them. A home that visitors find ugly may also suggest to them that something is wrong with the inhabitants. As Elsie de Wolfe, the famous interior decorator of the early twentieth century, warned her clients, "We attribute vulgar qualities to those who are content to live in ugly surroundings. We endow with refinement and charm the person who welcomes us in a delightful room, where the colors blend and the proportions are as perfect as in a picture." The implication, of course, was that you could hire Mrs. de Wolfe to do your drawing room up in such a way that visitors would (perhaps mistakenly) think well of you.

YOUTH AND AGE

Like any spoken or written language, the language of interior decoration includes variations that are felt to be appropriate at different ages and for different sexes. The room of a very young child is often a three-dimensional equivalent of baby talk: it will be painted and furnished in light, bright colors, and there may be wallpaper and curtains printed with pictures of happy animals or cartoon characters. Patterns will usually be simple, repetitive, and cheerful, suggesting and sometimes illustrating nursery rhymes and songs.

As babies become toddlers and then children, custom (and of course advertising) demands that their surroundings change, just as their speech does. Often gender will now have a dramatic effect on the appearance of the child's bedroom or playroom. The little girl's room will be pink and fluffy, with delicate, usually white furniture, and shelves for the display of dolls and toys. If the budget is large enough there will be a ruffled dressing table and a miniature canopied four-poster "princess" bed.

The little boy's room, at least as it appears in homemaking magazines and advertisements, tends to have a miniature macho theme: cowboys, space exploration, and sports are common. The furniture is sturdy and unadorned; patriotic red, white, and blue are the dominant colors, plus brown for the miniature cowboy and black and silver for the future space pilot. The bedding and curtains and sometimes even the wallpaper will feature related designs.

Merchandisers have done all they can to promote this sort of differentiation. In almost any large store that sells home furnishings there will be separate aisles for the latest fashions in girls' and boys' bedding and furniture. But children do not always develop or maintain the personalities that match the décor their parents have chosen for them. Once they learn to speak, and to whine, they may demand a pony-centered décor instead of a Mother Goose one. Even when their wishes are met, they may continue to change rapidly. The little girl who loved fashion dolls and wanted to be a fairy princess last Halloween may turn into a soccer player and a tomboy almost overnight; the little boy who loved *Sesame Street* action figures may become a skateboarder who likes punk rock and would not be seen dead with a Cookie Monster towel.

Teenagers often do their best to redecorate their rooms in ways that horrify their mothers and fathers, and their deliberately shocking décor may continue for several years, silently proclaiming that the messages broadcast by the other parts of the house are stupid or hateful, and do not define them. Yet, strangely enough, at some time in their twenties these same people often begin to revert to the styles of their parents, though in an up-to-date modified version, just as they abandon the foul-mouthed, semi-articulate language of their early adolescence. By the time they hit thirty, both their spoken vocabulary and the way their apartment or house looks will be recognizably adult, and there may even be a considerable migration of actual furniture from their parents' homes to their own—along, of course, with treasured objects from their own childhoods.

Typically, we begin life in a very small space: the rooms of babies are relatively tiny. As we grow up we occupy more and more square feet. Young working adults have their own apartments; the middle-aged often inhabit large, many-roomed houses. Then, gradually, our living space shrinks; we move from the family home into an apartment or condo, and finally, if we are unlucky, into a room in a retirement facility. Great economic success or failure, of course, may skew this progression, but even the well-to-do tend to begin and end their lives in a single room. The moves we make along the way are also eloquent: if a husband or wife rents a separate apartment in the same town (saying that he or she needs it to work in) we suspect an impending separation; when a young couple buys a four-bedroom house, we expect that they will soon produce or adopt a child.

In any couple, there is usually one whose taste will dominate, possibly throughout the house, possibly only in the principal sitting room or kitchen. Traditional ideas about masculinity and femininity may also operate, so that a house will have a rugged, outdoor look everywhere else—exposed beams, a stone fireplace, thick, wooly rugs, leather couches and chairs, for instance—while the bedroom is a dream of chintz and lace and delicate floral arrangements. Or possibly—though less likely—vice versa.

REGIONAL DIALECTS

Just as we can hear a Southern or New England or Texas accent, so most Americans will recognize regional styles in decoration. Sometimes, of course, the effect is the result of local availability: a native resident of Cape Cod who goes to buy furniture will find stores full of the kind of tables and chairs and lamps and pictures of sailing ships and ducks in flight that he or she grew up with, and may purchase them almost without thinking. All that can be understood from the result is that their owners of these houses are happy with the local style, or at least content. When these people move to another part of the country they may still display the same furniture and objects, which they have made considerable effort to transport across state lines. Now the cobbler's bench and the Winslow Homer print tell us that though they may be far from northern New England, they are still an important part of the owners' history and personality. Occasionally, of course, only a few objects will make it to the new home, especially if it is in a distant state or another country. Here an antique quilt and some Paul Revere candlesticks may have an almost spiritual meaning, and be cherished and cared for as ancestral totems.

Whether or not outside and inside match, we may often see in a house what might be called dialect objects, some of them authentically handmade, others manufactured recently in an Asian sweatshop. Such things may indicate regional origin or genuine love of a certain part of the country, especially when the objects themselves are not obviously attractive. This is the case, for example, with the heavy L.L.Bean blankets and maple sugar candy that suggest a northern New England past, or the fussy ruffled kitchen curtains and boxes of grits that are the equivalent of a Southern drawl.

FOREIGN ACCENTS

Not everyone, of course, can choose the style of their own homes, and it is quite possible that someone who lives in an adobe-style condo or an imitation Italian villa has never been to Taos or Rome and also has no wish to go there. Internal decoration, usually, is more informative. A house almost entirely furnished with objects of foreign origin or appearance, on the other hand, is a rare but striking phenomenon. It may be the equivalent of a foreign accent, a sign that the owner was born and brought up abroad, and regards these things as the natural and suitable contents of any home. This is especially true when a house contains foreign objects that have a practical use but are largely lacking in aesthetic appeal or social prestige: the giant jar of Vegemite on the counter of an Australian immigrant or the tawa pan and stainless-steel tea mugs of a family from India.

In general, the more items of furniture and decoration from any single location that are on display, the longer their owners have spent (or hope to spend) there, and the more important this culture is to them. In other cases, foreign objects do not function as trophies of travel, but rather declare that their owners' ancestors, or they themselves, come from another country or culture. These rugs and sculptures and vases may have been directly inherited, or may simply have been purchased to serve as symbols of origin. Many well-to-do African-American families, for instance, now prominently display genuine African wall hangings and sculptures.

Collections of foreign objects may also declare emotional loyalty to another country—possibly that of your ancestors, possibly one you have fallen in love with on your travels. If a visitor admires a set of French porcelain or a Greek bedspread that was acquired on site, its owners will be almost certain to explain where and when they found it, sometimes often at length. If they were not the original purchasers, they may tell us who gave it to them—often relatives or close friends.

Individual objects of varied foreign origin are much more common, and have functioned for many years as a three-dimensional proof of successful travel. This is true in literature as well as life. The home of Mr. and Mrs. Meagles, the confirmed tourists of Charles Dickens's *Little Dorrit*, for instance, bulges with real and imitation souvenirs:

There were antiquities from Central Italy, made by the best modern houses in that department of industry; bits of mummy from Egypt (and perhaps Birmingham); model gondolas from Venice; model villages from Switzerland; morsels of tesselated pavement from Herculaneum and Pompeii, like petrified minced veal; ashes out of tombs, and lava out of Vesuvius; Spanish fans, Spezzian straw hats, Moorish slippers, Tuscan hairpins, Carrara sculpture. . . .

The presence in a home of artifacts from many different nations announces that the people who live there—or their relatives—are experienced, acquisitive, and very likely indefatigable travelers. In Alan Bennett's *Untold Stories*, Bennett relates that his Aunty Myra, whose husband was regularly posted to the RAF, proudly displayed "an inlaid chest from Bombay, a nest of tables from Madras, bowls from Malta, linen from Singapore and a painted scroll from, Hong Kong." Today a visitor's attention may be called to the English Wedgwood vase on the chimneypiece, the possibly genuine African mask, or the Indian shawl draped over the end of the sofa.

HISTORICAL DÉCOR

Just as words and phrases from the past survive in contemporary speech and writing, so historical objects are often visible in contemporary homes. Semiotically speaking, actual or imitation antiques are the equivalent of out-of-date slang, or a slightly old-fashioned manner of speech. Like phrases such as "Jiminy Crickets," or "raining cats and dogs," they suggest a love of and nostalgia for the past. If the objects are actual heirlooms, they may also be a silent assertion that the owners of the home are from an old and well-established family that not only came to America a long time ago, but prospered here.

There are also people who deliberately and happily maintain what others would consider an outmoded style. David Sedaris has described an almost classic instance of decorative survival in a Southern boardinghouse in Chapel Hill, North Carolina:

The front door opened onto a living room, or, as Rosemary called it, the "parlor." The word was old-fashioned but fitting. Velvet curtains framed the windows. The walls were papered in a faint, floral pattern, and doilies were everywhere, laid flat on tabletops and sagging like cobwebs from the backs of overstuffed chairs. . . . Every available surface was crowded with objects: green glass candy dishes, framed photographs of movie stars, cigarette boxes with monogrammed lids.

Occasionally a particular historical or foreign style becomes fashionable among people who have little or no connection with its country of origin. In the late nineteenth and early twentieth centuries, the houses of the American rich were furnished with actual or imitation eighteenth- and early-nineteenth-century French antiques. Gold-framed mirrors and crystal chandeliers were everywhere; chests and tables developed curly, gilt legs; beds had silk brocade spreads; and wallpaper and curtains flourished fleur-de-lis and Napoleonic eagles. (For many years this remained the preferred style in expensive hotels.) According to some commentators, one purpose of all this elaborate elegance was not only to awe observers, but to confuse and disorient people who were not used to so many glittering lights and reflections and tromp l'oeil decorations.

In the mid and late twentieth century, Scandinavian modern furniture had a similar vogue; houses and apartments began to fill up with Swedish tables and bookcases, Dansk tableware, and hand-woven Finnish placemats. David Sedaris describes the effect of this style on him as a child: "Scandinavian, we learned, was the name of a region—a cold and forsaken place where people stayed indoors and plotted the death of knobs." In his family dining room the dinnerware was "charcoal-textured" and the walls were covered with cork: "It wasn't the kind you use on bulletin boards but something coarse and dark, the color of damp pine mulch."

Different historical or national styles often coexist, sometimes taking on opposed political and cultural meanings. At one time you could almost count on French interior décor as expressing conservative values, and Danish modern as a declaration of liberal or even socialist views. Today, they are more apt to be an indicator of generation. If expensive locations in the films you saw as a teenager featured curvy, gilded French furniture, you may even now long for a silk-canopied bed and dressing table in that style. But most people who are still in the market for household goods were born after 1940, and as a result every Target or Kmart is full of inexpensive semi-Scandinavian desks and chairs and dishes.

It is also possible to see a taste for the foreign and exotic in interior decoration as expressing a longing for what is lacking in our own lives. The confinement of Victorian women, who (except for the well-to-do) seldom left their native shores, may have led to the popularity of parlors full of Near Eastern draperies and ottomans, or Japanese screens and china brassware. Today, when what surrounds us is so often smooth, artificial, and plastic, we may compensate by filling our houses with rough hand-hewn salad bowls and scratchy hand-hooked rugs.

TRUTH AND FALSITY

Of course, just as it is possible to lie with words, it is possible (though usually much more expensive and complicated) to lie silently in the language of houses. The Picasso print or Tibetan prayer rug on the wall may be a fake, the Chippendale chest may be a cheap modern reproduction, and the gold-framed portrait of the Colonial ancestor may have been bought at an auction. On a larger scale, the luxurious seaside condo may be under foreclosure proceedings, or borrowed for a weekend from a friend for the purpose of financial or sexual seduction.

Inside buildings in a recognizable style we may find furnishings and decorative objects that do not match the exterior. A striking difference between styles may suggest that the owners of the house, too, are not what they seem from outside; in other cases it may only tell us that a householder with individual or unconventional tastes has been made to conform to local building ordinances. In a city apartment, discrepancies between exterior and interior are seldom very meaningful, though a pretentious lobby full of glittery chandeliers, marble statuary, and gilded urns of artificial exotic flowers may suggest a similar pretentiousness and artificiality and love of display in those who have chosen to live there but cannot yet afford to upgrade their own apartment.

Over time, certain styles of furniture have not only suggested reverence for the past, but also taken on social, political, and even moral meanings. In the mid-nineteenth century, American domestic décor might be evaluated in terms of its ethical influence. According to Deborah Cohen's *Household Gods*, "Urged on by clergymen who preached that beauty was holy, Victorians evaluated the merits of sideboards and chintzes according to a new standard of godliness. A correct purchase could elevate a household's moral tone; the wrong choice could exert a malevolent influence." Ethically elevating furniture often had ecclesiastical associations—hence the popularity of elaborate corner cupboards that looked like baptismal fonts, sideboards that resembled altars, pointed Gothic windows and chair backs, stained-glass panels, and religious statues and mottoes. Phony luxury was especially dangerous: false marble mantelpieces and imitation mahogany sideboards were pernicious because they were attempts to deceive. If you spent your life among such objects, you were in danger of being infected by their example: it was as "morally injurious to keep company with bad things, as it is to associate with bad people." Today such attitudes persist, though in different forms. Many people feel a deep suspicion and dislike of plastic flooring and furniture that imitates wood, or printed materials that pretend to be handwoven—and by extension of their owners. Some of us might even say, or at least think, that to be brought up among imitation marble counters and Oriental rugs made of vinyl could warp a child's moral sense.

STYLES AND SHAPES

Over the years, the shape of the female (and to some extent, the male) body, as disguised and altered by clothes, has tended to match fashionable interior décor. In mid-eighteenth-century Europe, the ideal woman was short, plump, and well upholstered, with delicate hands and feet, like the well-padded but thin-legged chairs and sofas of the time. In the early nineteenth century, a slimmer and paler type was admired, suitable to the elegant, slender Regency furniture of the time. Curves in both furniture and fashion came in with the Victorian era, and at one point were exaggerated in both cases. The voluptuous white-shouldered beauty of the time, sometimes described as "a fine woman," with her puffy sleeves and billowing skirts, matched the puffy, bouffant chairs and sofas, whose arms soon shrank back or became vestigial to accommodate hoop skirts. The boyish flat-chested flappers of the 1920s, with their short-cropped hair, by contrast, looked at home in elongated, attenuated Art Deco rooms.

Today well-to-do people, both women and men, tend to be taller and thinner than in the past, and their appearance is reflected in the high ceilings and rectangular, stripped-down furniture they prefer: the leather and metal sofas and chairs that suggest gym equipment, the spotlights and very visible electronic equipment. At the same time, the gain in weight at many levels of society, but particularly among those who cannot afford expensive low-calorie food and personal trainers, often causes a preference for, indeed a physical need for, thick carpets and huge, soft chairs and couches—the recliner, the elephantine sectional sofa, the king-sized bed piled with huge soft pillows. Furniture designers and interior decorators, who tend to be slim and fit themselves, do not care much for this kind of thing, but from a financial point of view they would do well to take note of it, at least until the current epidemic of obesity begins to diminish.

REFLECTIONS AND REACTIONS

One interesting piece of furniture that may dominate a home or be almost absent from it is the mirror. A mirror is always an ambiguous object, with many possible meanings. A bathroom lined with mirrors usually belongs to someone who does not mind or even enjoys seeing herself or himself naked; a bedroom with many looking glasses, some perhaps angled to give multiple views, suggests an unusually strong concern with personal appearance; while a mirror on the ceiling has strong erotic overtones. Large mirrors in a sitting room, dining room, or hall, however, do not necessarily belong to self-conscious narcissists. They may merely be there to brighten a dark room or increase its apparent size.

No matter what a house or apartment looks like, it will have a different effect on different people. If you feel you would be happy to live there yourself, it is a sign that you could probably have a real friendship, or perhaps something even closer, with at least one of the inhabitants. If you are seriously uncomfortable, you should probably meet these people elsewhere, in neutral territory. It is quite possible to maintain a good relationship with someone whose home does not appeal to you. But when you find the place very ugly or psychologically disturbing there may be trouble ahead and you should probably avoid entering into any kind of partnership with the principal inhabitant, especially one that involves sharing living or working space.

CHAPTER 6

Inside the Room

Within any contemporary dwelling there are three kinds of space. There is public space, which belongs to everyone who lives in the house; there is semi-private space, which belongs to subgroups of the family—a bedroom for the parents, and a play-room for the children, for instance; and there is private space, which belongs to a single person. These distinctions are not always obvious at first, but as time passes they will become clear, or be made clear, to any visitor.

SIZE AND CONTENT

As soon as we see the interior of any house, we immediately take in information about the people who live there. Some homes contain large, expensively furnished public rooms suitable for lavish enter-taining, and their inhabitants often have an elaborate public life—they may be, for instance, politicians or performers. In any case, they apparently want or need to impress others. There are also homes where the public rooms are small and uninteresting and the bed-rooms large and lavish; those who live there may have a rich, full private life into which very few outsiders are invited.

A big kitchen that contains a lot of cooking equipment, pots of herbs, and baskets of fruit or vegetables tells us that at least some of the those who live here care about preparing and eating meals; if the room also contains a table and chairs we know that they enjoy socializing informally. A very small, minimally equipped kitchen, on the other hand, is a sign of people who either eat out a lot or are not very interested in food.

In some houses there is little sign of anyone's presence in the sitting room, dining room, or kitchen: no toys, no open books or magazines, no discarded sweaters or half-finished cups of coffee or glasses of lemonade. What this house contains, we are silently informed, is not so much a family as a collection of semi-isolated individuals who live mostly in their own rooms. Recent studies have shown that the average American home now has at least three TV sets, and in some cases it may be possible for everyone in the house to spend much of their free time shut up in a room with their favorite programs. Or, perhaps even more likely, with their own computer, cell phone, iPod, and whatever other gadget is currently popular. People may come home from school or work and immediately establish electronic communication with invisible entities who live next door or thousands of miles away. In a fully wired household, physical, face-to-face contact is sometimes cut to a minimum, and close relatives may be more distant than office workers in adjoining cubicles.

In other houses, personal belongings and toys are everywhere, and it is clear that this is a closely integrated family in which the children have the run of the place, at least in the daytime. In the evenings or on weekends, everyone may gather in the sitting room or family room to talk or read, or to watch and comment on TV shows and films and sports events, with frequent trips to the kitchen for snacks. It is also possible, of course, that there may be little or no physical evidence in these comfortably cluttered main rooms of one or more people who actually live in this house. These individuals, who are usually but not always teenagers, do not leave anything around because they spend most of their time shut in their own rooms.

SIMPLE AND COMPLEX INTERIOR SPACES

Today, when you buy or rent a dwelling within any price range, you will often have a choice between a simple use of interior space or a complex one—that is, between many rooms and fewer but often relatively larger ones. In the Middle Ages, the poor often dwelt in one-room cottages, and the houses of the better off mainly consisted of a large multi-purpose area known as the great hall, where both owners and servants lived, worked, ate, and slept. In well-to-do homes there might be a separate bedchamber for the lord and lady, and perhaps for privileged relatives.

As time passed there was more and more differentiation. By the late eighteenth century even moderately sized homes often had many separate rooms, each with its special function. These rooms both divided their users from each other and made the division seem natural: masters and servants were together less often; parents and children met more seldom. Lives were physically and socially compartmentalized, and this was felt to be proper. Children might spend most of the day in a nursery or playroom, and enter the parlor or dining room only when invited to do so.

In the nineteenth and early twentieth centuries an upper-middle-class house could contain separate rooms for sewing, playing music, storing glass and china, reading, or paying bills and managing accounts. Among the well-to-do there were often different rooms for different meals: a breakfast room, a drawing room or parlor for tea, and possibly two dining rooms, one for the family and one for dinner parties. The children might occupy a whole floor or wing with its own bedrooms, playroom, and servants' rooms. For the rich, a billiard room, a ballroom, a conservatory, and a picture gallery were further possibilities.

The décor of each of these separate rooms often suggested or demanded the assumption of a different manner of speech and behavior. Both men and women sat up straighter in the parlor than they did in the kitchen, and children were not supposed to run or shout there. Sometimes different clothes were worn in different rooms: the mistress of the house would put on a more formal gown to greet guests in the drawing room, and her husband would wear a smoking jacket and slippers when he retreated to the study; the children might be "dressed up" before they were allowed to join their parents or shown off to visitors. In certain parts of society some of these customs are still in force.

Before World War II most middle-class families had at least one live-in servant with her own bedroom and bath. The servants' bedrooms and bath were located in the attic or near the kitchen, and tended to be very small, visibly indicating their occupant's inferior status. Sometimes there was also a set of back stairs so that visitors would not see the help as they moved about. During World War II, however, servants gradually disappeared from middle-class homes, and the presence of a maid's room or a flight of back stairs in a fairly modest house today just means that it was built many years ago.

Once the wife or other members of the family did most of the cooking, doors between the kitchen and the dining room began to be propped open, then removed; eventually whole walls might be torn down so that whoever was preparing the meal was not isolated from family life. The final result can be seen in many contemporary homes, where the sitting room, dining room, and kitchen have been collapsed into a multifunctional area that estate agents like to call a "family room." We may work in an office that is also our bedroom or spend most of our time in a space that combines sitting room and children's playroom.

In extremely modern houses, random sections of flooring between the first and second story may also disappear, so that it becomes possible, for instance, to stand in an upstairs hall and look down and see what is cooking in the kitchen. Developers favor this sort of open plan because it saves on construction costs by eliminating walls and doors; they usually promote it, however, as fostering communication and "togetherness." For some family members, especially the younger ones, it may produce the queasy feeling that Big Mommy or Big Daddy is constantly watching.

All this doubling up saves money for the developers, who do not have to build so many interior walls; it also allows every square foot of a house or apartment to be used for more hours a day. The fact that we have accepted or even welcomed these changes in interior planning has a lot to do with how we want to live now—or perhaps are forced to live now. In large cities, though, where space is very expensive, middle-income people are increasingly encouraged to take up less and less room, just as they are on airplanes.

In some cases the inhabitants of family rooms eventually began to complain that there was too much togetherness: the noise of video games and CD players and televisions, for instance, made conversation impossible and distracted the chef. One solution to this problem was the addition of what has come to be called the media room. This new space might simply contain basic equipment for watching television, playing video games, or listening to music; in really upmarket houses and apartments, it might take the form of a small movie theatre.

COME IN AND KEEP OUT

An important aspect of every entrance to a house is who uses it, why, when, and how. In some houses the family customarily enters and leaves through the kitchen or a side door. Close relatives and friends, especially children, may do the same thing. Strangers and acquaintances will come to the front door, which may be kept closed and locked even when other entrances stand open. Deliverymen and repairmen who appear there may be told to go around to the back door. People with petitions or religious pamphlets are also greeted or turned away at the front door. When those whom the inhabitants do not wish to get to know better appear at the kitchen or side entrance they are often met with only partly disguised coolness and asked to please ring the front doorbell next time.

Once you are inside a home you will be directed to one room or another. Someone calling on business may never get any farther than the front hall, or perhaps an office or study. Visiting children may be told to go up to their friend's bedrooms; or the child they have come to see may be called downstairs, when they may both be sent outside to play or given a snack in the kitchen. An acquaintance may be shown into a formal sitting room or study, a close friend or relative into the family room. When you are asked to come into the kitchen for the first time, it is a sign of increased intimacy. If you follow your host or hostess there without being invited, they may more or less politely suggest that you return to the sitting room, where you will be "more comfortable."

As a child, a teenager, and even a college student, you will usually be familiar with your friends' rooms and often spend time there. People who become close only as adults, however, may never set foot inside each other's bedrooms. As a result, part of their friends' lives may remains hidden, and can only be guessed at until some accident or illness breaks the invisible barrier.

Accessibility differs from one culture to another, however. In some European cities, people are unlikely to invite casual acquaintances to their houses or apartments; they prefer to entertain them in a restaurant. In small-town America, by contrast, even relative strangers may be invited to eat in the family room.

THE HALL AND THE STAIRS

By the end of the eighteenth century the former great hall had become mainly a reception area; life usually took place elsewhere. Later, in middle-class homes, the hall shrank even further, becoming merely an entryway, a place to store coats and hats and umbrellas and check one's appearance in the mirror before leaving the house. There was also sometimes a large, impressive piece of furniture known as a coat stand, incorporating a mirror, shelves, hooks or hangers for wraps and hats, and drawers for gloves and scarves and overshoes, as well as a bench on which to sit while changing indoor for outdoor wear. (In more modest homes, a single coatrack, like a large clumsy wooden flower, might bloom just inside the front door.)

When most people traveled on foot or in horse-drawn carriages, the hall had an important internal function as a kind of compression or decompression chamber where you prepared to face the exterior or interior world. The invention of the internal combustion engine changed this, especially outside of cities. From the mid-twentieth century on, many people usually left their houses by way of the garage or carport, sometime through what was often called a "mudroom," where there were hooks for coats and jackets and perhaps a rack for boots. As a result, in many middle- or upper-class homes today the front hall tends to have a formal, rather bare look. There will probably be a mirror or a painting on the wall, and a table that is essentially a repository for mail and a vase of flowers or a plant. If the hall is large there can be a couple of chairs or even a small sofa. These are often rather uncomfortable, but this doesn't really matter, since no one will sit on them for any length of time. Sometimes the hall will have shrunk to the point that there is room only for a shelf and a small coat closet. Low-end houses and apartments, motor homes, and trailers may have no hall whatsoever. This saves the builder money, but it has serious drawbacks, since the front door now admits cold air, mud, rain, and snow—as well as salesmen and unwanted guests—directly into the living area.

Most houses and apartments also have interior halls. The more of them there are, the more life in this home is apt to be compartmentalized. Such houses not only isolate visitors, they can separate family members from one another. If you have to open a door and walk down a corridor, climb a flight of stairs, go along another hallway, and knock on a second door to speak to one of your parents or siblings or children, you are less likely to do so. But if they are visible from the second-floor landing or through an archway between the sitting room and the kitchen, communication seems easy and natural.

In a grand house the front stairs have often been designed to impress visitors. They will be wide, often carpeted, and sometimes separated halfway up into two sub-staircases, allowing important people to make a grand entrance on important occasions. In the late nineteenth and early twentieth centuries there was a fashion for staircases that curved round the side of a circular wall, allowing for striking self-presentation but also making it hard to descend or ascend gracefully, especially in high heels. An even greater hazard was sometimes created by modernist architects whose staircases had treads but no risers and only a narrow handrail or none at all. These stairs were occasionally the cause of serious injury or even death both in films and in real life.

SITTING ROOM/DRAWING ROOM

The traditional nineteenth-century drawing room was designed to receive guests. It was generally the largest room in the house and contained the most impressive pieces of furniture, some of which appeared to have not quite completed a metamorphosis from animal or vegetable life: the chairs and tables had the legs and feet of birds and beasts, and their backs were often decorated with mahogany flowers and/or fruit. Nearby there would usually be vases of flowers and representational works of art, often depicting plants, birds, and animals. The implication of all this was that the room was a natural growth, almost a kind of transformed Eden. Usually there would be a working fireplace, often with an elaborate metal screen and brass-handled tools for managing the blaze; these too also often took the partial forms of plants, birds, or beasts.

With early-twentieth-century modernism the animal and vegetable aspects of furniture began to disappear; everything became flatter and more rectangular, and also less formal. The chairs no longer dictated an upright posture, and long, low coffee tables began to slide into place in front of sofas, silently encouraging people to put their feet up. The sofas also grew long and low, and both chairs and tables might take strange, abstract shapes made of molded plastic or treated plywood. Today some design magazines and advertisements for expensive apartments still feature this kind of stripped-down décor; other magazines and advertisements, however, present a softer and more rounded "country house" look. A compromise between these two styles is also common, and anyone who furnishes a home now has a choice as to what sort of impression they want to project, and can choose where their sitting room will fall on the continuum between contemporary and traditional. Political and social conservatives usually go for a traditional look, and radicals for a modern one, but not always. Ease and comfort are possible in both styles: a traditional room can look either formal and stiff or relaxed and welcoming, and the same is true of modernist décor.

In the sitting rooms of the past there was often an upright piano or parlor organ, sometimes covered with an expensive shawl and silver-framed family photographs. In the days before hi-fi, many children took piano lessons, and adults played for sing-alongs at parties. The invention of the phonograph and the radio gradually changed all this, and today the presence of a piano (often a baby grand) in a sitting room is usually a sign that someone who lives there is a serious musician.

HEARTH AND HOME

Once upon a time the fireplace was the essential center of every dwelling, the only source of heat and cooked food. But even after kitchen stoves and central heating were invented, the fireplace survived, gradually becoming a more or less symbolic object, a sign of family warmth and solidarity. Over time it also developed an elaborate frame, variously incorporating gilded mirrors, Dutch tiles, classical columns, and marble sculptures of nymphs and mythical beasts. Its mantel widened into a shelf for the display of significant photographs, souvenirs, small art objects, and invitation cards.

Today the fireplace survives in many homes, though it may be lit only on ceremonial occasions like Thanksgiving, Christmas, and Sunday dinner. Sometimes, however, the chimney is blocked and the fireplace does not actually work. The empty space may be filled with plants, or with an artificial log or coal fire with a fire screen and tools, to preserve the symbolic effect. In the latter case furniture may still be grouped around the hearth, which broadcasts artificial but emotionally effective warmth.

In second homes, especially in cool climates, a genuine fireplace is felt to provide a warm familial or romantic aura. Centrally heated country cottages and ski lodges often feature such fireplaces (or, occasionally, free-standing stoves), which can serve as the backdrop for family storytelling or erotic activity.

FRIENDLY AND UNFRIENDLY FURNITURE

Straight chairs and couches with stiff backs imply stiff, formal relationships. If they are also hard, slippery, or scratchy, the effect is increased. When you are invited into a room filled with such furniture, its underlying message is clear: even if you are treated politely, you may not be warmly welcomed. On the other hand, when sofas and chairs are soft and comfortable and heaped with cushions, you can relax and expect cordiality and perhaps intimacy.

In most sitting and dining rooms there is furniture that is the invisible property of certain family members. A particular chair, sometimes a large leather one, has been designated as Dad's, and another, usually smaller and more rounded, as Mom's. There may also be a rocking chair associated with a grandmother, grandfather, aunt, or uncle. It is also possible that someone in the family has an unseen claim on one end of a sofa. As a visitor you will not be invited to sit in any of these places, and if you do so unasked, a fog of discomfort will swirl round the room, and you may eventually be politely asked to move.

Furniture is full of information about its owner's role in the household. Studies have shown that the size and height of a chair influence how its occupant is seen; the larger a chair is, and the more it resembles a throne, with a high back and substantial arms, the more prestige and power its occupant appears to have. If you are invited to sit in such a piece of furniture, you are an honored guest. When you are directed to a small, low, armless chair, on the other hand, the intention, conscious or unconscious, is to put you in an inferior, less well-defended position.

In the main living area of any home the furniture suggests what ought to happen there—the kind of activities and relationships that should fill the space. Hard, formal couches and stiff chairs silently warn you to sit up straight and speak carefully. Cold, shiny floors discourage children from playing on them; thick carpets make it pleasant to do so, especially if there are floor cushions nearby. Comfortable chairs with good lamps nearby suggest that those who live there like to read. Big, soft sofas heaped with pillows tell us to relax and enjoy ourselves, while a love seat encourages intimate two-party conversations. In some nineteenth and early-twentieth-century sitting rooms, a padded and upholstered chaise lounge encouraged sitters to stretch out and put their feet up. This piece of furniture also had a slightly suggestive air: it was halfway to a bed, and could be used as one, at least temporarily. Today, the chaise lounge appears mostly in expensive bedrooms, and (in a much less elegant wood or plastic version) outdoors and beside pools, where it encourages relaxation and sunbathing.

PLACEMENT AND PSYCHOLOGY

No matter what shape and style furniture is, its placement continues to deliver strong messages. Most important, it silently informs both family members and visitors how to behave. As the sociologist Edward T. Hall has pointed out, the normal distance for close social interaction between Americans is 1½ to 2½ feet. A distance of 2½ to 4 feet keeps people at arm's length, but still allows for the discussion of personal subjects. Beyond 4 feet, conversation usually becomes reserved and impersonal. When chairs and sofas are placed at a considerable distance from one another, it is difficult to speak privately. Loud voices and communications on neutral topics such as the weather are encouraged; whispered asides are impossible to hear. The implicit message of this arrangement is that relationships both within the family and with outsiders are, or should be, cool and formal. Chairs and sofas that snuggle closely together, on the other hand, invite confidences.

STUDY / LIBRARY / DEN

In the past, well-to-do men might spend time in the sitting room or drawing room, but their natural habitat was the study or library, often paneled in wood and furnished in materials that echoed male clothing: the thick, smooth leather of their boots and shoes, the dark, durable fabrics of their suits. The furniture was heavy, strong, relatively free of decoration, and made for use. There would be a big desk, often with a tooled leather top that echoed the tooled leather of the books on the shelves, and several leather-upholstered chairs. The windows would be shielded by folding shutters, or dark, heavy curtains. This look survives today in the rooms of many men's clubs, even long after they have begun to admit females.

As time passed, the study or library often metamorphosed into what was known as a "den." This was a less formal room, more casually furnished, and allowing more casual clothing and conversation. Here you could take off your shoes and jacket and relax. At first the den was often exclusively the territory of the man of the house. Jokes were made implying that its occupant was a lion or a bear; children were told that Daddy sometimes had to go into it to hibernate, and that he would roar if interrupted there. Over time, however, the den tended to become available to other resident adults. In some cases it was eventually more or less taken over by television and used by the whole family. The furniture was still relatively simple and indestructible, but colors and materials often became lighter, and if there were curtains or blinds they were seldom elaborate.

THE DINING ROOM

The dining room was once a center of family gatherings and formal entertaining; it contained elaborate furniture and impressive works of art. Chests and cabinets held stacks of well-ironed linen and displayed fancy china and glassware. But ever since the middle of the last century it has been gradually vanishing. Families today often eat in the kitchen or family room, and may sit at a counter rather than a table even for supper. The separate dining room, if it survives, may be used only when relatives and friends come to visit. It may also become the location for a home business, hobbies like dressmaking and the compilation of scrapbooks, and a place for children to do their homework.

Dining room furniture varies from the informal to the oppressively ceremonial, depending on how much the meal resembles a formal, even ritual event. The shape of the table is often significant: round tables, as in the famous example at King Arthur's court, imply that every guest is equal, though there may be an invisible head seat, marked by a napkin holder or a set of carving knives. Square dining tables are rare, but also tend to produce an effect of relative equality between the diners. Rectangular tables suggest that whoever sits at the head is most important. At one time, it was customary for the father of the family to sit at the end of a long table farthest from the kitchen, with his wife at the other end, and this arrangement can still be observed, especially at large family gatherings. If the family is very large there will sometimes be a "children's table" set up to accommodate them and perhaps also some woman of lesser status to enforce good manners.

• • •

THE KITCHEN

Kitchens, in the past, were an essential but usually separate part of every middle-class house or apartment. They were also usually fairly large. So-called "convenience food" had not yet been invented, and the preparation of meals took a lot of time and space: bread and cakes were baked, chickens were plucked and stuffed, vegetables were washed and chopped. A well-to-do family would have both a cook and a kitchen maid; a woman with only one servant or none often spent much of her day in the kitchen. As a result the room was apt to be not only large but comfortable and well lit; there might be a sofa at one end, and a table and chairs where the housewife and her children and friends could sit. There was little thought of making the room efficient: often the stove, sink, and food storage were far apart, and getting a meal involved a lot of steps.

During World War II, however, household help disappeared from most middle-class houses. Most women with children and no outside jobs found themselves taking over those of their former servants, including cleaning, laundry, child care, and cooking. For a while, the family home became essentially a retreat for men and a workplace for women. Already in the nineteenth century, designers and scientific experts had begun to turn their attention to the kitchen, and now they increased their efforts. They found the standard American kitchen inefficient and wasteful of space. Their new scientific solution was a much smaller room, often merely a galley in which only one person at a time could function. Everything was within reach, and getting a meal together theoretically took fewer steps and fewer minutes.

Right from the start many women disliked the space-saving laboratory kitchen, which in effect cut them off from family activities and conversation, and they didn't think that the efficiency was worth it. As a result, doors between the kitchen and the dining room began to be propped open, then removed. In other cases part of the wall would be chopped away and converted into a "pass-through" so that whoever was preparing the meal was no longer isolated from family life. Another early-twentieth-century compromise was the so-called "breakfast nook." This was usually a kind of alcove in the kitchen with benches on two sides that made it unnecessary for the dining room table to be formally laid and food carried in and out. At first, only breakfast was eaten in this nook, but later on more and more family meals took place there.

Today many new homes still have a breakfast nook, but now it is seldom separate; instead it takes the form of an L-shaped padded bench and table, with chairs on the other sides, between the kitchen and the family room or sitting room. It may also metamorphose into a long counter with high stools, attached to one side of an open kitchen. All these arrangements make it possible for communication to flow easily between those who prepare food and those who eat it—and suggests that they are often the same people. The presence and constant use of a formal dining room has an opposite message; it does not encourage family and visitors to help prepare food, serve, or clear up, and often warns them to be on their best behavior.

The new kitchens, whatever their size, were at first usually all white, like laboratories, to suggest cleanliness and scientific management. The old black cast-iron stove and gray soapstone sink were regarded as outmoded and dirty. But in the later part of the twentieth century, possibly in part for commercial motives, psychologists and home decorating experts began to reject the all-white kitchen as bleak and unfriendly. Instead they recommended bright colors for kitchen furniture; and wallpapers, dish towels, and curtains with cheerful pictures of food and kitchen tools.

Still later there were often successful attempts to make the kitchen go through fashionable changes the way women's clothes did. At one point every up-to-date stove and fridge, including one in the first rented house of my married life, was autumn gold or avocado green; later these colors were identified as dreary and outmoded, and we were encouraged to replace them with copper-hued appliances and varnished wood cabinets, and then still later with stainless steel or black glass appliances and granite countertops. A surprising number of customers succumbed to these changes over and over again, often under pressure from housing magazines and TV shows, or from real estate agents who declared that a new kitchen would make their house sell for much more.

BATHROOMS

In the early twentieth century many middle-class homes had only one or two bathrooms, usually located upstairs, and anyone who came to the house could use them. Soon, however, architects added a "half bath" or "guest bath" downstairs, consisting only of a small sink and toilet, both for the convenience of the family and, according to some commentators, to keep visitors out of more private areas and make it impossible for them to inspect or steal from the family medicine cabinet.

Today, the messages broadcast by bathrooms vary widely. In England, for many years, it was customary to separate the place where you washed from the place where you relieved yourself. The bathroom contained only a sink and a tub and/or shower; the lavatory or "loo" was a separate closet, often at some distance away. Today the functions of cleanliness and elimination are usually combined in a single space, but a partial wall may separate the toilet from the sink. This arrangement is common in bed-and-breakfast accommodations, where the toilet and even the toilet paper may be further disguised by fluffy covers.

High-end bathrooms tend to be large and have an industrial aspect. Even when the rest of the house is full of Colonial or Victorian décor, the bathroom may be all polished porcelain, steel, and mirrored glass, with twin marble sinks, stark black or white towels, and a shower equipped with multiple nozzles like a Jacuzzi. The suggestion is that the care of the body is an act of scientific precision and considerable expense. Another expensive alternative is the neo-Baroque bathroom with flocked crimson wallpaper, gold-plated fixtures in the shape of dolphins, and a huge footed tub. It is here, in the most private of rooms, that the private fantasies of the owners often find expression.

BEDROOMS

The relative size and placement of bedrooms is always an important indicator of family relationships. A large, very grand master bedroom with en suite bath, combined with much smaller secondary bedrooms, announces that in this household adults are more important than children—or, possibly, that there are no children. When the children's bedrooms are close to those of their parents, we unconsciously assume that there is emotional closeness or at least concern. When they are very distant we may suspect an emotional distance. Occasionally a child will be exiled to a bedroom in the attic or basement, or to what was formerly a maid's room, as my present husband once was, causing him or her to feel rejected and lonely. For a teenager, on the other hand, the move may mean freedom and independence.

A bedroom that is seen only by its owner, or a romantic partner, may express a private self that remains invisible to others. The cool, efficient, perhaps slightly colorless stylishness of the rest of the house may be contradicted by a bright, comfortable, almost untidy clutter of magazines and ruffled pillows and crocheted afghans and framed photographs and children's paintings. The reverse situation, though rare, also occurs, notably in the interior décor of ascetics, who are happy to make their guests comfortable but sleep in a bare, undecorated, almost monastic cell.

At one time well-to-do homes, especially in Europe, often had separate bedrooms for the husband and wife, or a separate "dressing room" for one or both of them. The décor of the woman's dressing room was very feminine, with a mirrored dressing-table, while that of the man was obviously masculine and might include a single bed. These arrangements can occasionally still be observed among the rich on both sides of the Atlantic; but in working- and middle-class homes most couples will share a bedroom. A delicately feminine bedroom informs anyone who sees it that this is female territory, into which the male must enter as a visitor, though often a welcome one. A roughhewn bed covered with a checked blanket and chairs into which the antlers of deer are incorporated tells us that this space is truly a master bedroom, and belongs to a macho man.

The décor of a bedroom may also be neutral, or there may be a compromise between the tastes of the inhabitants. This can produce some odd juxtapositions: my flowered chintz armchair and your hippo-like black leather recliner, for instance. If this is a second marriage or partnership there may be two chests of drawers in different styles, each sometimes with a separate group of family photographs. The room may also contain valuable antique or foreign objects that do not match the décor, but need to be preserved from harm.

New development houses usually include a big, impressive master bedroom with its own large bathroom and walk-in closet. The other bedrooms, however, tend to be small, with few windows and minimal storage. This does not always mean that adults who live there are more important and valuable than the children. Builders may think, for instance, that making most of the bedrooms small saves on construction costs and that after all, children and guests don't buy houses. When explaining the discrepancy to prospective clients, however, they will probably say that the kids' rooms don't need to be very large, since they will spend most of their time in the family room, increasing communication and closeness. In a few cases they may be right, though not always. As the children become adolescents they may decide to shut themselves in their cramped, dark bedrooms to play music and video games; or they may simply leave the house.

THE ATTIC

According to some Freudian and Jungian psychologists, the psyche is structured like a house. The main floors are the ego, the conscious mind; the cellar is the id, or unconscious, where primitive impulses are stored; and the attic represents the superego, the repository of memory, morality, and tradition. This metaphor worked best in the past, when almost every house had an attic that contained old trunks, toys, books, clothes, and furniture, and often family letters and papers. Sometimes there was a box of Christmas tree ornaments and one of dress-up costumes. Children played in the attic on rainy days, and you could also go there to be alone—like Louisa May Alcott, the author of *Little Women*, who wrote her first stories lying on an old sofa in the family attic in Massachusetts. It was a private place: unless you were a visiting child or a roofer, you would probably never see anyone else's attic.

Today modernist architects and developers have usually done away with this useful space: the architects because of a love of flat roofs, the developers because of a love of money. But sometimes the attic survives in other forms. Possibly, as in my own house, a spare bedroom has effectively taken its place; in other cases the garage has become a kind of attic. Householders may also rent a self-storage locker to store excess possessions, often including objects that once belonged to their own parents and grandparents.

Things that are stored in a real or substitute attic, like memories from the past, may be more or less forgotten; they may also reappear with violent force, as in the most famous attic in English fiction, the one in *Jane Eyre* that houses Mr. Rochester's mad wife, Bertha, whose emergence represents the eruption of Rochester's guilty past and his bad conscience. In real life, though usually less dramatically, an old trunk may hold documents that will disrupt the lives of an entire family: unexpected wills and love letters, or newspaper clippings that expose some ancestor as a convicted criminal.

THE CELLAR

The cellar of most houses tends to be dim and shadowy, metaphorically suggesting the unconscious: the hidden, the dark, the concealed. In the past many basements contained a coal bin or stacks of firewood, and the furnace and hot water heater are usually still located there, suggesting that warmth and energy come from underground—but also, at least in legend, the fires of hell. The center of the earth, we are told, is dark and fearfully hot. In literature sinister things are discovered in basements: typically, imprisoned people and dead bodies. Stevenson's Dr. Jekyll, when he has become the bestial, violent Mr. Hyde, leaves his house by way of the cellar.

The general mood of the contemporary basement varies from neutral and well lit to gloomy, damp, and ominous. Some are bright and functional, with a washer and dryer, laundry tubs, and shelves for home-canned goods. Others are positively frightening; as a child I was sure that rats and goblins lived in the dark, earth-floored cellar of one friend's house. An extremely dark, dirty basement full of broken garden furniture, cracked storm windows, rusting tools, dried-up cans of paint, and stacks of moldy cardboard boxes containing God knows what can cause anxiety in adults as well as children. Even if one tries to suppress this primitive reaction, the place tends to suggest a side to family life that is best kept out of sight.

Some basements, of course, have been deliberately upgraded, converted into workrooms, playrooms, or recreation rooms with pine-paneled walls, Ping-Pong or pool tables, a television set, and even sometimes a wet bar. There will be lively posters (often travel, concert, or comic), sagging easy chairs, buzzing fluorescent fixtures, and maybe an old daybed piled with battered cushions. These transformations are reassuring, but not an absolute guarantee that the people who live in the house above have nothing to hide.

HAPPY AND UNHAPPY HOUSES

When two people live together, one of them may be largely responsible for the décor of any room, or it may be the result of collaboration or compromise. The true state of affairs can usually be determined by simply praising the way the place looks, and observing who takes credit for it. If both do, their relationship probably is (or recently was) a happy one. When one or both partner volubly refuses all acclaim, it may indicate either aesthetic indifference or emotional detachment, possibly both.

Sometimes different rooms will have very different atmospheres. There may be a bright, cheerful kitchen where one member of the family (not always the mother) is usually to be found, and a dark, closed-in office or study where someone else seems to work and live. The opposite situation is also possible: a bright, cheerful, orderly home office and a dismal, dirty kitchen. If there is only a single adult in the home, we may have the impression of a split personality: someone who loves work and hates cooking, or the reverse.

Houses can also seem to have personalities of their own. As Libbie Block puts it in her brilliant but now almost forgotten novel about Hollywood, *The Hills of Beverly*, "there were houses which made for laughter and some which made for tears, some which caused quarrels, and some which were so cold and emotionless that love froze in them and died." There are homes in which we instantly feel comfortable: something about the shape of the rooms, the furniture, the light, and the colors makes us happy. There are also dwellings like Shirley Jackson's Hill House, in the book of the same name, that feel wrong and make us uncomfortable. In Hill House, Jackson writes, "the walls seemed always in one direction a fraction longer than the eye could endure, and in another direction a fraction less." It is a sensation that some people have also had in certain office and school hallways, or in high-rise public housing where the buildings tend to be peculiarly tall and thin, with windswept exterior passageways blocked by wire fencing.

As Joyce Carol Oates has written in a memoir of her childhood, "The house contains the home but is not identical with it. The house anticipates the home and will very likely survive it." When we enter any residence we will be aware of it both as a house and as a home. In some cases, we will know or sense that there has been trouble there, and will therefore unconsciously see it as what sociologists call a broken home: a building symbolically split in half, as if by an explosion, with objects out of place and something wrong about the light. On other, better occasions we will feel a kind of euphoria, as if we have at last entered the Happy Home of our childhood dreams and drawings.

CHAPTER 7

Houses of God

Approaching a strange house, we will often start to form an impression of its inhabitants. The same thing is true of other types of buildings: apartment buildings, offices, schools, and—perhaps especially—churches and temples, which people of many faiths refer to as the House of God.

Visitors from another planet, taking this literally, but noticing that God is seldom visible in his designated dwellings, might attempt to discover his nature from an examination of these dwellings. It would soon be clear to them that the divinity takes many different forms. The God who resides in most of the great European cathedrals, for instance, is clearly very tall and very rich. He enjoys classical art and music, and is particularly fond of large pipe organs. In Britain and other parts of Northern Europe his taste is more restrained: he likes stone statues and wood carvings, but does not care for gold trim or nudes. Farther south he has a more dramatic personality, and appreciates luxury. His preference in decoration inclines towards the Baroque and even the rococo. Some churches in southern Germany and Austria, with their gilt barley-sugar pilasters and whipped-cream cupids and angels, suggest a highly romantic nature, with a craving for sweets.

Churches, of course, are erected by humans. Their architects construct what they think is beautiful, what is in fashion, what the authorities want—or a combination of these things. Often, they also tend to believe that their buildings will influence the people who use them. They see architecture as a cause of human action and feeling, rather than an effect. Andrew Jackson Downing, the famous landscape designer, thought that it was possible to control behavior through architecture, and that his buildings would make their inhabitants orderly and law-abiding.

Anthropologists and sociologists, on the other hand, view buildings as the outward manifestation of a society: an effect rather than a cause. Ebenezer Howard, the inventor of the garden city, believed that culture was embodied in architecture. Most Western houses, he thought, have separate rooms for sleeping, eating, and washing because we believe that these activities should be kept apart. Joanne Waghorne of Syracuse University sees a connection between the traditional multifamily Indian house, in which the son and his wife and children occupy separate quarters in his parents' home, and the design of Hindu temples that, though dedicated to a single deity, also usually contain smaller shrines to other gods.

Some experts on church architecture hold both views simultaneously. Michael DeSanctis, an architectural historian and design consultant, remarks that buildings "exert a subtle but real influence on those who inhabit them," but also that "[e]very house represents a self-portrait of its occupant."

Some writers have tried to explore the connections between the way buildings look and the lives of the people who use them, with special reference to religious architecture. Others have written impassioned studies recommending particular types of church design, with the avowed intent of changing the way people behave, believe, and worship.

During the nineteenth and twentieth centuries four types of religious architecture became popular in America, each with its distinctive appearance and perceived meaning. In chronological order, they were the neo-Colonial, the neo-Gothic, the neo-Medieval, and (after 1900) the modernist. Churches in all these styles can still be seen, and most are in current use.

The Colonial church, favored especially by evangelical Protestants, is often an actual example or copy of the traditional New England meetinghouse featured on countless New England calendars and in Grant Wood's famous painting, *The Midnight Ride of Paul Revere*. It is simple and rectangular, with a steeple and a shingled roof, and is built of wood and painted white. It has many windows and is usually almost without interior decoration except for an occasional curly brass or pewter sconce or chandelier. There may be a balcony running round one or more sides of the interior, supported by columns. The most striking feature is the large, impressive pulpit, which may have a canopy or sounding board and is usually elevated three to eight feet above floor level, silently indicating the dominance of the preacher, and of his sermons and prayers.

At first most of these churches contained parallel ranks of box pews whose sides were sometimes so high that few of the occupants could look at their neighbors: all they could see was the preacher. From a Puritan point of view this was not a disadvantage: worldly curiosity was a distraction from the divine. Though hymns might be sung, music was of minor importance: Martin Luther had stated that written and spoken language were the exclusive representations of God's power, and that the purpose of worship was to praise God and understand his word. Art was not in evidence: statues, paintings, and stained glass were considered popish.

To many Americans these Colonial and neo-Colonial churches now seem naturally beautiful, in part because of their elegant simplicity of construction, which appears to embody the moral qualities of the early settlers. They suggest Colonial American ideals and virtues: honesty, simplicity, thrift, seriousness, idealism, purity, and piety, and also a life somewhat lacking in material comforts: the seats in those pews were hard, especially after the customary one- or two-hour sermon.

Variants of the original meetinghouse church soon developed. There were larger and more impressive neoclassical versions, with a porch, pillars, and pediment, showing the influence of Christopher

Wren's London churches. There was also a Federalist or Colonial Williamsburg type, which reproduced the Colonial or neoclassical model in red brick with white trim, and tended to be more imposing. These churches almost always have tall Doric or Ionic pillars and an impressive steeple: they are especially common on New England and Middle Atlantic prep school and college campuses. In the course of the nineteenth century their box pews gradually gave way to bench pews, but for many years seats were still rented out at different prices depending on their proximity to the preacher, so that the comparative affluence and social prestige of the parishioners remained clear to all. These structures were what Richard Kieckhefer calls classic evangelical churches, which centered on verbal interchanges between a minister and a congregation.

From the 1840s on there was what Jeanne Halgren Kilde, in *When Church Became Theatre*, describes as a turn toward "more ecclesiastical worship practices and worship spaces." Well-do-do congregations began to move to the suburbs and erect churches in a neo-Gothic manner, which was now proclaimed in the England of the Oxford Movement as the only true Christian style. These buildings, especially popular with Catholics and Episcopalians, were usually constructed of dark gray stone, with imposing spires, tall pointed windows, and a cruciform ground plan. Some had stone buttresses and steeples decorated with crockets like rows of giant Brussels sprouts.

Inside the neo-Gothic church there was typically a long pillared nave with central and side aisles, a raised sanctuary and altar, and a communion rail that visibly separated the clergy from the laity. The ceiling was often made of dark varnished wood, like the hull of a ship, sometimes with the traditional protruding hammerhead beams. There might be a circular rose window over the entrance, and perhaps separate side chapels. The free-standing Colonial pulpit was replaced by a raised preaching platform in front of the altar, on which there was often an impressive reading desk supported by a ferocious brass or wooden eagle. Behind and above the altar there might be a reredos (a screen combining painted and sculptured images) or a display of the Ten Commandments. Many of these buildings were what Richard Kieckhefer calls classical sacramental churches, in which "movement takes place along a processional path"; the priest and his followers walk down the center aisle toward the altar, and members of the congregation also move forward to receive the sacrament.

These neo-Gothic churches, if large and grand enough, were also furnished with pipe organs and seats or stalls for a choir. Sculpture and painting proliferated, even in Protestant denominations that had previously banned them. But perhaps the most striking change was in the lighting. Colonial churches, with their many large windows, were full of light. The interior of the neo-Gothic church was shadowy and obscure: it had dark woodwork, thick stone walls, and narrow leaded windows filled with sheets of frosted or colored glass, or with multicolored images of angels and prophets and birds and flowers. All this created a mysterious, contemplative atmosphere— sometimes spiritually inspiring and uplifting, sometime merely melancholy and gloomy. It also preserved a view of God as tall and wealthy and wise, but essentially unfathomable, and not easily approached or understood by the layman.

Jeanne Kilde has suggested that these churches were the outward sign of a return to an older religious tradition and to a more visual and sensual sort of worship in which art, flowers, music, and even incense figured. She attributes the change in part to Americans' growing interest in high culture and high society, which was associated with Europe and especially with England. By the mid-nineteenth century Britain was no longer the wicked stepfather of a rebellious young nation, but the "mother country"—a source of tradition, refinement, and upper-class status.

There were also political changes at work. Many supporters of the neo-Gothic church had moved from downtown to expensive suburbs, leaving the less well-to-do behind. Out of sight became out of mind, and a new view of the church's mission developed. Conservative preachers and parishioners often no longer felt that their churches should look for converts among immigrants and the poor; instead they sought social connections and spiritual inspiration. The neo-Gothic church was also seen as a style suited to every Christian denomination—one that could unite respectable churchgoers in the North and the South as the country moved closer to the Civil War.

After the war, for many years, Catholics and Episcopalians continued to favor the traditional neo-Gothic style. This preference was responsible for the building of many neo-Gothic parish churches, and also some of American's most famous cathedrals, including New York's St. Patrick's (begun in 1853) and St. John the Divine (begun in 1907 and still under construction today).

For some American Protestants, however, the neo-Gothic churches seemed too European and too consciously artistic. In William Dean Howell's *A Hazard of New Fortunes* (1890, but set in 1886), the hero, Basil March, and his wife visit New York's fashionable Grace Episcopal Church on Broadway at Tenth Street. As Bostonians, they are both impressed and a little ashamed of their reaction to its aesthetic splendor.

> Rapt far from New York, if not from earth, in the dim richness of the painted light, the hallowed music took them with solemn ecstasy; the aerial, aspiring gothic forms seemed to lift them heavenward. They came out, reluctant, into the dazzle and bustle of the street, with a feeling that they were too good for it. . . .
>
> "But no matter how consecrated we feel now," [Basil] said, "we mustn't forget that we went into the church for precisely the same reason that we went to the Vienna Café for breakfast—to gratify an aesthetic sense. . . . It was a purely pagan impulse. . . ."

In the 1880s and 1890s some congregations, especially in rural New England and the Midwest, began to turn to a new, simpler, and less expensive architectural approach that mixed the Colonial and the traditional English, and thus combined piety and purity with aesthetic and spiritual inspiration. This style, now known as Carpenter Gothic, is probably most familiar from Grant Wood's famous painting, *American Gothic*. These churches typically have a basic rectangular Colonial shape, but with the addition of tall pointed windows and doors, sometimes set with colored glass. Some are painted or plastered with stucco over brick, but usually they are built of wood, and the exterior walls often have a simple board-and-batten construction, so that they seem to be striped vertically. These vertical pinstripes, and the tall, narrow, steeples that sometimes went with them, also carry out the directive of one of the first architects of American Gothic churches, Leopold Eidlitz, who claimed that the movement of Christian architecture must be continually upward.

After the Civil War, though neo-Gothic churches continued to be built, a new style based on Romanesque and medieval models began to dominate, especially in evangelical denominations—Baptist, Congregationalist, Methodist, and Presbyterian. Perhaps in part because they were so strongly constructed, most of these buildings are still standing. They typically have thick masonry walls made of big blocks of gray or tan or plum-brown stone, with "rusticated," or strongly emphasized, recessed joints, a style that my *Illustrated Dictionary of Historic Architecture* says is "used to create an appearance of impregnability." The overall impression is of a monumental medieval or early Renaissance castle, with heavy pillared porches, Romanesque arched doorways and windows, and massive square bell towers, the latter sometimes crowned with battlements that could have sheltered dozens of armed men.

Some of these churches were even more fanciful, with elaborate patterned brickwork, proliferating into all kinds of steeples and pinnacles and gables and domes. One of the most remarkable examples is Henry Hobson Richardson's Trinity Church in Boston's Copley Square, built in the 1870s. Though today it looks overdecorated and extravagant, at the time it was chosen by the American Institute of Architects for several years running as the finest building in the nation. It was tremendously influential, giving rise to hundreds of imitations all over the country, especially in the Northeast and Midwest.

Like the neo-Gothic church, neo-medieval churches appeared most often in the expensive sections of big cities and in prosperous suburbs. They were favored especially by the rich and the upwardly mobile middle class. These people wanted to worship in impressive buildings, and to hear the most famous preachers and musicians; and they could afford to pay for this privilege. Many of these churches were soon successful enough to invest in land, building up a considerable endowment. They competed for well-do-do parishioners, while discouraging the indigent through high pew rental fees and inconvenient locations; if you did not own a horse and carriage, it was hard to get to many of them on Sunday. Though these churches might generously fund missionary and charitable works, both at home and abroad, they did not want the objects of their charity at their services. Their preachers often deplored the moral condition of the unsaved working class; but it was also not unusual for them to suggest that if "laboring men" who grumbled about their lot would seek and find Jesus, they would forget their rage and envy of their betters.

These monumental churches, like the Romanesque forts and castles they resembled, conveyed an impression of wealth, dominance, order, and security. They not only looked like fortresses or banks; they were seen that way. In their sermons the resident preachers customarily used military or business metaphors. "Churches," pronounced the Reverend M. M. Dana of Minneapolis's First Congregational Church in 1886, "are spiritual recruiting agencies. . . . The church is not a hive for drones, it ought to be a hive of industry. . . . You are building a spiritual armory, and it rests with you to fill it with weapons." This was the era of muscular Christianity and the founding of the YMCA, one of whose original goals was the creation of pious and aggressively athletic young men.

Unlike the neo-Gothic church, the neo-medieval church did not stand out from its surroundings: instead it resembled many other public and private buildings of the period. Libraries, armories, colleges, city halls, and railway stations all across the country had begun to look like medieval fortresses, and the style was also adapted to the mansions of millionaires. (A striking example is the main building of the artists' colony in Saratoga Springs, New York, known as Yaddo.) One possible implication of these similarities was that the church was no longer a separate, spiritual place, but part of the material culture of the Gilded Age. Church, library, town hall, university, and mansion were united in preserving virtue and the social order.

Why did so many buildings of this period look like fortified castles? Who were the enemies, the besiegers? The period just after the Civil War was a time of great political and social unrest. There was a general fear of anarchists and revolutionaries. Crime was widespread; strikes and rioting were common. Masses of penniless immigrants were beginning to pour into the country; unemployment was high and police protection sporadic. As a result, American cities were often very dangerous places. No wonder that the rich should seek shelter in buildings that at least looked as if they could be defended against an angry mob.

Though the exterior of the neo-medieval church was massive, formidable, and extremely masculine, the interior conveyed a different message. Indoors the church was comfortable, cozy, and domestic—and (by Victorian standards) feminine. It was well heated, with facilities for socializing, cooking, eating, and child care: for church teas, church suppers, Bible study groups, and Sunday schools. Furnishings were usually elaborate: pews had plush cushions; floors were covered with thick carpet. Often the décor suggested that of a Gilded Age mansion: in contemporary photographs, some of these church interiors resemble expensive houses of the late Victorian period, and have the same luxurious, somewhat cluttered look.

At the same time, some private houses were beginning to resemble neo-medieval churches. They had arched windows, pilasters and balconies, religious paintings and statues, and parlor organs. Domestic chairs and tables and sideboards, like pews and pillars and pulpits, were made of dark oak or mahogany and carved with flowers, leaves, nuts, and vines; ceilings were painted with clouds or stars. Even fairly modest homes often had leaded stained-glass panels in the front door or a parlor window, depicting religious images—doves, harps, lilies, crosses—while a mansion might contain one or more large windows showing impossibly lush fruit, flowers, birds, and landscapes in shades of gold, royal purple, ruby red, and peacock green.

Though the family home was often seen as sacred, it was the church that remained the home or House of God. This was a fairly new idea: Colonial Calvinists did not think of God as actually dwelling in their churches. Of course, once you consider a church as the House of God, it is difficult not to imagine that in this incarnation He has the same fears and enjoys the same kind of expensive material comforts and music and art as his worshippers.

THE CHURCH AS THEATRE

The neo-medievalist church in America was not only a fortress and an expensive home: it was often also a theatre. By the 1860s the interiors of some of these churches began to look like auditoriums, with a raised stage and proscenium arch at one end. Usually they were wider and less elongated than those of the neo-Gothic church, and they often had a sloped floor and radiating aisles. Pews or padded chairs were arranged in curving rows, like the seats in a theatre, and there were often additional seats in a gallery overhead that sometimes ended in the equivalent of a private theatre box on either side. A large pipe organ usually stood next to or behind the preaching platform. Acoustics were taken seriously, and were usually good: the architects who built these churches also often designed theatres and concert halls.

For the Puritans the theatre was sinful, and music suspect. But by the 1870s people who attended the auditorium churches no longer considered the arts intrinsically evil. Some plays and paintings and songs might be corrupting, but others were seen as inspiring and uplifting. The auditorium churches rented out space to (and sometimes sponsored) lectures and plays with a moral message, and concerts that featured sacred music. Regular church services, too, were often quasi-theatrical events, with dramatic sermons, lantern slides, organ and choir numbers, and perhaps a paid soloist. Inside the fortress, the arts flourished, and the role of the audience was more active than it had been in the neo-Gothic church. They not only joined in the responses and sang hymns; at revival meetings they were encouraged to come to the front of the church and witness for God.

The acoustical qualities of a building can have an important effect on its use. Wood, soft materials, and human bodies reflect less than 25 percent of sounds; the result is dry and clear, excellent for preaching, especially if the shape of the room is regular and the ceiling relatively low. The wooden neo-Colonial church was ideal for services that centered on a sermon, as most once did. Stone walls, on the other hand, reflect nearly 100 percent of sound, and create what is known as "resonant space," particularly in buildings with high arching roofs. This sort of space is ideal for music, and accounts for the almost unearthly effect of voices and the organ in some cathedrals. In the long, narrow neo-Gothic church it might be harder to hear what was said from the pulpit, but music sounded splendid. This worked well in Catholic churches, where for centuries Mass had been said in Latin, and it was assumed that most of the congregation would not understand the words. The neo-medieval church, however, was suited for both preaching and music. The auditorium shape made the minister's voice more audible, but the size and height of the room and its stone walls favored music, though most of these buildings could not produce the supernatural resonant effects of a cathedral.

By the early twentieth century the neo-medieval church was beginning to lose some of its popularity. Society had become less puritanical, and more parishioners were attending secular theatres and concert halls. Meanwhile, improvements in police protection and the legal system were reducing crime, and the psychological need for the appearance of safety and invulnerability had diminished. For a while fewer auditorium-type churches were constructed. Aspects of their design, however, reappeared in the theatres of the period, and later in the movie palaces of the early twentieth century, which often included pipe organs and heavy Romanesque arches and columns.

During the revival movements of the 1920s and 1930s, when evangelical and inspirational speakers like Aimee Semple McPherson and Billy Sunday began to draw huge crowds, the auditorium church was also revived, though sometimes in strange forms. McPherson's Los Angeles Temple, for instance, was described by contemporaries as looking like a giant spaceship, and seated 5,300 worshippers.

In the years that followed, many even stranger religious buildings would appear in America. At the same time, admirers of the past would do their best to build churches that resembled as closely as possible the European cathedrals of the late Middle Ages; one famous example is Duke Chapel in Durham, North Carolina, completed in 1935, which is 210 feet tall, has three pipe organs, and looks almost brand-new, as if it had been created yesterday by supernatural forces.

THE MODERNIST CHURCH

Modern architecture was slow to move into religious buildings, and the first important International Style churches only appeared in Europe and South America in the 1920s and 1930s. Some were designed by the most famous architects of the time, including Oscar Niemeyer and Le Corbusier, and were remarkably innovative. Le Corbusier's Notre-Dame-du-Haut, at Ronchamp in eastern France, for instance, looks from some angles like a nun's headdress.

In America, famous modern architects such as Frank Lloyd Wright, Eero Saarinen, and Mies van der Rohe designed both churches and synagogues. These structures were always visually impressive, if occasionally impractical. (Wright's Unity Temple in Oak Park, Illinois, built in 1904, looks from outside like an almost windowless pre-Columbian tomb in gray concrete, and the benches in its interior, though handsome, are as square and uncomfortable as most of his early furniture.)

Many other architects were equally innovative though not always as impractical. Some, intoxicated by the possibilities of reinforced concrete, produced buildings that resembled flying saucers, rockets, pyramids, Mayan temples, A-frame ski lodges, hats, bread boxes, clams, and fish. At first there was often resistance from congregations: people complained that the new structures just did not look like churches. Occasionally parishioners were persuaded by the argument that, as the pastor of Trinity Lutheran Church in Walnut Creek, California—one of the bread boxes—put it, contemporary design costs less. Eventually some people became reconciled to this particular bread box or even began to admire it; others, especially older members of the congregation, left the church.

THE POSTMODERN CHURCH

Today religious architecture takes many forms. Traditional neo-Colonial, neo-Federalist, and neo-Gothic churches continue to be built; but most new churches, and almost all new synagogues, look modern—or, more often, postmodern, combining elements from many different traditions. Corinthian columns may support the semiclassical pediment of a church that otherwise resembles a big-box superstore, and pointed Gothic doors may appear on the flat end of a shingled A-frame building. Like the neo-medieval churches, they match their environment. They are almost always consciously simple and functional, with an emphasis on natural materials—stone, plaster, wood, and brick—and pale natural colors. The interiors tend to look rather empty, with high, bare walls and windows that (unless the church is located in a landscape of striking natural beauty) do not allow a view of the world outside. The floors are not always sloped as in a theatre, and the pulpit and altar or communion table may stand only a few steps above the rest of the room. It is not always possible to instantly identify the space as having a religious purpose, especially in the case of nonliturgical Protestant denominations. Usually there is a large plain cross somewhere, but it may be high on the wall or off to one side. Occasionally these buildings are readily identified as churches from the outside, though some still appear to be disguised as schools, corporation headquarters, or medical clinics. Inside, they often look like expensive concert auditoriums, or the lecture halls of a well-endowed university or a successful nonprofit foundation.

In some ways, contemporary church architects appear to have gone back to the Middle Ages for inspiration: not to the Gothic cathedral or the medieval fortress, but to the simplicity and use of light characteristic of the abbeys and nunneries of the late Middle Ages. Some new churches give the same impression of bare pale walls and echoing corridors, minimal but elegant benches and pulpits and altars, and light pouring down from above into the shadowy darkness below, in a religious metaphor made substance.

Several interesting books have been devoted to the celebration of American religious architecture. One outstanding example is Marilyn J. Chiat's survey of more than a hundred churches and synagogues, with a Zen temple or two thrown in. She includes classic examples of many styles, and also some fascinating freaks, including two churches in the northern Midwest with obvious faces: Immaculate Heart of Mary in Windthorst, Kansas, has the look of a prim and disapproving pioneer aunt, while St. Boniface in Menominee, Nebraska, strongly resembles a frightened puppy. She also includes a neo-Tudor Revival church in Atlanta that might be a set for a Shakespearian comedy, and a wildly extravagant Egyptian temple in Nashville—both of them Presbyterian.

Among more recent buildings, there are three churches that strongly resemble Hollywood versions of a small spaceship: La Ermita de La Caridad in Miami; Eero Saarinen's North Christian

Church in Columbus, Indiana; and, my favorite, the Tower of Prayer at Oral Roberts University in Tulsa, Oklahoma, which looks as if it were about to take off at any minute. God, these churches irresistibly suggest, is a being from outer space. All three of these spaceships, like many fundamentalist churches today, have what might be called a lightning-rod spire. The steeple or tower has always been one of the distinguishing marks of a church, its visible connection with the divine. The solid steeples and bell towers of Colonial, neo-Gothic, and neo-medieval churches are wide bridges between heaven and earth. The very slim, sharp lightning-rod spire, on the other hand, seems designed to transmit a kind of electrical or spiritual power, perhaps of the sort that strikes worshippers inside the building and causes them to sway and cry out to Jesus.

Michael J. Crosbie's *Architecture for the Gods* celebrates forty-three sophisticated modern and postmodern constructions. The plural title presumably refers to the fact that Crosbie includes several synagogues and the Islamic Center in New York City—but it also suggests that these diverse buildings house diverse divinities. The synagogues, for instance, make it clear that in Judaism the most sacred and important thing in the building is the ark in which the scrolls of the Torah are kept. It is always located front and center, clearly visible to everyone.

SACRED SPACES

According to Caroline Humphrey and Piers Vitebsky, all religious buildings contain levels of sacred space. The most private, holy, and powerful space "is often so sacred that it can be reached only by degrees. . . . Individuals must be purified before entering this space and entry to the inner area is often permitted only to special categories of people." The Orthodox Church, even today, "usually shelters the altar behind a screen of icons, beyond which no unbaptized person is allowed." For Roman Catholics and Anglicans the most holy part of the building is the tabernacle that contains the consecrated host.

In modernist churches, where many visual and psychological barriers between the clergy and the laity have been removed, the special sanctity of the tabernacle is sometimes preserved by moving it to a closed side chapel and bringing the bread and wine out only for Communion services.

Most other faiths also have characteristic and significant religious structures. The Quaker meetinghouse has no pulpit or stage; instead it is a simple square or rectangular room with rows of chairs or benches facing inward toward a central table. The windows are usually set high so that no one will be distracted by the activities of the world outside, though sometimes they give a view into a quiet garden. This plan announces that the Quakers are a group apart from the world, in which no one person has more religious authority than any other. If this is God's house, He is a person of modest ambitions and simple needs. He may be disguised, temporarily, as a member of the Society of Friends, since during meetings anyone who is moved to speak may do so—or, as sometimes happens, the whole group may sit in silence.

At the other end of the spectrum is Islam. Here religious services take place in a mosque, or *masajid*, which is often beautifully decorated with colored tiles and passages from the Koran. In large mosques there is usually a central dome that represent heaven, and there will always be a central hall without benches or chairs, often floored with Oriental carpets. Here believers can gather for the five daily prayers, usually led by an imam; they sit in rows facing toward Mecca, which is indicated by the *mihrab*, a tiled niche or depression in one wall. Usually the mosque also has an attached minaret, a very tall tower from which a muezzin calls the worshippers to prayer, and which also indicates the local presence of believers.

Most of the worshippers in any mosque are men. Women customarily pray at home: if they attend the mosque they are segregated in a much smaller space at the back or side of the central hall, separated by some sort of barrier. This arrangement sends a clear message about the peripheral place of women in public religious life—and, by extension, in public life in general. The design of the prayer hall also makes it clear that Islam does not encourage individual initiative; faith and ritual prayer and the study of the Koran are central.

THE WAR OVER CHURCH ARCHITECTURE

Recently there has been much disagreement about how Christian architecture should look. At the moment the controversy is hottest among Catholics and Episcopalians. Advocates of a new, simplified architecture, such as Richard Giles, complain that all too often "Christians are to be found worshipping in long Gothic tunnels, cowering beneath balconies and lurking behind pillars. . . . The buildings erected to serve them . . . now subdue them." They trace the change back to Pope Pius XII's 1947 encyclical letter, *Mediator Dei*, which declared that the arts should consider the needs of the Christian community more than the personal taste and judgment of the artist. This was sometimes taken to mean that, as Peter F. Anson puts it (adapting Le Corbusier's famous statement: "the house should be a machine for living," without achieving his laconic elegance), "Churches should be machines specially designed to make it easy for a number of people to worship in them."

Once Catholic services began to be conducted in the vernacular rather than in Latin, it seemed important that what went on at the altar should be fully audible and visible to everyone. One way of achieving this was to unite nave, chancel, and sanctuary in a single space and move the altar out toward the worshippers on what was now called a "bema platform." In many new Catholic and Episcopal churches this platform is surrounded on three sides with chairs or pews, so that during the service members of the congregation can see one another as well as the priest, and maintain awareness that they are members of what is now called a "church community."

Michael DeSanctis, whose book is largely addressed to Catholic congregations, believes that modern church buildings should strive for a noble simplicity and celebrate craftsmanship and artistic talent, while avoiding anything grandiose and lavishly ornamented. In America, he complains, it is difficult to express faith through architecture: too many people and organizations are involved in the planning of any new church, and controversy is often intense. Some Catholics, DeSanctis remarks, with the air of a weary survivor of many committee meetings, think that reforms in church design are part of a plan for the wholesale undoing of Catholic culture. It does not surprise him that many first-rate architectural firms now decline religious commissions.

Richard Giles, whose focus is on Protestant denominations, is considerably more militant. He points out that the church is now a center of activity all week long: "a home, a worship workshop, a source of inspiration, an oasis of prayer, a community college, an advice center, a typing pool, a soup kitchen and an operational HQ for a missionary organization." Giles recommends the construction of a large gathering place or narthex just inside the church entrance, equipped with chairs and tables, where members of the congregation can meet and mingle both before and after the service. He believes that churches can learn from the experience of supermarket chains, where goods that "have ceased to appeal to customers are promptly withdrawn." For him, and many modern architects, it is not always important that a building look like a church from outside. Indeed, some prefer that it fit into its surroundings in a more unobtrusive way, so that it will seem more "welcoming"—another favorite word—to potential members. The church, in other words, should consider itself as part of contemporary, even of commercial, culture.

For defenders of the traditional Gothic church, the important words are "inspiration" and "reverence." They are, if anything, even angrier than their opponents. Michael S. Rose's polemic against modernist church buildings is titled, uncompromisingly, *Ugly as Sin*.

Rose, who was trained as an architect, complains that these structures resemble conference centers and banks and nursing homes, and convey "a sense of ordinariness and cheapness." In his view, no one who enters them is awed or humbled. Imaginative modernist designs are even worse; as he remarks, "What passerby could look at Oakland's cathedral and think of anything but a giant clam?" Rose is appalled by the lack of religious paintings and sculptures in some new churches, and suggests that without Christian imagery they are like the temples to the goddess Reason established in the French Revolution. He even implies that those who want to alter or replace traditional churches are agents of the devil. "The fact is that ever since Christians have established holy places for sacred worship, there have been those who sought either to destroy these houses of God or to convert them for pagan or secular purpose."

These sentiments are not confined to architects and the clergy. In the town where I live there are two Catholic churches, one traditional and one very modern, and people who worship in each building have told me that nothing could induce them to set foot in the other. Meanwhile, all over the country, scornful epithets are hurled: modernist critics declare that traditional churches express "an extinct form of Christianity," while traditionalists claim that the new churches resemble drive-in hamburger restaurants or banks, and scornfully refer to them as "St. Wendy's" or "The First Presbyterian Trust."

Most established congregations do not have the resources to tear down a church that has served them for some time, whatever they may think of it. The solution has often been to remodel, and as a result there is now an ironic situation in which some designers are making traditional churches modern as fast as they can, while others are making modern churches traditional with equal speed. Modernists whitewash the walls and move the altar forward; they remove the reredos and put religious paintings and statues into storage. They may conceal the organ behind a screen, and replace windows that once portrayed saints and angels in lush late Victorian style with plain-colored or frosted white glass. Traditionalists reverse the process, raising the pulpit platform and moving it back, and restoring the paintings and sculptures and tapestries. Both sides often publish Before and After photographs in which, just as in homemaking magazines, the Before photo is ill-lit and dreary-looking, while the After glows with beauty and health.

THE MEGACHURCH

The newest development in American religious architecture of the late twentieth and early twenty-first century is the construction of vastly enlarged churches, with huge congregations (between 2,000 and 15,000) and charismatic preachers. In a way this expansion seems logical, even inevitable: a hundred years ago, Americans attended smaller schools, shopped in smaller stores, and worked for smaller organizations; today we are used to megaschools, megastores, and megacorporations. Megachurches are now appearing in increasing numbers, especially in the suburbs of large cities in the Midwest and South. They are the direct descendants of the nineteenth-century neo-medieval auditorium church, updated with lighting and sound systems, and with TV and video equipment. Their exteriors take many hybrid forms: they may look semi-Colonial or semi-Gothic or semi-modern—a few even resemble sports arenas. The Crystal Cathedral in Orange County, California, designed by Philip Johnson, might be a futuristic art museum.

Sometimes the general effect is still that of a medieval fortress, as with the Cathedral of Our Lady of the Angels, in Los Angeles. This is a looming edifice of tan concrete, with windows only at the very top of its walls. It has a huge separate bell tower and intimidating 25-ton bronze entrance gates. As with the neo-medievalist churches, its interior is more welcoming. The nave is 300 feet high and can seat 3,000 worshippers, and is decorated with somewhat over-the-top contemporary art: the altar, for example, is a six-ton slab of rose-colored marble supported by four big gold neo-Baroque angels.

Public reaction to the cathedral has been mixed: some visitors find it gloriously impressive, while others have compared it to the headquarters of an international corporation.

Like the neo-medieval churches of the nineteenth century, most megachurches provide comfortable seating and exciting entertainment. Video projection screens and microphones make it possible for huge congregations to see and hear everything in close-up: charismatic sermons, gospel choirs, organ music, Christian rock, and dramatic skits and films. Audience participation is frequent and often intense. Services in these churches can sometimes suggest a political convention, with banners, singing, chanting, cheering, and inspiring speeches. A visitor from outer space might well conclude that the God who lives in a megachurch is a politician, public official, or rock star, who loves loud music and big crowds. Also perhaps, considering the fortresslike exterior of many of these churches, he may have dangerous enemies.

The megachurch, like the neo-medieval church, is both inclusive and exclusive. It presents itself as a place of sanctuary from the world outside, which is represented by implication as alien and hazardous. At the same time, it extends a welcome to all, emphasizes the nuclear family, and encourages total involvement. There are groups for parishioners of both sexes and all ages, nursery schools, counseling services, medical clinics, and sports teams—and sometimes even coffee bars and gift shops. Brentwood Baptist Church in Houston incorporates a McDonald's restaurant, with golden arches and drive-in service; Southeast Christian Church in Louisville, Kentucky, is deliberately designed like a mall, with its auditorium in the place of the center court.

This last development has not escaped public notice. Several people I interviewed have compared the megachurch to the contemporary shopping mall, which also provides a safe, warm environment seven days a week, with multiple opportunities for social interaction, entertainment, and consumption—and is staffed with guards who can and do remove homeless people, political protesters, and unruly teenagers. In fact, both megachurch and mall, rather like America today, present themselves as welcoming to everyone, and at the same time work hard to exclude aliens, undesirables, and potential troublemakers.

CHAPTER 8

Houses of Art and Science

From a practical point of view, museums are unnecessary. Yet in 2012 there were more than 850 million visits to them in the United States. Many of us paid to get in, using money that we might otherwise have spent on food, shelter, or clothing. Why did we do this? Surely in part because we think that what these buildings contain is important. Today we live in a world of noisy confusion, in which we are constantly assaulted by exaggerated or false claims for the worth and meaning of objects. But museums, we seem to believe, preserve and display what is truly beautiful and admirable; they present the history of the world accurately, and explain history and science objectively.

Museums have always turned things that might in the past have had other uses—practical, social, or religious—into objects of contemplation and/or educational tools. Almost from the beginning, they have suggested that you could learn biblical and classical mythology from an art museum. Historical museums would reveal the impressive past of your country or city; natural history and science museums would acquaint you with great discoveries and great discoverers. Many authorities also asserted that the contemplation of great paintings and sculpture, historical documents and trophies, and scientific achievements would be morally and spiritually uplifting.

Whether the museum is seen as a schoolroom or a cathedral, from the start it has been essentially a container of valuable objects.

The design of the building always proclaimed this, and continues to do so. Basically there are three architectural types of museum: the classical temple, the palace or mansion, and what might be called the abstract box. Each has a different history, and each implies a different meaning for its contents and a different sort of experience for the visitor. All of the basic types have generated variants, and hybrid forms are sometimes created when an existing museum is remodeled or adds a new wing. Mansions may sprout porticos and pediments; temples, sometimes with the help of postmodern architects, may merge into abstract boxes.

THE TEMPLE

In the past, collections of significant objects were made by people who had the time, the money, and the energy to search out what seemed important or beautiful to them. Today most of these objects are in museums. The scientists who gathered rare plants and minerals often left them to public institutions, and the heirs of rich collectors donated works of art. The bulky buildings that were erected to shelter these treasures usually bore the name of a country, a state, a city, or a university. Such a museum was a manifestation of the power, wealth, and culture of this particular entity: it was a kind of secular church or temple, intended to arouse feelings of respect and awe.

In both Europe and America, many of these temple museums are neoclassical in style. Like many eighteenth- and nineteenth-century banks, universities, and government buildings, they resemble Greek or Roman temples and public buildings, with columns, pediments, porticos, domes, vaults, arches, and often a central sacred space or rotunda. Many of them are laterally symmetrical and have a classical rectangular floor plan in which long hallways extend in two or more directions from the entrance, with a series of interconnected galleries on one or both sides. Both the buildings themselves and the interior spaces are usually very large. They not only can accommodate many people; they can also make these people feel small and insignificant: the great height of the ceilings and doorways especially has this effect.

Typically, these neoclassical museums are separated from nearby commercial structures; they are well landscaped and often located in or near a park. Like Greek and Roman temples, they are usually reached by a broad flight of steps; lowly visitors must climb to enter the high and holy place. The Philadelphia Museum of Art, for instance, sits high above the city and is fronted by three almost ridiculously long flights of steps.

Public art museums tend to be relatively empty of furniture. The floors and windows are usually bare, and decorative household objects are isolated in glass cases. Like the dinosaurs and bears and exotic birds of the natural history museum, or the early steam engines and telescopes of the science museum, they are specimens. They are not meant to compete with the paintings and sculpture—or with what from the nineteenth century on was increasingly seen as the high educational, moral, and aesthetic purpose of the institution.

In a big public museum it was not important that visitors should be able to look out; indeed, it was not desirable, since this might distract them from the exhibits. The usual solution, as in many classical temples and Christian churches, was to let light and air in from high windows, skylights, and domes: illumination came from above both actually and spiritually. Once electrical light and air-conditioning were available, many temple museums blocked off these windows.

Visitors to temple museums are often encouraged to have what might be called a spiritual experience: to admire and feel awe. The great halls of natural history museums may feature the immense skeletons of dinosaurs or a giant floating stuffed whale; a science museum will display a rocket ship or a beautifully preserved antique railroad engine. In some art museums certain galleries have an ecclesiastical atmosphere, particularly when the paintings and sculptures displayed are of religious subjects and were originally created to hang in churches or assist devotion at home. At the Cloisters in New York, not only the name of the place but its pale walls, dark gray stone moldings and floors, and high barrel-vaulted ceilings strongly suggest that you are in a monastery.

Great works of art, even when their subjects are not religious, have always had a kind of spiritual aura. In the nineteenth century it was believed that exposure to such art was spiritually uplifting; the committee involved in the establishment of London's National Gallery thought "that the very sight of art could improve the morals and deportment of even the lowest social ranks." Today the visitor to a neoclassical public museum is still encouraged and even expected to feel awe in the presence of great art. The rooms in which it is displayed are huge, the lighting dramatic, the walls often hung with thick velvet or brocade, and the frames and pedestals rich with gold or marble—everything conspires to announce that these pictures and sculptures are, in a sense, sacred.

The work of certain modern painters such as Marc Chagall and Mark Rothko has also sometimes been presented as religious art. The huge murals by Chagall at the Metropolitan Opera House in New York are meant to inspire us, though the god they celebrate is music. The Rothko Chapel in Houston, opened in 1971, is a kind of shadowy space lit from above and containing fourteen of Rothko's last paintings. It is described on its website as "a place alive with religious ceremonies of all kinds." Weddings and memorial services are held there, as well as lectures on spiritual and social issues, and there are often people sitting on its benches in silent contemplation or meditation.

Science museums, too, may be deliberately designed to induce feelings of awe. Ceilings are high, galleries often immense. Huge sharks and luminous tropical fish swim in giant tanks, among which visitors walk in near darkness. Dramatic lighting, wall-sized video displays, and impressive music suggest the importance of the latest developments in physics, genetics, electronics, medicine, and astronomy. Meanwhile history museums have begun to reproduce the sounds and sights of the past dramatically through the use of the most up-to-date design and video techniques.

Even if they are not believers, many people visit a great museum in the same spirit in which they might attend church. We expect to be not only pleased and entertained, but also enlightened and uplifted. Though often a little weary from the efforts of the pilgrimage—bad weather, crowded trains or buses, climbing so many stairs and walking so far—we end up with a sense of virtue and moral achievement.

Long after they are purchased, objects from a museum shop often retain a special aura. A calendar or note card with a famous painting or historical poster on it seems more valuable than one with an anonymous design; scarves and teapots and jewelry have extra aesthetic prestige when they are museum reproductions. It is probably far-fetched to suggest that eating a sandwich in a museum restaurant is a form of communion, but as we pay our entrance fees we may sometimes have the feeling that we are dropping coins in a collection plate, and contributing to the preservations of the holy relics of art and science and national history.

THE MANSION

The palace or mansion museum is descended from the great royal and aristocratic collections of Europe, and in fact some European art museums were originally palaces—most notably the Louvre, which after the French Revolution was taken over by the Republican government and later used to house Napoleon's looted treasures. Most of the mansion museums that survive today were once the homes of rich and/or titled collectors, including kings and queens. Traditionally, their military, political, or financial victories were marked by the accumulation of trophies, which had been seized from their original owners and gathered in the dwellings of the victors.

As the art historian Carol Duncan remarks, the princely galleries of the sixteenth, seventeenth, and eighteenth centuries were designed "to dazzle and overwhelm both foreign visitors and local

dignitaries with the magnificence, luxury, and might of the sover-
eign, and, often—through special iconographies—the rightness or
legitimacy of his rule." This was also true, on a smaller scale, of the
homes of later American and European aristocrats and self-made
millionaires.

Most of the palaces and mansions that have become art museums still function as monuments to the wealth and taste (sometimes
good, sometimes not so good) of their original owners. They typically bear the names of their founders, and are often preserved in a
semblance of their former condition. To visit these museums is, as
many brochures boast, to step back into the past—not so much the
period of the art they contains, as the lifetime of their former owners. At the Gardner Museum in Boston, the three-story courtyard is
always filled with plants and flowers, and in April the balconies are
hung with eight-foot waterfalls of nasturtiums in honor of Isabella
Stewart Gardner's birthday.

The palace or mansion museum was originally a dwelling, and
its inhabitants needed light and air and windows that opened. Today
these windows may be sealed, and the galleries air-conditioned and
artificially lit, but they still often preserve the appearance of a luxurious private house, with furniture and draperies and carpets that
are either genuine or period reproductions. Usually there are courtyards and gardens to match. Mansion museums may have some of
the qualities of a mausoleum; indeed, in a few cases, as in London's
Dulwich Picture Gallery and the Sterling and Francine Clark Art Institute in Williamstown, Massachusetts, the donors are actually buried on the premises. Visiting these buildings, it is possible to see the
gilt chairs and tables, the gold-rimmed plates and gold-embroidered
tapestries—and even the paintings and sculptures—as the equivalent
of Egyptian or Anglo-Saxon grave goods chosen to accompany their
former owners on the voyage to another world.

In a way, of course, all museums are mausoleums, the final resting
places of things. But just as men and women may live relatively pri-

vate lives, but have funerals and memorials attended by multitudes, so works of art originally meant to be seen by a privileged few are now viewed by thousands. Yet a faint whisper of death and loss may still hang over them: to some visitors the huge and beautiful seasonal floral displays in many mansion museums suggest funeral tributes.

The sense of the past is even more striking in those great country houses that are open to the public on limited days. Sometimes rooms are arranged to suggest that the owner has just left and will soon return. The table in the grand dining room is set with antique china and silver and decorated with fresh flowers; open books and half-finished embroideries lie on the brocade sofas in the drawing room; pens and paper are ready on the tooled leather desk in the library. Such historical stage settings are also common in the houses of famous departed authors, artists, politicians, and entertainers that have been preserved as museums and shrines.

Some of the earliest museums were essentially undifferentiated assemblages of the rare and the unusual, both artistic and scientific. The Ashmolean in Oxford, for example, was built from 1678 to 1683 to house the miscellaneous collections that Elias Ashmole had donated to the University. "Cabinets of curiosities," like Charles Willson Peale's famous museum in eighteenth-century Philadelphia, might include not only paintings and sculpture, but also fossils, dinosaur bones, stuffed birds and alligators, lumps of rock crystal, meteorites, ancient musical instruments, and human or animal fetuses preserved in glass jars. Even today many mansion museums contain more furniture and bric-a-brac than paintings. Gold and silver and bronze, rare woods and ivories, colored glass, and semiprecious stones are shaped into statues and clocks and lamps and tableware—some of it remarkably ugly by modern standards. These collections are meant to impress us by their rarity and their obvious expense of manufacture. Like museums devoted to the decorative arts—for example, London's Victoria and Albert Museum—they have always had a special message for the visitor: that expenditure of time, money, and craftsmanship on amazingly expensive household goods is a worthy occupation, and one that should be honored.

Visitors to mansion museums may feel admiration, curiosity, envy, or any combination of these emotions. The setup of the rooms and the detailed information provided by guidebooks also encourage them in the fantasy that they have just arrived for a grand reception, ball, or dinner party, and that any moment now the host and hostess will sweep into the room to welcome them. Or, rather than thinking of themselves as honored visitors, they may imagine that they are the owners of these mansions.

The staffs of the mansion museum, however, tend to get in the way of these fantasies. Anyone who has been shown over a famous house will have noticed the proprietary attitude of the guides, who speak familiarly of the past or present owners, while warning you not to touch anything or go up the wrong staircase. The size and layout of the buildings may also be intimidating. Mansion museums often have huge rooms, long galleries, and steep flights of steps to the main entrance—though not usually as many steps as most temple museums: aristocrats are above the multitude, but not as far above them as gods. Also, though their publicity declares that these places are now open to everyone, the location of many big country houses, and their generally high entrance fees, tend to limit visitors to people who have a car and some excess income.

Many public and private museums have "period rooms" that resemble stage sets for a historical play or film. These rooms define us as outsiders: we may look into them, but are prevented from entering by metal railings or velvet ropes. The main galleries often also contain elegantly upholstered and cushioned thronelike chairs in which we are not allowed to sit. Instead, like parishioners in church or commoners in an aristocrat's reception room, we must stand or use a hard wooden bench.

• • •

As the popularity of the mansion museum demonstrates, the experience of stepping back into the past is seductive. But from the point of view of a curator, the dead hand of the donor may be very heavy. For one thing, the endowment often stipulates that nothing in the building can be changed or moved. Second-rate or even possibly fake art must remain on the wall, often in a prominent location, while great pictures are hung in dark corners. The mansion may also be relatively inaccessible to most members of the public, or very seldom open. As time passes, these problems can sometimes be solved, but the legal process is usually long and difficult, as in the recent case of the Barnes Foundation near Philadelphia.

The desire of wealthy people to preserve their collections, even when they have been willed to a public museum, can sometimes lead to strangely anachronistic experiences. The Lehman Wing at New York's Metropolitan Museum, for instance, looks both ultramodern and antiquated. Under a high modern ceiling, it contains exact reproductions of seven rooms from Robert Lehman's father's mansion on Fifty-Fourth Street. In the brochure they are referred to as period rooms—although, as Carol Duncan remarks, "it is doubtful that they represent any period other than late American robber baron." To some the Lehman Wing suggests a modernized Egyptian tomb, with a glass pyramid top and most of its internal space underground. According to Duncan it "is related to past structures in which the dead eternally receive the living and impress upon them their greatness," and in fact "the security guards who work this part of the building joke that Robert Lehman is buried somewhere under the floor."

Taste in the decorative arts, even more than taste in the fine arts, is apt to change radically over time. Photographs of the great private collections of the Victorian age may strike us today as cluttered or even vulgar. Yet the owners' admiration of and identification with these possessions was complete and even passionate. This phenomenon is brilliantly portrayed by Henry James in *The Spoils of Poynton* (1897). The country house of the title is presented by its owner,

Mrs. Gareth, as perfection. Her taste is typical of her time: she owns French eighteenth-century furniture, Venetian velvets, cases of enamels, and Oriental china. According to Mrs. Gareth, for her and her late husband these things "were our religion, they were our life, they were *us*!" It is not clear whether James shares Mrs. Gareth's admiration for these particular objects, though he clearly believes that identification with them is unwise and may even be somewhat insane. He remarks that Mrs. Gareth has a "strange, almost maniacal disposition to thrust in everywhere the question of 'things,' to read all behavior in the light of some fancied relation to them."

To a reader brought up in a twentieth-century home, *The Spoils of Poynton* may suggest not beauty and perfection, but clutter and pretension. We might prefer the house that Mrs. Gareth, shuddering with dismay, eventually has to move into, with its dark gray wallpaper sprigged with silver flowers (she despises wallpaper) and its white pots of geraniums on the terrace (she thinks them horribly ugly). In the same way, we may feel more at home in a simple, unadorned contemporary art gallery than in a mansion museum

THE ABSTRACT BOX

In the 1930s a new form of museum began to appear: a purpose-built, modernist (and later, postmodernist) structure of glass, steel, and concrete that eventually took many, sometimes fantastic forms. Inside, the new museum was an assemblage of what have been described as white cube galleries: "ideal spaces that, more than any single picture, may be the archetypal image of twentieth century art." So dominant was this new ideal that some galleries in older museums were converted into white cubes in order to display modern art.

The white cube gallery appeared along with several new developments in the fine arts, including a move toward greater and greater abstraction, and an increase in the size of both paintings and sculpture. It was accompanied by an increased emphasis on the artistic importance of the museum building itself, sometimes to the extent that architecture took precedence over the displays inside. The renovated and expanded Museum of Modern Art in New York, which reopened in 2008, is, technically speaking, a complicated collection of white boxes. At first it was greeted with almost effusive praise, but later comments were more critical. Some visitors missed the historical plan supported by Alfred H. Barr Jr., the director of MoMA from 1929 to 1967. Under his leadership, as James Hall comments, "there was only really one path through the collection, and Barr even placed a curtain over a fire exit to prevent viewers slipping sideways into another gallery." In the new MoMA most of the galleries have many alternative entrances. "The presence of all these apertures," Hall says, ". . . means that despite all the extra floor space hardly any more work can be shown. More space is wasted by the gargantuan size of the contemporary galleries, and by the atrium, where the drama of its surging verticality is muffled by the seemingly random intrusions of ungainly apertures and ceiling slabs."

The white cube gallery placed art in what was at first seen as a pure, neutral space, hospitable to a wide variety of work; but in fact it seems to have had a by no means neutral effect. This sort of interior space—big, brightly lit, uncluttered—favors large-scale works, simple shapes, and bright, intense colors. It does not usually suit older paintings, many of which were created for smaller, dimmer rooms. In a white box a Caravaggio or a Rembrandt can drown in the shine of its own varnish; even some more recent masterpieces, like those of Vuillard or Courbet, may look small and muddy.

As the big white box became standard gallery space, the typical artist's studio often also became a big white box. (Famous photographs and paintings of earlier studios, for instance those of Manet and Matisse, now surprise us by their relative darkness and clutter: we are used to seeing artists at work in large, bright, high-ceilinged lofts.) And as the gallery and the studio changed, art began to change. Consciously or unconsciously, many artists altered the scale and tone of their work, producing paintings that need and assume big, empty, white-walled spaces. A de Kooning or a Pollock, for instance, would seem strident and oversized in the sort of rooms that first held paintings by Vermeer or Whistler. Before 1900, sculpture was able to stand out in a gaslit Victorian gallery or private home only if it was very light; as a result, white marble or plaster was the favored medium. A contemporary all-white sculpture, however, may be difficult to see in a white-box gallery, though it still displays well outdoors in a garden.

Many museums built after the opening of New York's MoMA in 1938 are unadorned rectangular constructions of steel, glass, and concrete. Their entrances tend to be at ground level, or raised only by a few broad steps or a gradual ramp. These museums are easy of access, like stores; and in fact they sometimes resemble large, expensive stores, with their display windows, ranks of glass doors, and information and sales counters just inside. Some modern American museums also feature their names in large letters near the entrance, like big-box stores. They contain supersized shops that sell not only books and postcards and reproductions from the collection, but also a wide range of expensive household items that are promoted as "design objects." (Some contemporary upmarket stores, as if in reciprocity, now look like museums, with goods displayed as if they were unique works of art—and often with prices to match.)

Staff and trustees have protested that the commercialization of the museum has been necessary to save it. Today national, state, and local governments give less support, and institutions must find other sources of income if they are to survive. It is also true that many visitors today like to shop and eat as well as look at things. Assuming, of course, that they can afford it. The public museums of the nineteenth and early twentieth century often charged little or no admission, in line with their stated purpose of educating the public and bringing beauty and spiritual improvement into the lives of everyone. Even when they did charge there were usually many free days and evenings. Over time, however, entrance fees have risen, and the number of free hours has fallen. Without officially announcing it, some museums now seem to declare that they welcome only well-to-do visitors, and that even looking at art is or should be expensive.

BEYOND THE ABSTRACT BOX

Early in the history of the modernist museum, architects began to deviate from the standard box shape. The first and most famous experiment along these lines was probably Frank Lloyd Wright's Guggenheim Museum, which opened in 1959. Most people agree that the building looks great from the outside; but the main exhibition space, a huge spiral ramp open to an interior courtyard, has provoked criticism. Because the floor and the ceiling slope continually, looking down over the railing can be dizzying, and pictures can seem to be hung crookedly: a Mondrian show actually made some viewers I know nauseous. Nonrectangular and three-dimensional art works well in a space like this: some say that the best show they ever saw at the Guggenheim was of motorcycles—all placed facing up the ramp, as if about to take off into outer space.

In some ways the Guggenheim had few successors. Human beings are used to horizontal floors and vertical walls; we feel uneasy or even ill in a funhouse environment of tilted and skewed surfaces. As a result, even the most striking recent examples of museum design have confined their innovations to the exterior of the building. Within, whether the rooms are cubes, trapezoids, or cylinders, level floors and vertical walls are standard. Over the last thirty or forty years, architects have managed to create many original and striking museum buildings. They are full of soaring ramps and staircases, ingeniously shaped atriums, magnificently swooping roofs and walls. Yet all this frozen music, as Friedrich von Schelling called it, can take up so much space that there is not enough room for the art. Recently, critics have begun to notice this, but, as far as I know, no architect has ever complained that his or her museum building overshadows its contents.

Theoretically, galleries in a modern museum should be empty of anything that could distract from the art, and museum interiors are often photographed without visitors. But at most major shows the rooms are full of people, sometimes so many that it is almost impossible to see the exhibits, especially if you are below average height. (Of course, the people may be as interesting to some visitors as the Cézannes or the antique cars: current guides to meeting a romantic partner often recommend the museum as a happy hunting ground.)

One interesting feature of the new type of display space, as Brian O'Doherty points out, is the disappearance of the ceiling as a meaningful part of the building. He remarks that "in the history of indoor looking up, we rank low. Other ages put plenty up there to look at.... The Renaissance ceiling locked its painted figures into geometric cells. The Baroque ceiling . . . is really an arch, a dome, a sky, a vortex of swirling figures until they vanish through a celestial hole, . . . or it is a luxurious piece of hand-tooled furniture, stamped, gilded, an album for the family escutcheon. The Rococo ceiling is as embroidered as underwear. . . . The Georgian ceiling looks like a white carpet, . . . [with a] central rose, dimpled with shadow, from which descends the opulent chandelier." Examples of all these kinds of ceilings, including some masterpieces of the genre by Tiepolo, can still be seen, but seldom in anything built after 1920. As O'Doherty puts it, "Modern architecture simply ran the blank wall into the blank ceiling and lowered the lid."

As the abstract box museum expanded, it was also slowly becoming obsolete, as artists began to create work that was too large even for these spaces. Museum directors hastened to keep up: they erected new buildings to contain the minimalist but huge art works of the 1970s and 1980s, or adapted existing spaces—Tate Modern remodeled a former power plant, and the Dia Art Foundation took over a paper-box factory up the Hudson River, creating enormous rooms that could accommodate work by artists like Louise Bourgeois, Richard Serra, and John Chamberlain.

It is not all that much fun these days to be a museum director or curator. Government support is shrinking, making it necessary to court institutional and commercial donors, and the problems of display have been increased by new kinds of art that are difficult or impossible to exhibit. Visitors object to what they consider pornographic or violent or blasphemous subjects; politicians threaten to close exhibitions and/or withdraw funds. Meanwhile, artists are creating work that is too large even for the biggest indoor spaces, and may involve the alteration of large areas of the natural world. Video art and computer art are expensive and complicated to display, earth art messes up the galleries, and performance art vanishes completely at the end of the show.

LOOK AT THIS!

The architecture of a museum can suggest that we are having an educational, spiritual, or aesthetic experience, visiting a rich, powerful person, or going to a big store. But the way the objects are displayed inside may have more complex effects. Some curators tend to think of themselves as artists, and now that much of contemporary art is assemblage it is possible to see the logic of this belief. Silently and subtly, every museum display re-creates the world; it tells us what art and history and science are, and what is worthy of our attention. It does this both by selection and by arrangement. Most established public museums, and many private ones, own more objects than they can show at one time. If something has not only been collected and preserved, but is on permanent display, the implication is that it must be valuable.

Curators know how to make things look important. For one thing, any object that is isolated from other objects will draw attention, and the more empty space there is around it, the more attention it will draw. Theatre and opera directors follow the same strategy: the star stands alone, spotlit, while the chorus is bunched together under a dimmer light. In the museums of the eighteenth and nineteenth century, when the emphasis was on quantity as well as quality, the trophies of conquest and purchasing power were often crowded together; cases of birds and butterflies and minerals were jammed full, and paintings hung from floor to ceiling so that you could hardly see the wall behind them. Today pictures are usually displayed at eye level in a single row, with considerable space between them, making galleries of realistic painting into collections of imaginary windows, each revealing a different dramatic scene or figure.

In large public art museums the emphasis is usually on quality, and especially on the masterpiece. A famous picture sometimes has a whole wall to itself: in the Louvre the *Mona Lisa*, a relatively small portrait, is alone in its room. It is individually lit and further glorified (and, of course, protected) by bulletproof glass and a waist-high barrier. There are almost always crowds in front of it.

Most objects today must share space, but even then central placement will make visitors pay more attention. Studies have shown that as people move through a gallery, they look longer at things in the middle of a wall and spend less time on those in the corners. Unconsciously, they have received the message that these paintings or scientific displays are less significant. The placement of benches also encourages weary visitors to gaze for longer periods at whatever is directly in front of them. If there are benches, that is. In the past, most galleries contained one or more, and often they were comfortably padded. Today, as John Walsh, the former director of the Getty Museum, has pointed out, "seats are absent, or . . . are already sat on by the competition. What can we conclude from this?" There are two obvious answers: first, that we are supposed to move along rapidly, to glance at rather than study the works displayed; second, that we don't deserve to sit down.

Recent studies have shown that objects more than six or seven feet above the floor often go unnoticed, because people tend not to look up. Eighteenth- and nineteenth-century artists already knew this: they recognized that the most prestigious position was at eye level, and protested when their works had been "skied," or relegated to the top row, which in a grand gallery might be fifteen or twenty feet up. The yearly summer show of the Royal Academy in London is still hung on these principles, and artists still complain when their paintings are near the ceiling—or, almost as bad, right down by the floor.

In general, large objects and large paintings (like large houses and large cars and large people) attract more attention than small ones: psychologists report that when visitors enter a gallery they look first at the biggest exhibits. But when a valued object is small it can be made to look more important. Central placement and surrounding space will help, but there are other methods, such as elaborate cases and labels, and the inclusion of the work on an audio tour. Perhaps the most dramatic way of calling attention to an object, however, is through lighting. Meteorites and precious stones are illuminated in glass cases, and famous paintings sometimes have individual spotlights; glare and shadows (including the shadows of their own frames) fall on lesser works. Exhibitions of primitive or decorative art today often feature rooms painted black or some other dark color, with lights focused on isolated examples of sculpture, pottery, weapons, or textiles, as Emma Barker puts it, "so that they seem to glow of their own accord, endowing them with an air of mystery and preciousness."

In the past, the interior walls of most museums were seldom blank and white. Instead they often had dark or painted wainscoting, and their upper portions were covered with patterned silk, damask, brocade, or expensive wallpaper. In many neoclassical public museums today, the walls of galleries containing Renaissance, Baroque, and Romantic paintings are still hung with rich fabric, often red or gold—red for attention, gold for monetary worth—or painted in strong dark colors. Rooms devoted to Impressionist art, if not white, tend to be pale blue, green, or umber. Science museums, by contrast, usually prefer walls in black, white, and subtle shades of gray.

When artworks were hung one above the other or crowded close together, they had a lot to compete with. Presentation was important: for centuries almost every sculpture had its pedestal, and every picture its frame. A marble sculpture elevated well above eye level makes us look up, implicitly at something greater than us, calling perhaps on the experience of early childhood, when most people were taller than we were. A lower pedestal puts us on the same level as the work of art, while one on which we look down invites sympathy and pity: sculptures of sleeping children and dying saints are usually lower than those of kings and generals and gods.

A frame can not only separate each picture from its neighbors, but also advertise its individual importance. Medieval and Renaissance frames were often fairly simple constructions of dark wood, not always distinguishable from the paneled walls on which they might be hung. In the seventeenth century, however, frames began to swell and elaborate themselves in ruffles and ribbons of gold and plaster. Eventually they might include vines, flowers, fruit, and musical instruments, and the heads and bodies of cupids and satyrs; and in the so-called "trophy frame," game animals and weapons of war. A frame like this called attention to whatever it surrounded, even on a crowded wall, and proclaimed that the work was expensive and important.

In the late nineteenth century, when paintings became smaller and simpler, these elaborate gold frames tended to upstage the works they enclosed and make them look relatively unimpressive, especially when they were small. In reaction, artists like Whistler, Degas, and Gauguin often designed their own frames, fitting them to the subject and mood of the work. Later, in the white box gallery, when paintings were no longer threatened by busy backgrounds and encroaching neighbors, big, expensive frames became superfluous. But conventions in display change slowly, and in both public and private museums many Impressionist and modern paintings still have elaborate, stylistically inappropriate gold frames, and small sculptures are elevated on tall pedestals. The results are unfortunate: a Degas dancer in bronze on a marble plinth many times her size resembles a child's toy, and the beautiful little Rembrandt drawing seems dim and diminished inside its huge mat and gilt frame.

Today the competition for attention and wall space continues, intensified since the mid-twentieth century by an increase in the average size of artworks. Artists have complained about this, pointing out that, just as a parking lot can accommodate fewer trucks than it can bicycles, so when paintings and sculptures become the size of trucks, fewer artists can share in the available fame and fortune. Science museums, too, are often overwhelmed by the sheer size of telescopes and turbines, which prevents more than a few examples being shown at once.

FASHION AND FAME

Techniques of display tell us not only which works of art are important, but also how to think about them. In the eighteenth century, paintings were often hung according to subject, without regard for their date or national origin. But in the new public museums of the nineteenth and early twentieth centuries, the arrangement of the galleries was almost always on historical principles, by school and by country. As you walked through the building from one numbered room to the next you would involuntarily learn that art began in ancient Egypt, Greece, and Rome, fell into decline in the Middle Ages, was revived and became glorious in the Renaissance, and culminated in the masters of the recent past, who often were citizens of the country where the museum was located.

Many art museums and exhibitions are still arranged historically, but not all. When the Tate Modern organized some galleries by subject, public reaction was mixed. Some visitors were thrilled to see a room full of landscapes from widely different countries and periods; others preferred the familiar plan. As a compromise, some museums now have websites that allow you to view either all the paintings by a single artist (including those currently in storage), all those from a single period or school or country, or, for instance, every painting or sculpture of a cat in their collection.

Art is eternal, but taste changes. Henry James's *The American* (1877) opens with his hero, Christopher Newman, sitting in a gallery of the Louvre in rapt contemplation of Murillo's *Ascension of the*

Virgin, which, according to guidebooks of the time, was a great masterpiece. To modern viewers this painting—which shows the Virgin Mary gazing upward as she floats away above the heads of a group of men—may seem sentimental or melodramatic, or both. (The choice of this particular work may have been symbolic rather than aesthetic on James's part, since at the end of the novel the woman Newman loves retreats from him into a convent.)

In the contemporary world almost no installation is permanent. Fashions change, causing the circulation of work from the darkest corners of the museum basement to the full glare of the principal galleries and back again. In the nineteenth century people lined up to see huge contemporary panoramas like William Powell Frith's *The Derby Day* (1858) and Thomas Cole's *The Course of Empire* (1833–36) and *The Voyage of Life* (1840). Today, French Impressionism takes up the most prestigious space. In museums of contemporary art there were once mobs of brown and gray Cubist paintings; later the emphasis was on politically and socially conscious work, and much more space was devoted to members of the Ashcan School and artists like Jack Levine and Ben Shahn.

Paintings and sculpture may also vanish because they are away on loan, or have been "deaccessioned"—that is, sold. Or they may have turned out to be fakes, like the larger-than-life-size Etruscan warrior who used to dominate the south end of the Metropolitan Museum's Great Hall. Though it is now known to have been a forgery, I still miss it. Art may also be downgraded if it is later judged to be by the students of some famous painter rather than the master himself. After the Rembrandt Research Project cast doubt on the authenticity of certain paintings—including the beloved *Polish Rider*—museums revised their labels or moved works into storage.

The public has always been silently told what to admire through the amount of space allocated to any particular subject. In the eighteenth and early nineteenth century, there was a hierarchy: at the top of the list was the large dramatic portrayal of a violent historical, mythological, or religious scene, and huge paintings crowded with figures in classical costume were greatly admired. Portraits, especially full-length portraits of rich or famous people, came next, followed by landscapes and genre pictures (scenes from the private lives of the nonrich or nonfamous), and still-life was last. The modern movement upset or even reversed the hierarchy. As a result, the basements of many older museums are now crowded with immense panoramas full of writhing seminaked bodies and melodramatic weather, while relatively small paintings of a few pieces of fruit are installed in places of honor.

Economic necessity, as well as changes in taste, can affect what is on view. Now and then a major museum, usually with the financial help of a donor, mounts a big exhibition of the work of some fashion designer, or a collection of expensive automobiles, giving these products some of the status of fine art. Some critics object, suggesting that even if these shows are a success, the lines between art and merchandise have been blurred—though, after all, all art is, or once was, merchandise.

The paintings in a museum collection can suggest to us what was important in the world in which they were made, as well as what is valued today. Eighteenth-century British painting implicitly celebrated peaceful rural scenes full of fat cows and sheep; in the Romantic movement raging tempests and torrents and precipitous cliffs were seen as sublime. The Impressionists portrayed the charm of gardens, domestic life, and bourgeois entertainments: the theatre, the ballet, the picnic, and the racetrack. In the twentieth century, museum visitors were encouraged to find beauty and interest in industrial landscapes, tattered posters on a wall, and commercial signs and packaging.

The contents of a museum can please or annoy people. Feminists complain that too many paintings are of naked or nearly naked women presented as mindless sex objects; members of nonwhite ethnic groups become indignant at the lack of art by African-Americans,

Asians, or Latinos. Individual visitors may also be affected personally. If you are somewhat overweight, a room full of Rubenses or Renoirs may reassure you as to your essential attractiveness, while Modigliani's slim, pale models will cast you into gloom. Mothers of female infants have told me that they became depressed by the abundance of religious paintings featuring a woman and her male baby, but cheered up by Mary Cassatt's portraits of mothers with little girls. Even if we struggle against it, we cannot help but be influenced by what we see presented as worthy of our attention—as beautiful and admirable and natural.

HISTORY AND SCIENCE

In historical museums things often alter suddenly without any explanation. Shifts in political regime have caused the reshuffling and relabeling of exhibits, and sometimes the complete disappearance of formerly admired leaders and events. Panoramas of battles have been replaced by dioramas of village life; paintings of statesmen and writers and artists have been whisked on and off the walls of national portrait galleries as their public reputation rose and fell. Occasionally, too, a major donor has inspired an entire show featuring the life and work of his or her well-known ancestor.

In museums of science, changes may also be dramatic. For years new discoveries in physics, chemistry, medicine, electronics, and astronomy have demanded (or, some would say, usurped) more space, and in some cases led to the creation of separate museums concentrating on industrial design, photography, electronics, space travel, and computer science. Architecturally, these buildings often resemble laboratories and factories, with their stark rectangular lines and predominance of metal and glass.

In many cases, the relation of museumgoers to scientific exhibits has changed. Once, for instance, natural history museums featured dioramas of skillfully embalmed wild animals and birds in a "natural" habitat backed by real dried grass and dead tree trunks and realistic panoramas of their natural habitat. Visitors to these displays were essentially spectators, able to look but not to touch. Now interactive electronic presentations encourage us to help locate and save endangered species, and we are cautioned not to be destroyers rather than preservers of nature.

Lately the Darwinian theory of evolution—which for more than a hundred years inspired the creation of innumerable wall diagrams of a great tree with worms and bugs gathered at its roots and a man standing triumphant on the top branch—has been widely challenged. In the United States there are now thirteen institutions that promote the history of the earth outlined in the Old Testament, upholding what its proponents call "intelligent design." Perhaps the best known of these organizations is the Creation Museum in Petersburg, Kentucky, which, according to its website,

> brings the pages of the Bible to life, casting its characters and animals in dynamic form and placing them in familiar settings. Adam and Eve live in the Garden of Eden. Children play and dinosaurs roam near Eden's Rivers. The serpent coils cunningly in the Tree of the Knowledge of Good and Evil. Majestic murals, great masterpieces brimming with pulsating colors and details, provide a backdrop for many of the settings.

In Washington State, the "Mount St. Helens Creation Information Center" offers a display that "presents powerful evidence for Noah's Flood." Thousands of tourists have already visited such museums. Whether they will survive and continue to prosper in the future is anyone's guess, but we should remember that the Cardiff Giant, a fake "petrified man" made of gypsum and first exhibited in 1869, is still on view in Cooperstown, New York.

CHAPTER 9

Houses of Learning I: Grade Schools

As the cliché suggests when someone is described as the "product" of a certain school or college, every educational institution, from a toddlers' playgroup to graduate school, is a kind of factory. The building may resemble a well-landscaped country mansion or a run-down warehouse, but its function is the same. The raw materials (students) enter it and most of the time they are somehow transformed into the type of person conventionally associated with the institution.

In any factory both the employees and the physical plant are necessary to this process. Much has been written about the effect on students of different kinds of teachers and lesson plans, less about the influence of the school building itself. Recently, however, two British experts on school design, Catherine Burke and Ian Grosvenor, have looked at the educational factory structure as an active agent. In their study, titled simply *School*, they suggest that continually, though silently, a school building tells students who they are and how they should think about the world. It can help to manufacture rote obedience or independent activity; it can create high self-confidence or low self-esteem.

Of course there are wide variations within the educational factory system, visible both in America and in Europe, which is the main focus of Burke and Grosvenor's book. The lively, friendly, but determined three-year-old is a rather different product from the agreeable but politely ambitious prep school graduate. They may, however, be the same person, and the lessons learned in nursery school may be reinforced (or undermined) years later in a much bigger building. As a graduate student once said to me, describing his middle school: "All the windows were filthy, paint and plaster were scabbing off the walls in the cafeteria, and the playground was full of trash. The place looked like hell, and it made me feel like hell."

Teachers and staff also receive information from the buildings they work in. Dreary, overcrowded classrooms and cheap, shabby furniture and equipment, especially when combined with low salaries, tell adults as well as children that they are not worth very much. At the other end of the scale, the temporary increase in visible self-satisfaction, sometimes rising to smugness, in someone who has just moved into a large, thickly carpeted, oak-paneled study in an expensive prep school or college is often very striking.

PRESCHOOLS

For small children, the effects of school design may be huge and long-lasting. Any day-care center or nursery school gives toddlers a silent but dramatic message. Good, sturdy outdoor play equipment, bright, comfortable rooms, and lots of interesting toys not only make them happy but also tell them that they deserve the best. The treeless, nearly grassless backyard of the low-cost child-care facility, with its chipped swing set and cracked plastic pool, its stained and broken toys, delivers the opposite message, one that even the kindest and most skillful teacher cannot totally contradict. The building in which such a day-care center is located is also apt to have ill-lit, drab rooms, windows too high for small children to see out of, and door handles that they cannot reach, increasing their sense of imprisonment and disempowerment.

A good nursery school encourages children to think of themselves as unique and valuable individuals by providing them with cubbyholes marked with their names and walls decorated with their own artwork. (The effect may be even stronger for children who at home must share a room with other people.) It also gives them a wide choice of things to do: there are places for building with blocks, painting, playing house, and making music, and there are quiet corners for resting or looking at books. Outside there is room for running around wildly, swinging, climbing, or digging in a sandbox.

In a crowded low-budget day-care center there is usually no space or equipment for more than a few activities, and when the kids get bored the teacher is often tempted to turn on the Cartoon Network or pop in a DVD. As a result, children at the high-end nursery school learn that the world is full of new and interesting things to do, while those at the low-end center learn to watch television whenever they are bored or frustrated.

WHAT PUBLIC SCHOOLS SAY

Through architecture, schools can teach students (and possibly some adults, too) how to think about race and class. In the South, before the civil rights movement, the contrast between large, well-maintained public schools for whites and small, dilapidated, crowded schools for blacks quietly informed African-Americans that they were worth less. Even today, almost everywhere in the United States, schools in expensive suburbs are big, handsome, and well kept, in contrast to the run-down old buildings common in run-down urban areas. And, in spite of decades of legal and social effort, the students in these poor school buildings are often poor and either black or Latino.

Inside the building the contrast may be even greater. The upscale suburban public school is clean, well lit, and spacious; it has an attractive cafeteria and good food; and its library is full of new books and magazines and computers that always work. It tells the children who attend it that they are valuable, and worth spending money on. When students from a crowded inner-city school become aware of what they are missing, they are apt to become, according to their natures, depressed, resentful, or restless.

Educational architecture can also give out messages about religion. As Jonathan Zimmerman points out in his perceptive and original cultural history, *Small Wonder: The Little Red Schoolhouse in History and Memory*, many nineteenth-century elementary schools resembled rural churches: they had gabled front porches or stoops and a tower with a bell that was rung to call students to lessons, just as the church bell on Sunday called parishioners to worship. In some small towns, the school and the church were the same building.

Today schools run by separate denominations often resemble the churches or temples of that faith. But even when they do not, they usually display religious emblems, paintings, or statuary, both outside and inside, and they are often physically attached to a church, synagogue, or mosque, or are located next door to one. To attend such a school is to be reminded many times every day that you are, for example, a Catholic, a Jew, or a Muslim.

SEPARATION AND CONSOLIDATION

Children may also learn in school that they ought to be separated by age and gender. In the one-room schools of the past, kids from six to sixteen or eighteen shared the same space, and could study or play together. If they were especially good at reading or arithmetic, or skilled at games, it was easy for them to join their intellectual or physical peers. If they fell behind, an older student was often assigned to help them catch up.

The classic "little red schoolhouse" (which, as Jonathan Zimmerman points out, was more often white or gray) not only resembled a country church, but also—as its name suggests—looked a lot like a small farmhouse. The students knew each other, and often knew each other's families. Usually the school was also a kind of community center: town meetings, concerts, debates, dances, and seasonal festivals like Arbor Day, Memorial Day, and Fourth of July were held there, and in November it often became a local polling place. Inside, the decorative theme was simple and patriotic: probably there would be an American flag on a stand and a portrait of George Washington, but otherwise the walls were often bare, to avoid distraction from lessons. A woodstove in the middle of the room was flanked by rows of desks and benches.

The invention of the automobile, and the intensified road building that followed, gradually altered all this. In the early twentieth century there was a move toward rural school consolidation all over the United States. The change was intended to save money, and improve the quality of instruction and discipline: teachers would be better trained, and more able to handle sometimes unruly students. As time went on, fewer children walked to small local schools, while more and more were driven in big yellow buses to buildings that might hold up to a thousand students. In these new consolidated schools, classrooms, lunch, and recess periods were organized by age. The result, in many cases, was boredom or frustration for anyone who was ahead or behind in some skill.

The consolidated school was usually an imposing multi-story brick building in a modified neoclassical or Romanesque style, with large windows and an impressive entrance. It looked like a town hall or a late-nineteenth-century factory rather than a church or a home, and because many students came from a considerable distance, there was much less sense of community. In its classrooms, as well as the American flag and portraits of local or national political figures, there would be maps on rollers and possibly posters of state flowers and birds and animals. Sometimes there were several rooms for each grade, and in this case competition between classrooms often supplemented competition between individual students, creating pressure to succeed not only for one's own sake but so that Miss Smith's class could be announced at the end of the term as having defeated that of Mr. Jones.

The generally age-segregated classrooms of the consolidated school also suggested that all the children in a room were essentially similar: that most eight-year-olds, for instance, had similar abilities, skills, and interests. The unconscious lesson was that one should identify with and mainly associate with one's age mates, rather than with older or younger people, a pattern that now often continues throughout life, limiting our possibilities for love and friendship.

In Britain, as Catherine Burke and Ian Grosvenor explain, school design followed a somewhat different pattern. Unlike the one-room schoolhouse in America, built to serve everyone in the neighborhood, state schools in the United Kingdom were mostly established for poor working-class children. The ragged schools and dame schools of the early nineteenth century were generally unsystematic and unregulated, and their teachers, as many Victorian novels attest, were often incompetent and cruel.

After the Industrial Revolution these informal institutions were supplemented by Sunday schools, originally intended for children who worked in the local factories and mines six days a week. These schools were usually run by clergymen and staffed largely by unpaid lady volunteers, and were in session only one day a week in whatever space was available. All they usually taught was Bible reading and simple arithmetic. Meanwhile many religious denominations had begun to establish schools for the children of their members, some free or relatively inexpensive and some affordable only by the well-to-do.

In the later nineteenth century, following horrified protests against child labor, and its gradual decline, nondenominational board schools were established under the British Education Act of 1870. Like the American consolidated schools, they were usually large, substantial brick edifices with big windows and imposing entrances. In Britain they often resembled late Victorian or Edwardian town halls and government offices—a style consciously chosen, according to Burke and Grosvenor, to differentiate them from Anglican Gothic and Nonconformist classicist buildings. The British schools and their playgrounds also tended to be enclosed by high brick walls, which, as Burke and Grosvenor point out, institutionalized the separation of children from society. (In fact, in late-nineteenth- and early-twentieth-century Britain, middle- and upper-class children often lived in a nursery world of their own, eating separately from their parents and sometimes seeing them only once a day.)

MODERN SCHOOL DESIGN

The modernist movement in architecture had a powerful and, some would say, unfortunate effect on school architecture after World War II. In Britain many schools had been destroyed by bombing, and, according to Burke and Grosvenor, "there was a moral panic about war children being out of control." More classrooms were needed immediately, and radical modernist architects welcomed the opportunity to design them. This was the period of what is now known as "the New Brutalism" in European architecture, with its heavy, blocklike construction and rough surfaces—its effects can be seen most easily today in the National Theatre on London's South Bank. Rushed schedules and limited funds, combined with these new ideas, led to the creation of low-cost, cheaply built schools with rough concrete floors and walls, asbestos ceilings, and "not one single piece of soft material anywhere." Some architects and educators welcomed these schools, declaring with enthusiasm that in them "there is an utter and refreshing absence of conscious detailing. There are no materials except glass, steel, and plaster." Many American architects also created these kinds of ultramodernist schools, though less often, partly because of the opposition of local school boards and citizens, especially in rural and suburban areas. They can still be seen here and there.

The new stripped-down schools, though impressive in photographs, had serious practical problems. The huge expanses of glass made them hot in the summer and icily cold in the winter, and they were often intolerably noisy and echoing. In the damp gray weather so common in Britain, Canada, and the American Northeast, the rough concrete walls looked dark and hostile, especially when they were soaked with rain, and though advertised as vandal-proof, they were vulnerable to graffiti.

Fortunately, perhaps, lack of funding and cultural conservatism ensured that these schools were relatively rare. Large institutions change slowly, and only a minority of educational authorities will ever have the desire, or the budget, to go all the way with any new design. Teachers began to complain that it was impossible to teach in the new buildings because of the heat or cold, and that they were unpleasantly institutional. Architects began to suggest that, especially for younger children, a school should not resemble a military fort; rather it should look like a private home, with soft carpets and furniture. Changes along these lines began to be made in the later years of the twentieth century, and have continued into the present. Today, though cost-conscious accountants still demand simple, cheap, fixed designs and industrial materials, many American and British classrooms, especially in the early grades, look relatively cheerful and comfortable.

BOYS AND GIRLS APART

What we think children are like tends to determine how we educate them, and in what sort of environment. One persistent belief, for example, has been that boys and girls, as well as men and women, are very different—in some cases almost different species.

The British began to separate the sexes in education earlier, and continued more often and for much longer than the Americans did. The American one-room schoolhouse and consolidated school were usually coed. But until the mid-twentieth century many elementary and secondary schools in Britain were single-sex, and this was especially true if they had been established by some religious authority, or were what we would call private schools. (One of the many ways in which Harry Potter's Hogwarts is a fantasy is that though it reproduces the look of the classic British all-male or all-female "public" school, it is coed.) Mixed-sex schools, in America as well as in Britain, often had separate classrooms and separate playgrounds for boys and girls. Typically, the boys' playground was (and often still is) much bigger than the girls', silently conveying the message that females ought to take up less space than males. Even today, many British schools and classrooms are single-sex. The results of this history can still be seen in public places, where large groups of men often sit or stand together, and take up the greater part of the available area.

Both in Britain and in America a girls' school, whether public or private, often looked most unlike a boys' school. It was more apt to resemble a large family home surrounded by porches and gardens, and its playing fields tended to be fewer and more discreetly placed. The implication was that girls were less physically active, more sensitive to beauty and nature, and more attached to home, a message often reinforced by a curriculum that emphasized music, fine art, and courses in the domestic sciences. Laboratories tended to be less well equipped and sometimes even absent.

For many years, even in American consolidated public schools, boys and girls often entered through different doors, sat on different sides of the classroom, and had different areas or times for lunch and recess. In secondary school, girls took home economics and typing and dressmaking; boys took shop and auto mechanics. Boys were also more apt to be encouraged to study math, chemistry, biology, and physics, since girls were thought naturally less able to learn these subjects—a view that still persists even in some of our most renowned institutions.

Over the course of the twentieth century, most American public and private schools became coeducational. Recently, however, there has been a counter-reformation. In part, it seems to have been a reaction to the discovery that for the first time in our history more girls than boys are graduating from both high school and college. There have been different explanations for this unsettling development. Some feminists have declared that it proves that women are and have always been superior; other experts, however, have concluded that it is the result of the "over-feminization" of contemporary education, which, they believe, has become hostile to the natural needs and abilities of boys.

One solution proposed has been to separate the sexes again; as a result, at the beginning of 2008, as reported by Elizabeth Weil in the *New York Times Magazine*, there were forty-nine new single-sex elementary schools in the United States, and many more were being planned. They were promoted as a means of improving the performance of poor black and Latino children, especially boys, in areas where de facto segregation still existed. In these new single-sex schools and classrooms, not only teaching methods but also the physical environment is very different for boys and girls. Following the recommendations of Leonard Sax, a former family doctor, the "walls of the boys' classroom in one Alabama school, for instance, are painted blue, the light bulbs emit a cool white light, and the thermostat is set to 69 degrees. In the girls' room, by contrast, the walls are yellow, the light bulbs emit a warm yellow light, and the temperature is kept six degrees warmer."

Though these schools will perhaps convince some boys and girls that they are intrinsically and hopelessly different, with unfortunate results (think only of the thousands of future marital quarrels over the proper setting of the thermostat), it is not clear whether they will increase happiness and educational performance in the long run. The reported gains in morale and test scores may be partly due to the selection process: children in most experimental schools have usually applied for admission, that is, they have parents who care about their education. There may also be what sociologists know as the Hawthorne effect—the fact that if you pay more attention to people they tend to do better. New school programs that attract dedicated, enthusiastic teachers and press coverage often succeed—though sometimes only temporarily.

FREEDOM AND CONTROL

In the past, when both boys and girls were often regarded as naturally wild and uncivilized, and in the extreme case as potential imps of Satan, it seemed right that they should be confined and controlled. Most classrooms had fixed rows of desks, sometimes bolted to the floor, facing a platform on which there was a much larger desk and chair for the teacher, who could thus always be on the lookout for bad behavior and ready with a reprimand or, in some cases, physical punishment. The design of the room implied that if kids were not restrained and supervised they would act up, and to judge from novels and memoirs of the time, many of them did.

A more neutral view, often associated with eighteenth-century rationality and the writings of John Locke, saw the child as a tabula rasa, a blank sheet upon which a parent or teacher could inscribe not only knowledge but also morals, manners, and ideals. Yet even where these views became popular, classroom design usually remained unchanged. The teacher now had even more potential power, since his or her job was to write upon the children's minds and souls as well as on the blackboard: to watch, direct, question, and judge. The job of the children was to absorb factual and moral lessons and repeat them when called on. Today, in classrooms that still follow the traditional model, some children may also learn that if they refuse to sit quietly and follow instructions, they may be diagnosed with attention deficiency and treated with mood-altering drugs.

The grid-pattern classroom limited action and freedom of association. The teacher had room to move about, but the straight rows of separate desks told the students that they were supposed to face forward and pay attention, not squirm around and talk to their friends. This arrangement made it hard for them to help each other and also often discouraged individual assistance from the teacher, since whenever he or she left the supervisory position at the front of the room, all the suppressed energy in the place tended to break loose. The grid-pattern classroom implied that you were on your own in the world and could not expect much aid either from your peers or from the instructor. It also suggested that you should strive for individual success, winning spelling bees and gold stars and year-end prizes—in other words, that you had both the opportunity and the duty to compete and achieve.

As Sharon Sutton points out in *Weaving a Tapestry of Resistance*, "public space teaches children their roles in society." In many American schools children learned that it was natural for them to be classified by their intellectual aptitude, which was usually seen as the ability to pass written tests. Today kids who do poorly on such tests, or seem to learn more slowly, may still be assigned to a special classroom where they receive "special education" and are seen by their peers and also sometimes by adults as not only different but inferior. This sort of placement is relatively new: in a small nineteenth- or early-twentieth-century school, students were more likely to be allowed to learn at their own pace without being marked out as slow and separated from the others.

THE PROGRESSIVE SCHOOL

The Romantic movement of the late eighteenth and early nineteenth centuries cast the child as a Wordsworthian innocent, naturally good and eager to learn; it also had important and lasting, though far from universal, effects on the physical form of schools. One of the earliest fictional manifestations of these new ideas occurs in Louisa May Alcott's *Little Men* and *Jo's Boy's*. Both books take place at Plumfield, the boarding school run by Jo and her husband, which was based largely on the radical educational theories of Ralph Waldo Emerson and his friend Bronson Alcott, Louisa's father, who once ran a short-lived day school in Boston on similar principles. At Plumfield it is assumed that all children are potentially good, and that if they are educated with kindness and according to their individual needs (as well as getting lots of exercise and fresh air and frequent moral lessons), they will grow up to be worthy citizens of a democracy. Plumfield looks like a large, comfortable family house, which it once was, and is surrounded by orchards and woods. The children have their own garden plots, keep pets, and go on educational nature walks, possibly inspired by the works of Henry Thoreau, on whom Louisa May Alcott once had a serious crush.

Over the last hundred years there have been many other Romantic-inspired attempts to change the way traditional elementary schools look and operate. The Waldorf movement, founded in Europe in 1919 and based in part of the ideas of Rudolf Steiner, emphasized individuality and imagination not only in children but in architecture. Its schools today, in many parts of the world, still tend to be rambling, informal-looking buildings that sometimes recall Alpine chalets, with their steep overhanging roofs and peaked gables; a few look rather like the fantasy houses of Oz. Montessori schools, which also date from the early twentieth century, encourage self-directed learning and physical activity and stress the importance of a child's relation to nature; they may refer to their staff members as "guides" rather than teachers. These schools, too, tend to look like large, comfortable houses surrounded by lawns and trees. Inside, their classrooms are full of samples of the natural world—ant farms and chickens and white mice—and the walls are papered with the children's drawings and paintings.

A related European movement, the open-air school of the 1920s and 1930s, emphasized the idea that students should spend as much time as possible outdoors. As Catherine Burke and Ian Grosvenor point out in *School*, many of these institutions were founded for children who either had or were seen as in danger of acquiring tuberculosis; they were the juvenile equivalent of the sanatorium in Thomas Mann's *The Magic Mountain*. Their walls often had folding glass doors so that each dormitory and classroom could be open to the elements on at least one side. Occasionally the open-air movement crossed the ocean. My boarding school in Connecticut, whose directors were aristocratic European refugees, was partly built on these principles. Our daily assembly took place in a long, unheated open shed, and some of our classes were held outside even in the dead of winter: if it snowed or rained we merely moved under the shed roof. I vividly recall stamping my rubber boots on the frozen ground to keep my feet from going numb, and trying to take notes on European history in woolly green mittens.

The architecture of all these innovative systems, and the progressive school movement of the mid-twentieth century in general, suggested that children were innocent, unique, and valuable, and that the world was endlessly fascinating. Children needed small classes, interesting and enthusiastic teachers, and healthy, comfortable, and varied surroundings. Unfortunately, all these good things were expensive, and as a result most of the schools based on progressive principles, both in America and Europe, were not free. Usually, therefore, their message only reached children with prosperous parents.

OPEN CLASSROOMS AND OPEN SCHOOLS

In America in the late 1960s and early 1970s a new educational development, the open-classroom movement, had a significant though not always lasting effect on school design. One of its central texts was Herbert R. Kohl's *The Open Classroom* (1969). In his view, "rooms represent in physical form the spirit and soul of places and institutions. A teacher's room tells us something about who he is and a great deal about what he is doing." Kohl criticized the hierarchal structure of contemporary schools, which, he believed, consciously or unconsciously taught obedience to authority and suppression of new ideas and opinions. "Most of all, they teach people to be silent about what they think and feel. . . ." He complained that in the first school where he worked the whole staff "was obsessed by 'control,' and beneath the rhetoric of faculty meetings was the clear implication that students were a reckless, unpredictable, immoral, and dangerous enemy."

Kohl wanted to give his students the freedom to think and speak, and to follow their own interests. To this end, he recommended replacing the standard classroom setup (in which rows of desks face the teacher's larger desk and the blackboard) with small, informal groupings of chairs and tables, and separate areas for reading, writing, discussion, and other activities. He also suggested moving the teacher's desk into a corner and letting students choose their own seats, rather than having them assigned.

All this was in many ways a manifestation of the current countercultural revival of Romanticism, which included the belief that children and young people were naturally good, spontaneous, and free-spirited, and should not be closely confined and controlled. The most radical educational theorists, following earlier British experiments in "schools without walls," recommended not only a change in individual classroom design, but the removal of fixed, separate classrooms in both schools and colleges. Some of the new open-space schools had few or no interior walls, while in less extreme versions these walls were replaced with movable partitions between classrooms.

Along with the campaign for open classrooms and open-space schools went demands for more comfortable learning areas. The sociologist Robert Sommer, for instance, criticized what he called "hard classrooms," with tile floors, institutional furniture, dull colors, and overhead fluorescent lighting. He recommended instead, a "soft classroom," furnished with carpets, upholstered benches and hassocks, floor pillows, and spot lighting. (In studies, college students and teachers also turned out to prefer this type of classroom, and to report that the amount of discussion increased.) As a result of this and similar proposals, many open-classroom floors were carpeted and strewn with large, colorful pillows, mimicking the standard interior décor of an encounter group.

There were advantages to the open school: building and maintenance and heating costs were greatly reduced, spaces could be altered to accommodate kids with diverse interests and abilities, and teachers could move easily from one group to another. Children of different ages could be brought together for a lesson that wouldn't bore or discourage any of them. They could sit on the floor close to the teacher, and at the same time interact with one another.

The movement of teachers between subject and skill groups also meant that no child was stuck for a whole year with an adult whose personality may have been antipathetic to theirs—or vice versa. Older children could work one-on-one with younger children, providing individual tutoring that, according to studies, kids of all ages enjoyed and benefited from. The overall message of the open-space school was that education (and also, by implication, life) was not only fun but a varied and interesting experience, involving association with people of different ages and personalities.

But like the other innovative movements, the open school turned out to have disadvantages. As anyone who has ever furnished an apartment knows, comfort has a price: soft furniture and cushions and carpets may be cheaper to begin with, but they are harder to keep clean and far less durable than metal and wood and hard plastic. According to many experienced teachers I have spoken to, order is difficult to maintain in an open-space school, and it is easy for children who become restless or bored to wander away from a group. The lack of walls also increases the noise level tremendously, and distracts both students and teachers. It can become impossible, for instance, to concentrate on multiplication tables when other kids a few feet away are singing or telling stories; and any kind of explosion, whether from a fifth-grade chemical experiment or a kindergarten temper tantrum, is apt to draw the attention of everyone in the building. Another problem was that there was no obvious limit on the number of students an open school could accommodate: all the school board had to do was add a few more pillows. Overcrowding became common, and groups of children could sometimes be seen huddling together around their teacher at the far end of a hallway in order to get away from the general hullabaloo. Over the years studies have seemed to suggest that open-space education is most successful in the earliest grades, and that most teachers prefer a closed classroom. As a result, many former open-space schools have now installed interior walls, though kindergarten and first-grade classes still often have a large carpeted play area, soft furniture, and piles of floor pillows.

In Europe the extreme innovations of the American 1970s were rarer and more short-lived. In some schools, particularly those designed by the architects David and Mary Medd, there was an attempt to make the environment look more like a home, with movable walls and furniture and areas for different activities, so that teachers could easily move from one group to another. But from the late 1970s on most open-space schools were subdivided into separate classrooms.

The influence of the progressive movement of the 1920s and 1930s, however, can still be seen everywhere on both sides of the Atlantic. Today most elementary schools try to bring the natural world indoors, and classroom walls are decorated with juvenile artwork. The rooms contain plants and often also animals: tanks of fish, colonies of ants, cages of birds, and occasionally even hamsters or rabbits or mice. In some cases children are allowed to bring their pets to school, or borrow a guinea pig for the weekend. Classes are taken on trips to museums and to local sights. When these kinds of activities are not possible, usually because of budget restrictions, drawings and paintings of animals and plants and objects outside the classroom are often encouraged and exhibited, implying that the children's own experience of the world is valued. (Posters of types of animals and plants and scenes from real life, however, while probably better than bare walls, suggest that experts always know how to visualize reality most correctly. Unfortunately there is not much in common between a scientifically accurate two-dimensional colored drawing of a gerbil and the actual fuzzy, moving, eating and squeaking creature; in fact, a child's version may be nearer in some ways to the reality.)

Today, though the bare, traditional classroom with its rows of fixed desks can still be seen, it is becoming rarer. In many modern American elementary schools, classrooms are now equipped with lightweight rectangular or hexagonal tables rather than desks. According to Burke and Grosvenor the same thing is true in England, where the traditional oak and cast-iron double desks with attached seats have now often been replaced by tables and chairs made of plastic and tubular steel. In both countries children are assigned to work on projects at these tables in groups of three to six, while the teacher moves from one group to the next.

This kind of classroom plan suggests that it is natural for teams or groups rather than individuals to compete, and that you will belong to different groups at different times. (A similar unstable setup, of course, is more and more common in contemporary businesses and professions; whether as a result or a cause of the team approach in elementary school it is hard to say.) Another implied lesson appears to be that now and in the future outside oversight and correction will be intermittent but frequent, and also that you may have no permanent place to work and to keep your possessions, since where there are no individually assigned desks, books and papers and lunchboxes are often stored in knapsacks or in labeled bins.

Movable furniture and group projects, however, are less common in understaffed and overcrowded schools. It is not easy to control twenty-five to thirty-five active children who are free to move about, and teachers who lack assistants may need all the help they can get from classroom design. They often prefer a more traditional room, along with the support for authority that it implies. The current emphasis on written exams and memorization encourages what is referred to bitterly by many educators as "teaching to the test." Some of them point out that what is actually rewarded is not the general level of achievement, but rather improvement of test scores from year to year; thus a very good school may receive a low rating because its students continue to do well. More than one teacher has complained that this system encourages deceit in frightened and harassed faculty and school administrators, since it is now no longer students or classes that are competing, but individual schools. As a result there is a new tendency to favor rote learning and nineteenth-century classroom design—and also sometimes to expel low-performing students or somehow ignore their scores so as to raise school averages.

BACK TO THE PAST

The continuing problems of school design in America have led some experts to call for a return to an imagined past. As Jonathan Zimmerman reports in *Small Wonder*, by the 1950s most one-room schools had closed, but the "little red schoolhouse" had become a sentimental icon. Soon many of these deserted buildings began to be preserved as tourist destinations, and sometimes as "living museums" with imitation teachers and students in old-fashioned costumes. By the end of the 1990s there were more than 450 restored one-room schoolhouses open to the public, most of them much cleaner and prettier and redder than they had been in the past.

Meanwhile, perhaps partly as a result of the idealized rural schools portrayed in many memoirs and in popular children's books like Carol Ryrie Brink's *Carrie Woodlawn* (1936) and Laura Ingalls Wilder's *On the Banks of Plum Creek* (1937), both conservatives and liberals had begun to present the rural school of the past as an educational model. But as Zimmerman remarks, left-wingers and right-wingers emphasized different aspects of the nostalgic ideal. Liberals liked the small classes, the mixing of ages and skills, the informal scheduling, and the individual attention. Conservatives praised the one-room schoolhouse for its basic no-nonsense curriculum of "readin' and 'ritin' and 'rithmetic" and its emphasis on order, discipline, and obedience to the teacher. They also pointed out that in many one-room schools daily prayer and Bible reading were part of the curriculum.

Both liberals and conservatives, however, spoke with admiration of the rural school as a quaintly beautiful institution that encouraged individual initiative and self-reliance, drew local citizens together, and protected students from the confusion, corruption, and commercialism of the big city. But, as Zimmerman says, "when conservatives imagine a schoolhouse of quiet obedience, they distort the past every bit as much as liberals who celebrate freedom and cooperative learning." In fact, the history of the one-room schoolhouse is full of rundown, disorganized classrooms and incompetent or overwhelmed teachers, and the most common form of lessons was rote recitation.

• • •

SCHOOLS TODAY

Experts in school design and architecture now tend to write and speak as if their goal is to make school buildings as attractive and comfortable as possible, and education as much fun. But it has also been argued that school (and indeed childhood in general) should not be made too wonderful. Some American private boarding schools based on the British public school model have operated on this principle; bare dormitories, hard beds, cold showers, muddy playing fields, and monotonous food were seen as building character—and, of course, they also reduced expenses considerably. It is sometimes proposed even today that childhood should be presented as a lesser and more limited and uncomfortable state of being, while adulthood is shown to have far greater rewards and privileges. Otherwise, children will never want to grow up, and college students won't want to graduate, take jobs, or sometimes even leave home. With the best intentions in the world, we will have created a population of sulky, disappointed adults who will long all their lives for the lost paradises of their youth that well-meaning but misguided school architects, educational experts, and parents created.

Today two new developments are in the process of radically changing both school design and education in general. One is the computer, which is already beginning to crowd out both desks and books in many classrooms and school libraries. Potentially, the Internet can bring education into every home and make school buildings as we know them obsolete, as it has already done for the homeschooling movement. Some teachers welcome the amazing access to information that the Web can give. Others hate and fear computers because they interfere with group learning and bonding, and make it all too easy to patch together school assignments out of other people's words, or to access what are in fact lies. For them, a classroom full of computer terminals looks like a factory or a prison workshop in which workers are isolated and discouraged from speaking to one another, and competition replaces cooperation.

The other great contemporary change in school design is at least partly the result of the coming of a new kind of "Age of Anxiety" in which physical fear has replaced the metaphysical unease described in Auden's poem of the same name. Today not only are many of us afraid of all kinds of threats from without; we are afraid of one another. We feel vulnerable, and consider our children even more vulnerable. Some commentators attribute this to our greater awareness of international terrorism, others to television, the Internet, and computer games, which send a constant stream of images of violence and destruction into our homes.

In the past it was possible to walk right into almost any American public school while it was in session. Today, more and more schools, especially in big cities, have locked doors and gates with speaker-phones, guards (sometimes armed), and even metal detectors and surveillance cameras. Both in America and Britain the number of entrances and exits to many schools has been deliberately reduced, and walls around playgrounds have been erected or reinforced.

For centuries, even after the invention of electricity, schools customarily had large, tall windows to provide as much free natural light as possible. In every classroom, the desks were arranged so that this light came from the left to minimize shadows on the paper for right-handed students. In some cases, however, windows were placed so high that children sitting down could see nothing but sky and trees or a blank wall. Occasionally a school would deliberately block the view from its windows with frosted glass, especially if it was thought to be ugly or distracting. More informally, classroom windows were often partially hidden by commercial decorations or the students' own artwork: the rows of paper pumpkins and turkeys that appear every fall, and the flowers and butterflies of the spring. Today windows are more often blocked with bars or unbreakable glass, or simply not installed in the first place.

New levels of windowlessness have been achieved in the United States with the conversion of commercial buildings into schools, especially charter schools. As Julia Christensen explains in *Big Box Reuse*, many charter schools, whose operating costs come from public funding supplemented by donations, involve commercial real estate transactions. They may be constructed from scratch on vacant lots, or set up within unused or underused buildings, not only actual public schools, but abandoned big-box stores (often Kmarts or Wal-Marts). Using a former store, the larger the better, can save money and avoid expensive changes for handicap access, and costs may be reduced by cutting few or no new windows on the outside walls. The implied message is that education is a kind of consumerism—a message reinforced by the fact that many charter schools actively market themselves or even advertise for students.

For years the blocking or removal of windows was justified as a way to minimize distraction from lessons, and there seems to be some sense, though of a depressing sort, in this argument. After all, dozens of memoirs have reported how as a child the author would forget to listen to the teacher or work on an assignment, instead gazing idly out of the window and watching clouds, birds, trees, animals, or people. Later on, the walled-in, artificially lit school building was more often explained as necessary to protect children from possible intruders. Over the past decade, however, terrible events in which the perpetrators of violence in American schools have been the students themselves have cast doubt on this argument. The closing in of the American school is now intended not only to keep out dangerous adult trespassers, but to stop armed students from going on murderous rampages. Many schools in America now have a resident social worker or psychologist to watch out for possible internal catastrophes and provide counseling after they occur.

In England, though there have been fewer instances of violence in schools, Burke and Grosvenor report the same sort of architectural developments: the reduction of entrances and exterior windows, the building of gates and security fences, and the suspicion of strangers. As a result, they write, "A recent poll of schoolchildren . . . returned a surprisingly large number of respondents who felt over-protected and that their schools were beginning to resemble prisons."

Whether or not walled-in education is safer, it always sends the message that there is danger outside. A room without a view tells students that school is and should be separate from the world. Also, as studies have shown, the completely locked-in school can have a depressing effect. The result may be alienation from or total rejection of education, which is seen as both oppressive and irrelevant to "real life," with students increasingly staying away and perhaps eventually dropping out entirely.

THE PLAYGROUND

In *Children's Spaces*, Mark Dudek suggests that a climate of generalized fear has also changed the way their world looks to kids even when they are not in class. Most people over thirty can remember getting home from school, scarfing down milk and cookies, and then going out to play unsupervised until suppertime. Now, if they are not ferried about to a series of lessons and organized athletic contests, many children are taken to supervised playgrounds in which nothing dangerous—and also nothing interesting—can possibly occur. As David Harsanyi puts it in *Nanny State*, these places are "nothing like the playgrounds I so fondly remember: towering jungle gyms with blacktop floors; sky-high slides that would burn your skin as you slid down; swings . . . that swung so high you felt like you might go all the way around."

It was not always like this. The progressive school movements of the mid-twentieth century saw children not only as naturally innocent and creative, but as free spirits who should be encouraged to explore the world on their own. As a result, in the countercultual 1960s and 1970s many old-fashioned parks, especially in cities, sprouted what were known as "adventure playgrounds." Children were presented with inventive and original wooden structures to climb about in, augmented by piles of movable building material: boxes and boards of all sizes, logs and sticks, concrete blocks, and rubber tires. There were piles of pebbles and rocks, and dirt and sand to dig in. Often there was also a fountain or a stream of running water. The implication was that the world was full of possibility, and you could change it.

Today, a few such playgrounds still exist, but they are becoming less common because of concerns about health and safety. Children are increasingly seen as vulnerable, and apt to get hurt in an adventure playground; boards may have splinters and boxes can be piled too high; you can fall off an improvised tower, or get cold and wet in a fountain. Experts have also begun to question the safety of traditional playground equipment: swings and slides and jungle gyms, they point out, sometimes cause serious injury, and therefore should be removed.

It is not clear why these fears for the dangers of both school and playground have become so intense lately. One explanation sometimes offered is that when both mothers and fathers work away from home, they often become more anxious, and possibly feel guilty because they do not really trust the substitute parents they have hired. As a result, they want to protect their kids from every real or imagined danger, and especially from strange adults. They are reassured by fenced-in, rubber-surfaced or shredded-bark-heaped playgrounds in which nothing heavy moves or can be moved, and there is no equipment that could possibly hurt anyone or get them dirty. Natural materials—sticks, stones, plants, grass, and dirt—are replaced with manufactured plastic "play equipment," and a grown-up is always present to supervise and organize play.

Critics of these super-safe contemporary playgrounds, like Mark Dudek, remark that they are boring and unchallenging. These places also suggest to children who spend much time there that the world is very dangerous, and that they themselves are fragile and vulnerable and need to be watched constantly. At times, these oversupervised children may be seriously affected by the lack of opportunity for active and creative play. This is especially true if at home you are given dolls and stuffed animals that talk, so that you do not have to invent dialogue for them; plastic figures that turn into other shapes, so that you do not have to imagine for yourself how they might change; and cars and planes that you do not have to move but can control with a handheld gadget. Interaction with such toys eventually becomes repetitive and uninteresting, especially if an adult is constantly there overseeing your play. As a result, you may not only become soft and fat from lack of exercise; you may conclude that excitement, adventure, invention, and freedom from supervision are only available secondhand, on expensive little game-playing devices—a dismal lesson that unfortunately sometimes persists into adolescence and adulthood. After all, whether you are six or sixty, if you never leave the house or turn off your computer, nothing really bad will probably ever happen to you—and also, very likely, nothing really good.

CHAPTER 10

Houses of Learning II:
High Schools and Colleges

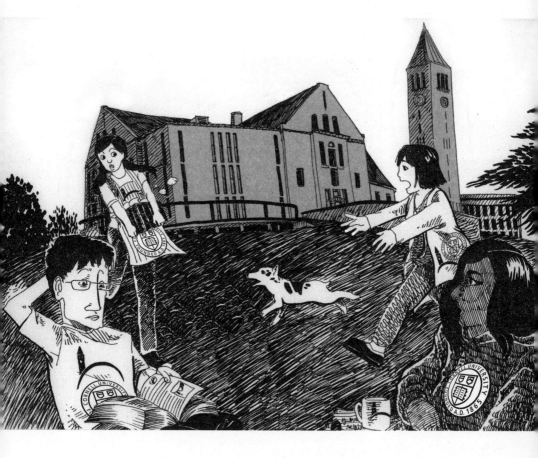

Most nineteenth- and early-twentieth-century secondary school and college buildings visibly proclaimed the importance and dignity of education. Some followed a classical model, with porches, pillars, and pediments; others had an impressive Romanesque look, featuring heavy, solid stonework and arched windows and doors. After World War II, however, things began to change. As the babies of the baby boom became teenagers they put a heavy strain on existing buildings and budgets. Wealthy, well-established institutions still might go in for expensive traditional styles, but the average public high school or community college could not keep up.

HIGH SCHOOLS

When there were just too many kids, the existing facilities had to be expanded somehow. If there was not enough space on school grounds to extend an old building, the land it sat on was often valuable. One result was that, as the architectural critic Philip Langdon puts it, "Countless public high school and middle schools slunk out of the center of town, gaining sites that were several times larger— the better to accommodate parking, athletic fields, and fleets of school buses."

The new buildings erected on these sites tended to be fairly basic and functional. They might have a classical front entrance, with fake pillars and a pediment, but their sides and back were often unrelieved expanses of brick and stock windows. Once you went around the corner, the place looked like some kind of factory.

Even when a public high school was handsome and well built, the new middle schools that fed into it were apt to be undistinguished and sometimes unpleasant to look at or work in. It is often said that junior high students are the hardest to teach, because they are just hitting adolescence and the transition from primary school is often traumatic for them. I can remember this trauma vividly. Suddenly, instead of knowing everyone in my class well and spending most of the day in the same pleasant room, I had to find my way around a big ugly building in which loud bells or buzzers constantly sounded, and the corridors and stairs were blocked by the tramping feet and shoving bodies of noisy strangers. When I drove past this terrifying place a few years later I was amazed to see how small it actually was.

Essentially my bad experience was the result of economics. Private schools can afford to keep their buildings and classes small, and spend money on architecture that suggests that education is a pleasure and a privilege. Even when private schools are quite large, they tend to be collections of relatively small and attractive buildings, each with its own purpose. There may be a science laboratory, a dining hall, a gym, a theatre, and several groups of classrooms, usually arranged around one or more green lawns. The overall effect often suggests a country village.

Public high schools, on the other hand, are usually big and all-inclusive, since it is cheaper to build and maintain one huge school rather than two or three medium-sized ones that might encourage a sense of community. Studies show that a small high school tends to creates a cohesive society, while a large one tends to subdivide into groups and cliques—and sometimes into rival gangs, each with its unofficial territories. A small high school also gives more people a chance to excel. Whether it has a hundred or several thousand students, a school can only have one top baseball and basketball team, one orchestra, one newspaper editor, one senior class president, and one valedictorian. In a really big school, relatively few students will fill these roles. Many more will be lost in the crowd, often becoming discouraged and alienated, and sometimes just dropping out.

When a large secondary school is open-plan, with no separate classrooms, things become even more problematic. One study found that teachers in an open-plan middle school had higher levels of tension than those in a conventional building, and that their students suffered from greater homework anxiety and spent much more time in "off-task" behavior—that is, in not doing whatever they were supposed to be doing.

THE ELECTRONIC CLASSROOM

More and more secondary schools, both public and private, now depend on electronic devices. In many classrooms every student sits in front of a computer and logs into the official program for their course. The teacher posts readings and assignments online, and students type in their questions, answers, and comments, which instantly appear on all the other computers. Group discussion may be carried on silently, as in an Internet chat room, or it may switch to ordinary speech, which still feels more natural to many teachers. Others prefer the chat-room format because it prevents especially articulate or aggressive kids from dominating every conversation, and gives equal time to the shy and inhibited. Small-group projects are easy to set up in a computer lab, and students who miss class can log on at home.

At present electronic teaching is limited by the fact that some public schools cannot afford to equip every classroom with computers, but more and more of them probably soon will. Often the machines will be donated by companies that hope to promote their products and habituate students to their particular hardware and software. There is still the problem that some teachers are not very quick with the mouse, while their students may be too quick. My stepdaughter, Lana Hower, who has taught English in several New

York State high schools, says that whenever she gives an online lesson she has to keep walking round the room to intercept kids who call up other and more exciting Internet sites whenever they think themselves unobserved. Often someone may have two or three outside programs running at once, while text-messaging on a cell phone under the table. As a result of situations like this, cell phones are not allowed in many classrooms, and they are banned from examination rooms almost everywhere because they make cheating so easy.

The lesson of the new electronic classroom is that disembodied communication, including constant and elaborate multitasking, is the preferred life style. Studies show that students who have learned this lesson no longer watch much television; they see fewer films; and they almost never read a book. Instead, even when not in school, they spend three to six hours a day online, checking their own and their friends' blogs, sending instant messages, visiting popular websites and watching music videos on YouTube. According to some commentators, students today are actually becoming a new and different type of human being for whom the three-dimensional world is a kind of shadow of the two-dimensional one. For these people, silence and solitude are either irrelevant or frightening or both; they expect and need to be in constant touch with other disembodied entities. To be alone and totally disconnected is to be in a sort of suspended animation or coma state—a kind of temporary death.

COLLEGES

Colleges and universities, like private schools, are theoretically not only factories but also stores: like the museums of today, they need to sell themselves. If they are attractive and distinctive they will pull in many applicants, some of whom who will become paying customers, and perhaps eventually donors, both individual and corporate. If a college seems run-down and obscure, few people will want to attend it or give it money, and it may eventually be forced to close.

This terrifying if remote possibility may be one of the reasons why even the richest and most famous universities are reluctant to spend more than a small percentage of their endowments.

According to Richard P. Dober, our foremost authority on the architecture of higher education, campuses can be classified as Formal: "regular, symmetrical, rectilinear"; or Informal: "picturesque, irregular, unsymmetrical." In practice, of course, many campuses contain both formal and informal areas. Some campuses, however, like the University of the South at Sewanee, Tennessee, are *monoform*, with most of the buildings in more or less the same style: even the modernist new student dining hall looks like a classic Sewanee building on speed. Other campuses are *multiform*: collections of wildly different styles, like architectural zoos. Most often there is a prevailing model with, as time goes on, one or more unmatched buildings that have produced both public awards and considerable indignation among nostalgic alumni.

Traditionally, most American colleges and universities have been built to look like older institutions of learning, following either a European model or an American one. The four dominant styles are Collegiate Gothic, Collegiate Georgian or Federal, Collegiate Beaux-Arts, and Modern, though there are also many other, sometimes entertainingly eccentric, stylistic possibilities.

The Gothic style, all else being equal, is the most expensive. Many well-endowed institutions, like Princeton and Duke, have spared no expense to imitate the stone towers and arches and cloisters of Oxford and Cambridge, which derive ultimately from the monastic and ecclesiastical buildings of the Middle Ages. As Dober notes, such buildings recall a pre-industrial, more spiritual age, and suggest "a separation of the world of the mind from the world of real life." The visible signs of this separation have sometimes been felt to be indispensable, especially when a university is established in a city, among large commercial buildings. According to the well-known and gifted American architect Henry J. Cobb, the University

of Chicago, founded in 1891, was deliberately designed to "remove
the mind of the student from the busy mercantile conditions of Chicago and surround him with a peculiar air of quiet dignity."

Other universities, especially in New England and the Southeast-
ern states, chose the red bricks and white wood trim of Georgian
and Federal design, often with Greek Revival additions, such as ped-
imented porticos and tall white columns, with their suggestions of
classical learning, purity, and civic virtue. In some cases, the Puritan ascetic tradition was also continued indoors—dorm rooms were
small, and there were few amenities; the lack of privacy and comfort
was supposed to inform students that they should work hard and not
expect to enjoy themselves. This sort of cramped, minimalist design
saved money, but as time passed it also tended to repel students and
cause them to move to off-campus housing. College administrators
were left with empty rooms and the loss of potential income, and as
a result more time and effort is now spent in making dormitories
agreeable, especially at expensive institutions.

Sometimes the religious preferences of the founders appear to
have affected architectural choice. Episcopalian colleges tended to
prefer Gothic stone, and Calvinists and Unitarians Georgian brick. In
America these choices had equal prestige; in England, however, stone
dominated, and more recent British universities, like Sussex, Notting-
ham, and Warwick, were distinguished from Oxford, Cambridge, Ed-
inburgh, and London by the denigrating epithet "redbrick."

In the mid-nineteenth century a new style, referred to as "Beaux
Arts," began to dominate campus architecture. Deriving originally
from the French Empire, whose traces are still visible everywhere in
many European cities, it featured large, impressive stone buildings
with mansard roofs, dormer windows, arched entries, and center halls.
The message of this style was that education is a serious, imposing,
and expensive pursuit, one that can make you both wise and powerful.
In a wealthier and less puritanical era, these Collegiate Romanesque
dormitories were more comfortable than Gothic or Georgian ones,

and the heating was better. Today, buildings like these still dominate quadrangles in many American colleges and universities.

MODERNIST CAMPUSES

Modernist college buildings tend to project an elegant, stripped-down simplicity, continuing to proclaim (like Colonial Georgian and Colonial Gothic) that education is a rigorous and intellectual pursuit. Engineering schools and science buildings especially favor this sort of architecture: hard-edged, urban, formal. Typically, it features poured concrete and a great deal of metal and glass, with flattened roofs, sharp-edged verticals and horizontals, and a simple geometric internal design. Such a building needs not only a good architect but also first-rate construction and maintenance. Without them, as Richard Dober says, "The pride of using modern materials [gives] way to the depression of seeing stained, flaking, cracking concrete surfaces. . . . When the site is wet and cloud-covered, . . . dampened concrete is dreary and dismal." The result in terms of public opinion may be disastrous, since all university buildings, whether traditional or modern, must look prosperous and solid—they must announce silently that if you attend this institution, you will acquire these qualities. The message is always that this university is worth your tuition and will be around for a long time.

Occasionally a bad modernist building can destroy the psychological effect of a beautiful old quadrangle. When the social critic James Howard Kunstler attended a conference at the University of Texas in Austin, he was depressed to find that it was held in "a 1960s-vintage monstrosity dropped onto the campus like a refrigerator on a croquet court." This refrigerator also seemed to have no apparent entrance. Because the entire ground floor was composed of identical glass wall panels, it took Kunstler ten minutes to find his way in, making him feel both unwelcome and undignified.

Several American campuses have gone in for vernacular or regional styles, sometimes with unusual results. At the University of New Mexico, where many students are Native American, the architecture recalls Pueblo dwellings. Two buildings at the University of Iowa suggest grain silos; the U.S. Air Force Academy favors wing and arrow shapes, and its famous chapel looks as if it were about to take off at any moment. Meanwhile, the University of Colorado at Boulder has adopted an architectural style that resembles that of Tuscany, with steep tiled roofs and heavy stonework, while the University of Texas at El Paso, set among rocky hills, bears a strange resemblance to Bhutan or Tibet. As Dober remarks, its buildings "feature massive gently sloping walls, high indented windows, projecting roof eaves, and dark bands of brick and stone at the high window levels." The campus has been called a Western Shangri-la. There are also some odd mixed forms, like the Cathedral of Learning at the University of Pittsburgh, which is essentially a forty-two-story Gothic skyscraper crammed with small, dark offices and often extremely crowded elevators. The unfortunate message of this building appears to be that an impressive exterior, whether architectural or human, can conceal a shabby and cluttered interior.

COLLEGE AND LANDSCAPE

In the eighteenth and nineteenth centuries many colleges were built at the top of a steep hill above the nearest town, where everyone would have to look up at them, receiving the message that higher education is a higher thing. This system also economically made use of land that was less fertile and not as well adapted to farming. Even now, colleges tend to be built on high, steep ground where it is available.

Green lawns, towering deciduous trees, and lakes or rivers are part of the ideal campus, but in many parts of the United States grass goes brown in the summer and ponds dry up. Where there are problems with natural vegetation the sensible solution is to create regional plantings: pines in New England, cacti at Arizona State, palms at the University of Miami. Ivied or Virginia-creeper-covered walls also have great metaphoric value, especially in the Ivy League, and are popular with students and alumni. Most maintenance departments, however, hate vines because of their slow but relentless destruction of not only old brickwork and stonework, but the newest high-grade concrete. In many cases, the solution has been to maintain a few old ivy-covered buildings for the look of the thing, and scrape the rest raw.

Other problems face campus architects, among them the need for all new buildings to be handicapped accessible, with ramps and elevators. Older buildings can and do put off code compliance for an amazing length of time, with the result that handicapped students are silently told to get lost. Parking is a problem everywhere: the faculty and staff want it, but cars ruin the look of a beautiful campus, and parking structures are expensive and usually ugly.

MONEY AND METAPHOR

From a cynical point of view, colleges can be seen as corporations, devoted to profit and image maintenance. As Robert A. M. Stern, the designer of the student center at the Harvard Business School, puts it, "a university needs to have its own brand." Stern's Spangler Campus Center follows this rule: it is a Georgian brick building with white trim and white Ionic columns in the traditional Harvard style. Though now glaringly new, it will presumably weather into a semblance of authenticity. New buildings in old styles generally succeed, but attempts to connect the new with the old by incorporating materials from older buildings can misfire badly. Henry Cobb's elegant Center for Government and International Studies, though modern in design, successfully retains the connection through the use of Harvard's basic construction material, red brick. The new student center at Duke University, on the other hand, has tried to keep up appearances by including thin slices of the stone used in Duke's older buildings laid flat on concrete surfaces. The result, as Richard Dober puts it, looks very much like the peanut brittle that can be purchased inside.

Most American colleges and universities contain at least one iconic building, a stylized image of which appears on their website, letterhead, backpacks, and T-shirts. Often it is one of the oldest structures on campus, frequently the library or administration building. Occasionally, a relatively new institution appears to have erected some kind of semifunctional architectural object, such as a gate or a clock tower, in order to have a recognizable symbol. The University of North Carolina at Wilmington, for instance, has built a very tall classical gateway, with eight columns and a pediment, between two of its buildings. It looks beautiful, but does not open or shut and is not attached to any wall.

The plan of a campus is often initially haphazard, but as time goes on and the institution expands, certain characteristic arrangements tend to emerge. An old, central, architecturally distinguished building with good parking, no matter what its original purpose, will often be taken over by the administration. Meanwhile, dormitories, athletic buildings, and playing fields will naturally tend to migrate to the periphery of the campus, while the library and the student union remain in the center.

Different university departments are often arranged in a symbolic manner, from the fine arts at one end of the campus to the applied sciences and business school at the other. The music department and the art studios tend to be close to each other, but a long way from the engineering buildings. The social sciences are grouped together, and so are the nonsocial sciences. There are practical reasons for this arrangement, but it also tends to compartmentalize the disciplines. A painter who wants to study marketing or an engineer who would also like to write fiction may find it almost impossible to get from one of his or her classes to another in the standard fifteen-minute break: this difficulty was notoriously experienced by the engineering physics major and novelist Thomas Pynchon at Cornell. Less motivated students, simply as a result of the campus layout, may absorb the message that their oddly varied interests are not supposed to coexist, and give one of them up.

Well-established, well-endowed American colleges and universities usually provide attractive accommodations for every department, but it is sometimes possible to judge the importance of a subject by the size and importance of the building in which it is housed. These differences are clear to students, parents, and teachers, and can sometimes influence the choice of a major. A newer institution, which is more dependent on the preferences of individual donors, may end up with a truly impressive physics building, prominently labeled with the surname of its benefactor, and a shabby old ill-equipped theatre—or, of course, vice versa. Favored sports like football, basketball, and hockey attract glamorous stadiums and gymnasiums and rinks named after the alumni who endowed them; less popular sports must make do with smaller and less attractive accommodations. Such obvious material differences cannot help but influence both students and alumni in their choice of what sports to play, watch, and fund, in a manner that tends to snowball as time goes on. In Europe sports tend to be less important and attract fewer big donations, especially in newer universities.

INSIDE THE ARCHITECTURE

College classrooms tend to be of two types, the lecture hall and the seminar room, and each produces a different type of student behavior. An experienced teacher will already know something about his or her students the first week of classes by observing where they choose to sit in a lecture hall. People in the first few rows, toward the center, will be more interested in the material and will work harder. Those in the back, especially at the sides, will be less committed, and they will drop out more often. They will also have more friendly—and occasionally, unfriendly—interactions with their neighbors than those nearer to the instructor.

Experiments have confirmed these intuitions: at a Pennsylvania university, for instance, students who sat near the front and center of a room got better grades and liked the instructor better than those who sat at the back or at the sides. At the University of Rochester, students who felt vulnerable and inadequate "showed a marked tendency to be located in the rear and far-side regions of the classroom. Students with the most positive self-concepts tended to sit in the front." It may be true that students with poorer self-esteem are predisposed to choose low-risk seats. It is also possible that certain seats cause certain behaviors since, rather amazingly, even when seats were assigned alphabetically the students who sat front and center did better.

One study at a Pennsylvania college found "that women sat in the front of the classroom more often than men, and also obtained higher grades and cut class fewer times than men." Today, college students usually get to choose their own seats. If women prefer to sit front and center, this might help to explain the recent unsettling discovery that female undergraduates are doing better in college than males. Though none of these studies mentions the possibility, choice of seat in a lecture hall might also be connected to the students' relationship to the subject being taught. English majors such as I once was will sit right up front in English classes, while in biology lectures they will choose to huddle in the back, hoping not to be noticed or called on.

In a seminar room different rules apply. Experienced instructors know that friendly students and potential teacher's pets will choose the chairs next to them; potential opponents will sit directly opposite. Friends and lovers will naturally choose to sit beside each other, and enemies on opposite sides of the table. Students who want to avoid being called on, either because they are shy or because they haven't read the assignment, will try to place themselves where they are hard for the teacher to see. The longer the seminar table is, the more all these differences will be exaggerated. A long, narrow table makes it hard for students on the same side to see and speak to each other; a wide, short table brings the group together. Teachers who prefer to do most of the talking in a seminar will feel comfortable with a long table; those who want to encourage conversation will dislike it. Sometimes these preferences are so strong that instructors will, with the help of the class, move the furniture every time the class meets to achieve the plan they like best—I have done this myself. No matter how the tables and chairs are moved, however, the alteration itself has a strong message: it tells the students that if they are dissatisfied with the way the world is arranged, they may be able to change it.

An instructor who wants to convey that he or she is just one of the gang rather than a know-it-all authority may sit on one of the long sides of the seminar table, a choice that also tends to increase the amount of student participation. But wherever the teacher sits, those who identify with and agree with him or her will soon be found nearby, while those who disagree will appear on the opposite side of the table. Of course, as the semester progresses, individual students may change their opinions, their friendships, and therefore their seats, providing the observant instructor with valuable information. The one thing that no prudent teacher will do is to change his or her seat frequently during the term; this produces confusion and alienation, and sometimes only partially suppressed hostility.

In every college, according to studies, the more homelike the environment the happier students are, the more often they join in discussions, and the better they do on tests. Researchers at St. Cloud State University in Minnesota changed a college classroom by adding softer lighting, plants, posters, cushions, and rugs, while an identical control classroom was left as is. The students in the "soft" classroom got higher scores on tests, and liked both the room and the teacher much better—even though the teacher was the same person for both rooms. In the over twenty-five years since this and similar studies were done, however, relatively few classrooms have been remodeled along these lines. From the point of view of most college financial officers the expense is unnecessary or even misguided: learning is not supposed to be too pleasurable, and students should not be coddled with cushions or distracted by posters. Though there has been a steady movement toward making dormitories more comfortable and homelike, the monastic and puritan traditions that are the inheritance of American education often remain in force in the classroom.

CHAPTER 11

Houses of Confinement: Prisons, Hospitals, Asylums, Nursing Homes

There are some buildings that we enter reluctantly, aware that we may not be able to leave when we choose. This may be obvious from the appearance of the structure, as in a maximum-security prison, or it may be deeply disguised, as in a psychiatric hospital that looks like an expensive country club. But once you are an inmate of such a building, the physical signs of incarceration soon become apparent.

PRISONS

Almost any enclosed space may feel like a prison. Even buildings that give comfort and joy to many—a church, a theatre, an art museum, a sports stadium—have at some time, to someone, seemed intolerably confining. Deep in most of our unconscious memories is the experience of being shut in a playpen or crib, behind the vertical bars that appear as the symbol for a jail cell in cartoons. (Today, in reality, cell windows are usually made of unbreakable glass with heavy wire embedded in it.)

When we were children there were times when our own homes, however comfortable, felt like prisons, especially if we had been forbidden to go out and play until we finished our homework. Educational institutions could also feel like prison. In a day school the sensation was temporary, but probably there is no boarding school in Europe or the United States—no matter how excellent its staff and facilities—that does not have a few ghosts of homesick or bullied children wandering its corridors. Nineteenth- and twentieth-century fiction and memoirs are full of such imprisoning schools, from *Jane Eyre*'s Longwood to George Orwell's Eton.

There are also schools that are virtual prisons: the classic fictional example is Dotheboys Hall in Dickens's *Nicholas Nickleby*, a malevolent for-profit institution with locked doors and barred windows, designed to house unwanted or rebellious boys as cheaply as possible. Today a military academy for adolescents, with its tall spiked iron fences and gates, may serve a similar purpose. Though some students may enter freely and enjoy the order and discipline, others will have been sent there against their will, as incipient juvenile delinquents.

A workplace, too, may seem like a prison. Usually the constraint is economic rather than physical, but not always. Early factories and sweatshops often literally imprisoned their workers; one of the scandals of the Triangle Shirtwaist Factory fire in New York in 1911 was that the door to the stairway had been locked, preventing the escape and causing the death of 146 women and girls, some of them as young as twelve or thirteen. Today many large office buildings have windows that do not open, doors that you need to swipe a card to enter or leave by, and reception desks staffed by security personnel.

There are also buildings whose main purpose is confinement. Some are forthrightly called prisons—others go by terms like "detention center." The most common current justification of our huge prison system is that it removes those who have been classified as criminals from the general population, keeping the rest of us safe. A building with this purpose must appear impregnable from outside, to reassure local law-abiding citizens and frighten possible evildoers. It must also look and be impregnable from within, not only to make escape difficult, but to discourage inmates from even trying to break out.

For many years prison architecture echoed the medieval tradition of the castle and its dungeon—the thick stone walls, squat towers, crenellated battlements, and iron gates ending in iron spikes. The most famous surviving example is the Tower of London. Today walls may be brick or concrete, but they are often supplemented by heavy-gauge chain-link fencing and shiny coils of razor wire. The message is the same: You cannot get out of here. The type of enclosure, however, depends on the type of inmate, and different kinds of jails can usually be recognized from outside.

Around a maximum-security prison there is often a high wall, its base sunk from eight to fifteen feet belowground to discourage the digging of tunnels, surrounded by two high rows of fencing, each with a garnish of barbed or razor wire. There may also be an electrical fence, wired to sound an alarm and sometimes charged with enough current to stun or even kill anyone who touches it. There are watchtowers with armed guards, and the walls of the buildings are thick and solid, with few or no exterior windows. A medium-security prison will probably have double fencing, regularly patrolled by guards. A minimum-security jail or juvenile detention center will usually have only one fence, often without razor wire on top and only occasionally patrolled. At a distance many of these institutions look like factories or community colleges; it is only when you come close that you can see the wall or the cyclone fencing.

In the nineteenth century, many prisons around the world were built on the panopticon ("all-seeing") system designed by the British economist and philosopher Jeremy Bentham. The idea was to locate an armed tower in the center of an open area surrounded by a ring of single cells. The guard in the tower could see into all the cells, and thus every inmate remained both isolated and under constant supervision. At one time there were more than three hundred active prisons in the world built on this system. Its effects, however, were unfortunate: deprived of exercise and companionship, many inmates went mad or became violent.

Today only a few panopticon prisons are still in operation, none of them in the United States. But there are many organized on a modification of the system, in which buildings contain triangular or trapezoidal units called "pods" or "modules," designed to hold from fifteen to fifty prisoners. There is a central control station, with tiers of cells around it, and inmates eat and exercise within the pod. The goal of the design is to restrict movement around the prison, separate violent from less violent criminals, and reduce staffing.

In a maximum-security prison today the message of separation and confinement is expressed by high, sheer interior walls, armed guards, and spotlights. There are locked cells, reinforced windows, and heavy gates that can only be opened by an electric switch. As far as possible, inmates are kept under constant surveillance, either by guards or by closed-circuit TV. Often one wall of every cell or dining hall or exercise room is an open metal grid, so that what goes on inside can be seen at a glance. The silent message to inmates is not only that they cannot leave, but that they are dangerous and, if not constantly watched, might try to injure others and steal or destroy property.

Inside, prisons are usually unattractive. The cells and corridors and dining halls are made of rough, hard materials; the walls are painted in drab colors, and sometimes streaked and stained. Rooms may be lit by fluorescent tubes or low-wattage bulbs in wire cages, and the clumsy, battered metal and plastic furniture is bolted to the floor. There is seldom a view from the windows, which may be filled with frosted glass; the message to the inmate is that he or she no longer deserves even to see the world outside, let alone enter it. Though safety and budget restrictions may have something to do with this ugliness, it often seems almost intentional.

The two-man bunk-bed cell of cartoons is by no means standard issue. Maximum-security prisoners are often housed in single cells, since they are assumed to be a threat to everyone, including possible roommates, while in minimum-security and juvenile facilities, inmates may live in large dormitories, where the apparent assumption is that no one is really dangerous. But in fact violence is not uncommon in these dormitories, and noise is constant; as a result both prisoners and guards are under constant stress. In the United States, the recent increase in the prison population has put a strain on housing, and in some cases inmates who have committed serious crimes are crowded into former gyms filled with rows or tiers of bunks.

THE PURPOSE OF PRISON

The removal of criminals from society has not always been the only—or even the main—declared aim of the prison system. At times, four other objectives, sometimes reinforcing and sometimes contradicting one another, have been proposed: punishment, safety, rehabilitation, and profit. All of them are visible in the physical structure of prisons, though not always to a casual visitor.

In the past, crime was primarily linked to punishment, that is, to revenge. Injuries to persons or property, or to the state, were requited by injury to the guilty person. Not only murders, but also many lesser crimes, were punished with execution, often involving great cruelty. Even a petty thief might be branded with the letter *T* or lose his hand. But long after such penalties began to seem barbaric, the idea that criminals should be comfortably housed and fed at the expense of the state met with opposition. Today some offenders are still seen as intrinsically evil. As David Garland puts it in *The Culture of Control*, they are regarded as "dangerous others who threaten our safety and have no calls on our fellow feeling."

Confinement of dangerous persons rather than their punishment is now usually given as the main justification for the American prison system. Of course if separation from society is primary, there is no reason why prisoners should not be relatively well housed, well fed, and provided with ordinary comforts. But in general the present system appears to have been designed to make imprisonment disagreeable, though now and then people who have a great deal of money or powerful connections, like Martha Stewart or Bernard Madoff, have managed to live fairly well behind bars.

REFORM AND REHABILITATION

In the nineteenth century, members of the so-called Progressive movement broke with tradition by proposing that the true purpose of prison was the reform of inmates. Most criminals, it was argued, were not naturally evil. Rather, they were unfortunate people who had received neither a secular nor a spiritual education; they were often functionally illiterate and cut off from morality and religion. They should be taught to read and write and pray; they also needed regular exercise and a nourishing diet, and if possible they should learn a trade. If, when they were released, they were literate, healthy, skilled, and saved, they might eventually, like Dickens's convict Magwitch in *Great Expectations*, become useful members of society.

Such ideas led to the replacement of the words "prison" and "jail" by the euphemisms "reformatory" and "correctional facility." Occasionally there were changes in building design that are still visible today. Most prisons now have classrooms where inmates can learn to read and write and eventually earn a high-school equivalency degree; some offer college-level courses and computer training. There is almost always a place where religious services can be held and a collection of exercise equipment. In some cases visiting rooms have been expanded and made more attractive and comfortable: inmates are allowed face-to-face contact with family and friends, and vending machines for snacks and soft drinks have been installed, incidentally providing profits for the institution.

Visitors, educational programs, psalm singing, and pumping iron make prisoners less restless and bored, and thus more manageable, especially when participation must be earned by good behavior. As a result, there are fewer riots and escape attempts. Some experts, however, as well as many members of the public, still consider efforts to rehabilitate criminals useless and misguided. They cite statistics to show that only a minority of prisoners are ever reformed, and maintain that they should merely be confined and punished, rather than given opportunities and privileges that might not be available outside the walls.

This struggle between the liberal and conservative points of view sometimes takes ambiguous physical shape, resulting in classrooms that are crowded and poorly lit, and exercise equipment and TV sets that are located outdoors even in harsh climates. I will never forget crossing the icy, stone-walled exercise yard at the state prison in Auburn, New York, on a freezing cold night. The menacing darkness was broken only by an occasional harsh spotlight in which flakes of snow whirled, and it was populated by half-visible groups of men muffled in heavy coats, most of them huddled around a row of outdoor television sets, each one of which was under the control of a different inmate gang.

PROFIT AND LOSS

The final reason for the existence of prisons, financial profit, is invisible unless you are an inmate or a guard; but, some believe, it has come to be the real motive behind the almost terrifying expansion of our prison system. Prisoners have always worked, and at one time their labor was obvious: convicts in striped uniforms could be seen digging ditches along roads or hoeing and picking crops in a field, especially in the South. Their visibility was seen as both a punishment and a warning to observers.

Today most prisoners still work, but usually inside the walls in shops and factories that outsiders seldom see. They make office furniture, license plates, uniforms, and many other commodities, in conditions and at pay scales that often compare unfavorably with those in Asian sweatshops: average wages are from one to two dollars day. In some cases the factories run around the clock, and prisoners sleep and eat on different shifts. Their labor is supposed to be voluntary, but in fact many inmates are encouraged to work by promises of reduced sentences, or by threats of solitary confinement or loss of privileges. Inmates are ideal employees, since they do not have to be paid minimum wage or given health insurance, and they are always available. As a result, convict labor is attractive to many companies, and some eventually abandon their outside factories and operate wholly within prisons. This system also generously rewards prison administrators, who often lobby and compete for business contracts. Teenagers in juvenile detention centers may also work, often outdoors on government lands or in state parks. This system not only helps to reduce the cost of incarceration; it tells the public that those who have behaved badly are both paying for their crimes and producing useful goods.

From the outside, prison factories are more or less invisible, but prisons themselves are easier than ever to see, mostly because there are so many more of them. The United States now has the highest incarceration rate and also the highest total prison population in the world: with 5 percent of the world population, we have 25 percent of its prisoners. Of course, the more people there are in prison, whether or not they are working, the greater the profits for companies providing food, equipment, transportation, and telephone and medical services, often of a very low quality. Prisons also provide jobs in construction and maintenance, as well as employment for correctional officers. As a natural result, lobbyists for all these companies and organizations are working for stricter drug laws, longer sentences, and more cells. If they succeed, as you travel around the country you will see more and more prison buildings; it is not clear whether or not this will make you feel safer.

THE HOSPITAL

Before the mid-nineteenth century almost nobody went to a hospital if they could possibly avoid it. When middle- and upper-class

Europeans and Americans were ill or injured, they stayed at home and the doctor came to them. The idea of joining the poor and destitute in a public ward horrified the well-to-do; they were also, quite reasonably, afraid of infection.

The earliest European hospitals were charitable institutions, often attached to almshouses and affiliated with some religious organization; they were built to serve pilgrims, plague victims, and lepers, or to confine those with contagious diseases. They offered little effective medical care except for bone setting and the lancing of boils, but the best of them could provide fresh air, simple food, religious consolation, and a relatively warm, clean place to rest while waiting to recover or die. But during epidemics the death rate in these institutions was terrifyingly high, and even the poor considered them a last resort.

Early almshouses were extremely basic buildings, but by the eighteenth and nineteenth centuries a more elaborate façade in a currently fashionable style was sometimes slapped onto a hospital to show the importance and generosity of its founders. At first glance these buildings are impressive, but their back and side walls are often unadorned. An early- or mid-nineteenth-century hospital was essentially a warehouse for the poor: a two-to-four-story stack of public wards—long, bare rooms with a row of beds down each side. This austerity was justified first on moral grounds (the seriously ill should be thinking of heaven, not of material comforts); later it was explained as hygienic (the fewer objects there were in a ward, the easier it would be to keep clean). Even today a stripped-down, scrubbed look is characteristic of many hospitals.

The introduction of anesthesia, antiseptic surgery, and antibiotics in the mid-nineteenth and twentieth centuries changed hospitals drastically. Middle- and upper-class patients began to realize that they had a better chance of getting well if they left home, and hospital directors soon found that they could charge for more comfortable facilities. Profit-making hospitals run by corporations or by groups of doctors began to appear in the 1890s, and by the middle of the twentieth century there were also separate hospitals for women, for children, for members of different religious faiths, and for those with many different common diseases. Large wards, which could and often did become sinks of infection, were gradually replaced by two- or four-bed rooms, and patients with contagious diseases and those who needed or could pay for special care had single rooms. It was no longer necessary to be kept awake at night by the groans and cries of strangers, especially if you were well-off.

Though the function of the hospital had altered, its physical appearance was slow to change, and for many years something of the bleakness of the charity ward survived in its design. Early-twentieth-century hospital architects favored simple abstract shapes, and the internal spaces they created were bare and basic, with long, wide, featureless corridors and blank interior walls. The exterior was almost always white, the color of purity. Inside, designers favored dull pastels, especially dusty peach and tan, which were supposed to calm and reassure patients and improve morale. Operating rooms, on the other hand, were and still are usually light green, since blood shows up best on this color; operating room scrubs are often light green for the same reason.

Eighteenth- and nineteenth-century hospitals were often set among lawns and gardens, contemplation of which was thought to encourage recovery or ensure a peaceful death; later on, as medicine and surgery became more effective, architects and administrators saved money by eliminating these amenities. Hospitals were not presented as comfortable or attractive places to recover or die in, but as well-organized repair shops. Even today, as Sarah Hosking and Liz Haggard remark in *Healing the Hospital Environment*, they are often conceived of as "garages where people are taken to be checked and repaired before being sent off to resume their journey."

Almost anyone who has ever gone to a public clinic or convenient care center will have waited at least twice for attention: first, often in a line before the receptionist, then among other obviously ill and anxious people and their relatives in an area that rather resembles a bus station, and finally alone in a room with a hard, paper-covered examination table, a sink, and a straight chair. A particularly busy clinic may have many such rooms, in which sick and injured people are condemned to anxiety mixed with boredom unless they have thought to bring a book with them or snatched up a magazine from the rack outside. In a hospital emergency ward things may be even more unpleasant: if your situation is not desperate you may sometimes have to wait a long time in a cubicle behind a canvas curtain, under a buzzing fluorescent light, listening to incomprehensible sounds and cries while suffering pain and fear.

Whether or not you enter a hospital via the emergency ward, eventually you will be shown into a room with a hospital bed, two or three chairs, and numerous electrical outlets. Possibly there will be a second bed in this room, containing a complete stranger who may be seriously ill or in pain. You will be told to undress and put on a hospital gown, and the door will be firmly shut behind you. You may be instructed to get into a high bed that may have bars on the side like a crib. If you go out into the hall you will be scolded and told to return to your room. (Sometimes, in your weakened and frightened condition, you will be physically or psychologically unable to get up and drag the heavy door open anyhow.) The dominant sensation is that of having been reduced to helpless infancy. The hospital gown is shaped like a baby's wrapper, made of flimsy cotton and fastened at the back with tapes; it is designed so that it can be put on by someone else rather than by its wearer. This costume makes you totally vulnerable, and is a signal that your body will soon be exposed to observation and invasion by strangers.

Social and moral force, as well as pain and fear and hope, and the sensation of being a very small child again, keep patients from leaving a hospital. But the structure of the building also helps. Today public hospitals are usually large, impressive buildings, which in some ways resemble old-fashioned public high schools. They have the same strict schedules and bleak, efficient décor, constantly ringing bells and broadcast announcements, long, bare corridors, and heavy doors, each with its observation window. Many hospitals still assign patients to two-bed or four-bed rooms, where it may be impossible to sleep because your roommates have noisy visitors, listen to television programs you hate, or (more forgivably, but just as exhaustingly) groan and cry out with pain much of the day and night.

An informal survey of former patients revealed that almost nobody likes hospitals except for women who have had babies, and even they confine their approval to the maternity ward. As one mother put it,

> After I had each of my children I had very happy associations with hospitals. I still associate the top of the buildings with babies and sunshine, but the lower floors I think of as increasingly dark and grim. I think of hospitals as being big boxes of life and death, and that you have to be careful to stay in the good, life-giving areas.

Another interviewee said that hospitals made him "think of big gravestones. Especially if they're made of that shiny granite. I wonder if I'm going to get out alive." Many informants reported that they often got lost in hospitals, and felt helpless and not in control. "The TV was at an awkward angle and too far away to see clearly. The lighting was bad and I couldn't do anything about it." Some people reported that the smells of antiseptic and blood and the noise of the machines frightened them. Others, however, said that the technological and mechanical aspect of a big hospital, though strange and scary, made them feel that they were getting the most advanced care.

At times, some people said, being in a hospital felt like being in prison. They pointed out that the hospital gown, like the prisoner's uniform, enforces anonymity, and that a hospital stay, like many prison sentences, is usually open-ended. You may be released in a few hours, or you may never leave the building alive. And though hospitals are not surrounded by electric fences and guard towers, they are not easy to get out of, and what happens to you there is generally unpleasant and undignified. There is also the question of loss of status. Though the ill are pitied, they are also sometimes looked down upon; like people in jail, they are not full members of society. Of course, if you are in a hospital briefly for something like appendicitis or a sports injury, it does your reputation little harm; a stay for childbirth or plastic surgery may enhance it, by demonstrating that you are fertile or wealthy. But longer and recurring visits, for more serious diseases, have been found in studies to have a lowering effect on status.

Lack of control over your own life is built into hospital design, and, according to Ann Sloan Devlin and Allison B. Arneill, has "been found to be associated with depression, passivity, . . . and reduced immune system functioning." They also point out that what nurses and doctors call the good patient—the compliant one—"may actually be in a state of anxious or depressed helplessness, . . . while the bad patient is angry and resistant." Worse still are intensive care units, which seldom have windows and suffer from continuous noise and harsh lighting that makes no difference between day and night, causing temporal disorientation. Hospital administrators now recognize what is called ICU syndrome, which involves delirium, hallucinations, and delusions in previously psychologically normal patients.

Hospital architecture is also hard on the people who work there. The constant noise, the ugliness, the unpleasant smells, the sense of confusion and enclosure, the sudden emergencies, the long hours, and the great distances from one part of a huge building to another make the jobs of nurses, doctors, and support staff difficult. They get headaches and become exhausted; they suffer from depression, anxiety, and stress, and often contract infections. As Devlin and Arneill put it, "The statement that prison guards do more time than the inmates applies to health care settings as well."

• • •

As a result of both public and private complaints, hospitals are beginning to change. Some have followed the advice of experts who say
that a hospital should look more like a hotel; it should suggest that
you will have a comfortable and pleasant experience. In hospitals
that have been built or remodeled along these lines, a well-to-do patient can now pay for attractive surroundings and good food. There
are more and more single rooms, many with a pleasant view. Often
both rooms and corridors have been painted in cheerful colors and
decorated with pictures, plants, curtains, and comfortable furniture
for visitors. In children's wards there will be toys and books and a
daybed in each room so that parents can stay overnight without having to sleep upright in a stiff leather chair, as I did several times years
ago. All these things, according to studies, lead to faster recovery;
they also increase yearly income and market share.

Some experts, however, believe that what patients want from
a hospital is a high-tech image that will assure them that they are
about to receive the latest and best medical treatments. A hospital,
they remind us, is essentially devoted to the cure of disease. They
recommend advertising that announces survival rates and stresses
the presence of state-of-the-art diagnostic machines and procedures. From this point of view, a hospital room should not look too
comfortable or informal; patients and their families should be aware
at all times that they are surrounded by high-tech equipment and
highly trained doctors. Today, both hotel-type and laboratory-type
hospitals are common; often, a building appears to be trying to combine the two forms.

What these opposing views have in common is the belief that the
design of a hospital should both project and justify expense. Many
big hospitals now advertise, and compete with each other for patients who have money or generous insurance. The very rich can
stay in luxurious suites with guest rooms for their relatives, Internet connections, and a complete kitchen. Special care is devoted to

the admissions desk, which hospitals are now advised to refer to as "the customer service center." The term "customer," experts explain, should be seen as including not only the patient, but also visitors, family members, employers, physicians, staff, and vendors. What is now called the "intake area" may look like a hotel lobby, with a reception counter, pictures, plants, and comfortable chairs. It may include a gift shop, coffee shop, flower shop, pharmacy, bookstore and newsstand, and an ATM machine. The planning expert Cynthia Hayward warns hospital administrators against neglecting these profitable additions. "Undersized and inappropriate visitor support space, a lack of amenities, and outdated interior décor and furnishings may promote a negative first impression among the organization's customers and defeat efforts to increase volume and expand market share."

It is not only in the intake area that the contemporary hospital is focused on economics. For maximum profit, all beds must be filled at all times. The ideal patient demands nothing and requires many expensive procedures and drugs and monitoring devices—ideally, he or she is very ill, with complex disabilities, possibly in a coma. Today new mothers now often spend only a day or two in the hospital instead of the week I and my friends were allowed for rest and recovery back in in the 1950s and 1960s. Maternity wards and delivery rooms have been made more cheerful and comfortable, and more welcoming to family members, but after the first twenty-four hours they do not bring in much money. An otherwise healthy patient who just hangs around eating full meals is unprofitable; the sooner you can get rid of her or him, the better. Presumably it was for this reason that I was once discharged with a compound fracture of the leg after only a few days, though I could not walk even with crutches and there was no one at home to take care of me.

One new market-driven development is the building of satellite clinics, open only during the day, to give tests, take care of minor illness, and shunt more seriously ill and remunerative patients to a particular hospital. Another possibility is for hospitals and clinics to add "wellness centers" where outpatients and people who are recovering can use expensive exercise equipment and receive massage and beauty treatments. All these amenities, of course, are largely available only to the rich and those with generous health insurance. The poor, meanwhile, spend hours waiting in the bleak, germ-filled emergency rooms of overworked and underfunded public hospitals.

The resemblance of the hospital to both the prison and the hotel has sometimes been noted. As Abram de Swaan remarks,

> From an architectural perspective, hospitals, hotels, and prisons pose similar problems, and in fact these buildings tend to look somewhat like one another. On the one hand, they all hold a transient population that must, however, be cared for twenty-four hours a day, seven days a week; and, on the other hand, they all accommodate a permanent population that does the care-taking, often for many years at a stretch, in daily eight-hour shifts, according to a fixed daily rhythm. . . .

Prisons and hospitals sometimes try to look and operate somewhat like hotels, while hotels for their part naturally seek to avoid any association with the other two.

THE MENTALLY ILL

Two institutions that today try hard not to resemble prisons or hospitals are those once known as the madhouse and the old-age home. Later the preferred terms were "insane asylum" and "nursing home"; the current euphemisms are "psychiatric hospital" and "senior living center" or "assisted living facility." The degree to which these places succeed in resembling upmarket hotels or country clubs depends largely on economic factors.

In early modern Europe and America, mentally afflicted people were highly visible: every village had its fools and half-wits and its Mad Tom or Crazy Jane. But from the late seventeenth century on, there was a growing attempt to remove such people from public view so that they would not threaten or offend the sensibilities of the general population. In the eighteenth and early nineteenth centuries, curious spectators could pay to visit London's Bethlehem Hospital, known as Bedlam, in the same spirit in which we might visit a zoo today: a famous illustration in Hogarth's *The Rake's Progress* shows well-dressed ladies and gentlemen observing the ranting and deluded patients. Though this sort of tourism ended in the mid-nineteenth century, society continued to kept the insane confined: if they were well-off, usually in private homes, like the madwoman in the attic of *Jane Eyre*—if not, in public institutions.

The psychiatric hospitals of the nineteenth and early twentieth centuries were huge, warehouse-like buildings, or collections of buildings, into which indigent patients, or those whose families did not wish to pay for their care, were sorted according to the degree of their disability. At first, the most confused and violent inmates caused a lot of trouble, but by the mid-twentieth century most of them had been made docile and dim by drugs, or by lobotomy and electric shock treatment. Efforts on the part of patients to leave were generally unsuccessful unless they had relatives and doctors on their side.

Sometimes there were serious efforts to make these new mental hospitals attractive, at least from outside. Thirty years ago, Willard Asylum for the Chronic Insane (now closed), not far from where I live in upstate New York, resembled a redbrick college campus with extensive lawns and gardens, enclosed by a high, spike-topped iron fence; there was also an artificial lake, heavily fenced to prevent suicides. Inside the buildings, amenities were fewer. The most seriously afflicted patients lived in bare, locked wards, and spent their time in shabby dayrooms where a black-and-white television set, mounted high on the wall so that it could not be damaged, played constantly. Below it badly dressed, stunned-looking people sat in rows of chairs, few or none of them watching TV. Less troubled patients were housed in almost equally bare but unlocked wards, which they could sometimes leave to go to the dining hall or to walk on the grounds. Patient labor saved money: many inmates worked in the gardens, where they grew fruit and vegetables for their own meals.

The efforts of patient advocates, and the desire of state governments to save money, gradually closed many of these hospitals and sent thousands of confused, anxious, and depressed people out into the community, where it was claimed that they would be better off. Unfortunately, safe places for them to live, with someone on hand to make sure they took their prescriptions, were not always available. As a result, Mad Tom and Crazy Jane can now be seen everywhere again, sleeping on park benches or in cardboard boxes, or wandering about the streets.

At the other end of the economic scale, the rich now have wide access to "therapeutic communities" in which to place their disturbed or difficult relatives. An expensive psychiatric hospital may be almost indistinguishable from a country club or resort hotel. It will have gardens, tennis courts, a swimming pool, and possibly even a golf course. The architect and interior designer will have made efforts to provide a soothing and calming atmosphere by the use of pale soft colors for walls, carpets, and curtains; they will have avoided odd angles, sharply contrasting surfaces, busy patterns, and bright hues, as well as shadowy, mysterious, and possibly threatening spaces. Often there will be no mirrors in the public rooms. If there are any long corridors, they will be softly lit and broken up with plants and pictures. Everything will combine to suggest peacefulness, safety, and relaxation.

Because most mental patients are now on mood-altering and tranquilizing drugs, the atmosphere in psychiatric hospitals is often strangely quiet, and everyone may seem to move in slow motion. Patients will have wide choices of walks on the grounds, but some may prefer to stay in their rooms, or even be encouraged to do so. The sociologist Erving Goffman wrote in *Asylums* that "to rest immobile in bed is, after all, defined as what one does in our society when one is sick, and in some cases the patient may feel physically incapable of doing anything else."

THE OLD

The contemporary retirement community or senior living center usually tries to look as little as possible like a hospital or a prison, and the more expensive it is, the more often it succeeds. A really upmarket retirement home may resemble a large, luxurious country-house hotel, though it is a hotel that most guests will never leave. As a result of extensive surveys of what potential customers and their families want, most designers have deliberately opted for a comforting old-fashioned look. They have tried to balance their clients' need for care against their fear of being cut off from the world; white picket fences will be preferred to solid walls.

The buildings of an upscale retirement community are often surrounded by extensive grounds, with flowering shrubbery and large old trees; they have peaked roofs, shutters, dormer windows, wide porches with rocking chairs, and hanging baskets of old-fashioned flowers. Natural materials—wood and stone and brick—usually predominate. The exterior doors all have windows so that residents can see in and out. Inside there are attractive private rooms and public spaces that suggest a domestic interior of fifty years ago. There are curtains and carpets and flowering plants everywhere, and the dining room resembles a high-end hotel restaurant of the past, with chandeliers, tablecloths, linen napkins, and menus. Often there is a library, meeting rooms, a pool, and an exercise room. At the same time ramps have replaced steps; the hallways have discreet handrails and are wide enough to accommodate wheelchairs, and it is possible to sit down in the showers.

New arrivals will be able to take advantage of all these amenities. At first they may live in so-called "cottages" and continue to drive and, if they like, make their own meals. Some of them, relieved from shopping, gardening, cleaning, cooking, home repairs, climbing flights of stairs, and shoveling their own driveways, will experience an increase of energy and find new friends and new interests. But gradually they will begin to feel the physical and mental effects of old age. The institution will be prepared for this, and will at some point suggest that they move into an attached "assisted living facility" or "long-term-care wing." Here there will be fewer recreational opportunities and more nursing staff; there will also be architectural provision for loss of physical and mental capacity. There may be large signs reading DINING ROOM and OFFICE, and photographs of patients on the doors of their rooms to prevent them getting lost. Though some people with dementia often have an almost uncontrollable urge to wander off, none of the windows will have bars—but they will also not open more than four or five inches, and if you want to go for a walk you will have to ask a staff member to unlock the outer door and accompany you.

In an inexpensive old-age home there is less disguise. The buildings will be constructed of reinforced concrete, or of imitation stone and wood and brick. There may be a flat roof and vinyl shingles. Inside, the curtains and carpets will be cheaper, most of the flowers and plants will be artificial, and there may be visible bars on the windows. Rooms will be smaller, and possibly shared, and the staff-to-patient ratio will be less generous. A badly funded public old-age facility will look even more like a prison, with cell-like rooms or wards, steel and glass doors, and vinyl flooring, and the ill-paid attendants will not be disguised as friendly receptionists. In such a place it is more obvious that the very old are serving a life sentence; their crime is simply that they have ceased to function productively and may cause trouble for the able-bodied, or at least make them feel uncomfortable.

There is an odd aesthetic and psychological component in our society's wish to conceal what are called "senior citizens." We admire old buildings and old trees; some of our most celebrated landscapes and poems celebrate the beauty of classical ruins. Yet we do not really want to look at or think about old people. American television seldom shows anyone over seventy, and when it does there has usually been a lot of plastic surgery and makeup involved. The old frighten us with the thought that we will one day resemble them; we too will eventually be old, then ill, and then dead.

LIFE INSIDE

The more time you spend in any building, the greater its influence on you will be. An hour in a good restaurant can lift your spirits; an hour in an ugly, crowded, noisy airport terminal, waiting for your flight to be announced or canceled, can make you anxious and depressed—but in both cases the effect soon wears off. To be confined anywhere twenty-four hours a day for a long, perhaps indefinite number of days is deeply disturbing. It is like hearing the same song over and over again; even if the tune is attractive and apparently harmless, it bores its way into your brain.

The effect of being permanently housed in any building, whether it looks like an expensive hotel or a prison cell block, can be severe. In some ways being in jail may be less disruptive to the psyche, because there is no pretense that you are really at an upscale resort and can depart whenever you like. It is sometimes possible, of course, to leave a psychiatric hospital or a nursing home, either on a chaperoned excursion or in the company of family or friends who will take you out to lunch or dinner; but you will always be returned afterward. If you leave permanently, it will usually only be to move to another facility of the same sort. Chances of getting out of a psychiatric hospital permanently are better, but there is always the threat that you will have to go back, and if you do not you will often have to face what Goffman called stigmatization—in this case, the assumption of others that you are perhaps only temporarily or partially sane.

Goffman also wrote extensively of the process known as institutionalization, which eventually afflicts almost everyone who is shut up for a long time in a prison, hospital, or old-age home—or in some boarding schools and army barracks. After a period of stress and confusion caused by the loss of their past freedoms, people often adjust. They make friends; they learn how to survive and get on in their new circumstances. The institution, with its rules and customs and routines, gradually becomes their whole world, and what is outside comes to be regarded as irrelevant or even, in some cases, as frightening. As a result, long-term prisoners or patients in mental hospitals may "mess up," as their discharge date approaches. And your aged parent, who angrily or pitifully protested the move to a senior living center, may even, if you try to bring him or her home to live with you, refuse to come.

CHAPTER 12

Houses of Hospitality:
Hotels and Restaurants

I n any American town or city, many commercial buildings are versions of two of the oldest businesses—the roadside inn and the tavern. They are designed not only to attract our attention but also to draw us in with the promise of food, drink, and rest. Once there, we are encouraged to stay—though usually for a limited amount of time—and to leave poorer than when we arrived.

The skills of restaurant owners and innkeepers, and of their architects and designers, have been developed over centuries to produce this effect, though the finished product varies widely according to the kind of customers the business wants to attract. A sidewalk café may deliberately interrupt our progress down a city street with tables and chairs and tubs of flowers; a very expensive restaurant may conceal itself inside a hotel or behind heavy curtains.

THE HOSPITALITY BUSINESS

Some enterprises descend ultimately from another very early type of commercial establishment, the whorehouse. Instead of (or in addition to) selling things that we can take away, they market what their publicity calls an "experience"—a dining experience, a travel experience, or a vacation experience. The phrase is usually qualified with a positive adjective: we are told that we will, for instance, have a

satisfying, superior, or unique dining experience. The implied promise is that in this restaurant or hotel we will eat better or sleep more
comfortably than we do at home. We will also be treated with more
consideration and deference than we usually get from our family,
friends, and fellow workers.

Unlike a prison, which physically informs the inmates that they
are dubious, undesirable persons, even a low-end motel is designed
to make customers feel cared for and valued. Some experts recommend that houses of hospitality think of themselves as providing
a theatrical experience, and in fact a successful hotel or restaurant
usually has an elaborately designed set, professional lighting, and
well-trained and costumed actors who work together to create a performance for customers. Patrons of an expensive hotel will be subtly
encouraged to imagine themselves, for a day or two, as millionaire
celebrities who deserve only the best accommodations and services;
participants in a convention will be given the illusion that they are
successful and important in their chosen field. A couple who choose
to spend a weekend at a bed-and-breakfast will ideally be treated as
welcome family members: the ruffled, densely pillowed four-poster
bed, shelves of china knickknacks, and breakfast pancakes are meant
to suggest visits to the home of loving parents or grandparents.

Though people who go to hotels and restaurants know they
are paying for the privilege, the essentially economic nature of
the transaction is often disguised. Hotels and restaurants almost
always refer to their customers as "guests," and money is seldom
mentioned, though we may be encouraged to "save" by spending, at
special off-season rates. The pretense that we are welcomed for our
own sake is maintained until the bill slides under the door of our
room, or onto the restaurant table in a discreet dark folder.

The amount of these bills is apt to come as an unwelcome surprise. There may be charges and taxes that we did not expect, especially if we unknowingly ordered bottled water in a restaurant or
made phone calls from the hotel room. It is an axiom of the hospi-

tality industry that people should be encouraged to live more expensively when traveling than they do back home. The difference may be small or huge. In a budget motel or restaurant, your only—or at least most obvious—luxury is the freedom from menial tasks: though your bed may not be very comfortable, you do not have to make it yourself; the breakfast coffee may be weak, and the pastry stale, but you do not have to prepare them or wash up.

In a high-end vacation resort, on the other hand, you will often far exceed your usual standard of living—especially if you are on your honeymoon, or if some company that has designs on your wallet or your professional influence is paying for the trip. A free weekend at a resort may soften you up with lavish buffets and tropical drinks and the attentions of attractive strangers until, overfed, overflattered, and somewhat dizzy, you are persuaded to buy a time-share, vote for a certain bill, or agree to recommend a new drug to your patients.

The way a hotel or motel is designed to look from the outside tells the experienced traveler what sort of guests it expects to attract. Businesses that cater mainly to tourists will try to suggest ease and relaxation through rounded shapes and lavish floral plantings, while an establishment that serves mostly business clients will usually stick to no-nonsense rectangular shapes, though allowing a few curves for their in-house bars and restaurants. Price, too, can be calculated from a quick look. The larger the sign, especially if it is trimmed with neon or surrounded by blinking bulbs, the cheaper the place will be; very low-end roadside hotels and motels may even announce their low room rate in lights. Expensive establishments, on the other hand, tend to have only a small, discreet sign set into an exterior wall or planted among flowers beside the entrance.

Exterior walkways and stairs, instead of interior corridors and elevators, reduce building costs, and are often a low-price indicator. They also make your stay less safe, because anyone who wants to can reach your room without passing the reception desk. Persons engaged in the sale of drugs or sex naturally favor this kind of architecture, and so do thieves, some of whom may be employees of the motel or their friends. The separate cottages of the old-fashioned "tourist court" and the luxury palm-roofed bungalows of resorts are vulnerable in the same way. In both cases, what you gain in terms of privacy you give up in terms of security. A resort may have high walls and gates and guards, but its relaxed and sometimes intoxicated customers are tempting targets, especially since they are often having such a good time that they forget to put their valuables in the safe.

Most American travelers, when not splurging on a wedding or holiday, stay in low- or mid-priced chain hotels and motels, which can also be easily recognized from outside. They are usually large, blocklike buildings of brick or stucco, with drive-up portico entrances, surrounded by uninteresting hardy local trees and shrubs. If they are in city centers they may have an underground garage, which will charge for parking. Farther out, where land is cheaper, there will be minimally landscaped parking lots.

An inexpensive hotel or motel will clearly inform travelers that a stay there will be reasonably comfortable and pleasant. Well-kept shrubbery and lots full of clean, fairly new cars are a good sign. Low ceilings are almost always an indication of low prices: indeed, the higher the ceiling in any hotel lobby, the higher its prices usually are. If the lobby is small and plain, your stay will be less expensive, but not necessarily uncomfortable; nevertheless, experienced travelers will ask to see the room before they hand over their credit cards. Piles of clean towels in the bathroom are promising—plastic glasses are not. A selection of free shampoo, conditioner, and lotion is a standard amenity: their lack announces that the place is on the skids. A TV or air-conditioning unit that does not work, or makes a loud rattling noise, is another ill omen.

According to an informal survey, the most repellent features of undesirable hotels and motels are, in ascending order, noise, darkness, disorder, and dirt. Even the most comfortable room became intolerable when the walls were so thin that the travelers were kept awake all night by a quarreling or loudly passionate couple next door, or by their TV set. Dark-colored walls and carpets and bedspreads were depressing to many people, and seemed soiled even when they were possibly clean; sheets and towels that were stained or torn suggested the presence of bugs and germs. When the carpeting and furniture were visibly worn or soiled, the revulsion of interviewees was even stronger. Low-watt bulbs, presumably chosen to save money or disguise the shabbiness of rooms and corridors, made people think that the hotels or motel was dirty. The absence or malfunction of bathtub plugs and showerheads also repelled many informants, and brown stains on the fixtures were even worse. "I felt as if centipedes were about to crawl out of the drain," one disgusted guest reported.

A high-end hotel or motel announces itself immediately from outside. There will be lots of expensive landscaping, and cars will be discreetly concealed by shrubbery. Even if the building is essentially a block of brick or concrete, it will be disguised with porches, columns, archways, towers, or bay windows that attempt to suggest a Hudson River mansion, a Southern plantation house, or a millionaire's vacation home.

In the lobby of an upscale hotel there will be luxuriously comfortable furniture, lush houseplants, and lavish fresh flower arrangements. The rooms will be well furnished, possibly with real antiques, and a basket of huge, artificial-looking, but in fact real fruit will appear on the coffee table in your room, along with a fulsome welcoming letter assuring you of the manager's respect and his appreciation of your patronage. The bathroom will be full of fancy sample toiletries, which are not as expensive for the hotel as you might think, since they are often provided for a nominal fee by their manufacturers in the hope of future sales, and many well-to-do guests will not use them, preferring their own favorite brands. Guests will also seldom steal the big, fluffy white towels, because they already have plenty at home—though in the past, when fancy hotels had monogrammed linens, they were sometimes removed as souvenirs. Yet since kleptomania has no class limit, even in luxury hotels expensive lamps and clocks are often firmly attached to the bedside table.

The cheapest and the most expensive lodgings are strangely alike in some ways. For one thing, both often have guests who stay for more than a few nights at a time. A run-down motel room may be home to someone of dubious occupation, or a whole family on welfare, for many weeks or months, while a suite in a high-end city hotel may be the year-round pied-à-terre of a billionaire. Both high- and low-end hotels also tend to have small lobbies, and in an upscale so-called "boutique hotel" the rooms may be no larger than they are in a low-priced motel—though, of course, very differently furnished: multiple telephones, huge mirrors, and Jacuzzi-type tubs will try to suggest that you have attained celebrity status.

CONVENTION AND CONFERENCE HOTELS

Some midprice hotels and motels are deliberately planned to attract business conventions and conferences. Individual travelers may stay there, but they will tend to be crowded aside by mobs of orthodontists, insurance agents, New Age spiritualists, college teachers, or political candidates and their supporters, often with identifying labels pinned to them. The lobbies will be very large, full of small groups of furniture, and there may be more than one bar or restaurant. A convention hotel may have as many as two thousand rooms, which will usually take up no more than 75 percent of the total square footage; much of the remainder will be occupied by meeting rooms, dining rooms, and exhibition halls. A conference center, with 100 to 300 rooms, will usually assign only 55–65 percent of its total space to guest rooms and corridors.

Convention hotels, which are usually large and centrally located, are often used as meeting places by people who are not staying there, and by shoppers who need a place to rest and relax. If you are reasonably well dressed you can use the washroom of this type of hotel without being challenged, and sit in the lobby for up to two hours even if you don't buy any food or drink. The hotel staff will probably know that you are not a guest, but they will not care as long as your appearance maintains its image.

Other upscale hotels and resorts are designed to attract large social functions: weddings, banquets, retirement parties, and charity balls. (Typically, these functions take place in a hotel at least one level up from where the participants would normally stay when traveling.) In these places the public rooms will be more lavishly furnished, with lush plants and flower arrangements. Casual travelers will be crowded into elevators with giggling bridesmaids and drunken senior citizens rather than with ambitious lawyers, pharmaceutical representatives, and collectors of vintage Barbie dolls.

TOURIST HOTELS AND RESORTS

Some hotels and motels cater mostly to tourists. If a place is called a "lodge," it will usually be associated with some strenuous activity like rafting, fishing, or skiing, while less exhausting sports such as golf and tennis tend to use the term "inn." Gambling announces itself with extravagant décor and signage, flashing lights, ringing slot machines, gold-framed mirrors, shiny marble floors, and glittering chandeliers. Casinos also tend to have themes, and in some cases the entire hotel may look like a giant fantasy castle or a black glass pyramid. All this excitement is consciously deployed to stimulate and confuse patrons, inducing a kind of artificial high and making them feel that they have stepped into a magical world in which life is full of careless fun and it is perfectly all right to lose your inhibitions— and, of course, your money.

Another specialized type of hotel is what is known in the business as a "destination resort." These places, often in exotic locations, are advertised as containing everything that a tourist might want or more; they may include game rooms, exercise rooms, tennis courts, golf courses, and access to beaches, ski slopes, or hiking trails. Largely for economic reasons, guests are subtly but strongly persuaded to stay on the hotel grounds, where sanitized samples of, for example, Fijian dancers or overpriced Appalachian arts and crafts will be brought in. Group tours of local attractions may be available, but if you want to visit a nearby town on your own you may be discouraged, and even frightened, by stories of undependable transportation and local crime.

Some expensive hotels and resorts have a deliberate fantasy or historical theme: they will, for instance, pretend to be Western ranches or Colonial villages. This does not always go down well with guests. One informant complained bitterly of "a faux-castle inn" in Iowa that "was dark and dank and not very clean and stank of mildew," not appreciating the fact that real medieval castles were very likely to have had the same characteristics. There are also hotels, often patronized by honeymooners and lovers, in which each room or suite has its own particular theme. In one, for instance you can choose from Roman Spa, Log Cabin, Tree House, Jungle, and Love Shack (this one has a heart-shaped bed, a mirror on the ceiling, and a basket of sex toys). In an Edmonton, Alberta, hotel you can sleep in an imitation stagecoach or the back of a pickup truck. Hotels like this attract romantic couples of every age; according to some friends, they often have a good effect on the relationship. One interviewee remarked that the nature and even the future of a love affair can be determined by the sort of hotel someone takes you to. If it is both beautiful and comfortable, you have seriously charmed him or her; and may expect a happy future together. A cheap, shabby motel, especially if it is chosen largely because it affords secrecy and anonymity, predicts a cheap love affair with a shabby ending.

Hotels get upset when people occupy space without spending money. One common solution is to make the lounges small and the cafés big. Airport terminals, according to Robert Sommer, act from similar motives when they furnish waiting areas with rows of hard seats in which "it is virtually impossible for two people sitting down to converse comfortably for any length of time. . . . The motive . . . appears to be the same as . . . in hotels and other commercial places—to drive people out of the waiting area into cafés, bars, and shops."

RESTAURANTS

In a midlevel or high-end restaurant, just as in a hotel, there is usually a willing, if unconscious, collusion in the drama of hospitality. Customers do not think that their waiter sincerely admires and cares for them, but they enjoy the sensation of being honored, served, and deferred to. Patrons of a Chinese or Italian eatery do not believe themselves to be in Beijing or Rome, but the more authentic the décor and menu, the more satisfied they will be. If the staff seem to be Chinese or Italian, so much the better. A French restaurant whose chef is actually from Paris will encourage him to make himself visible to the diners, especially if he has a charming accent. If in fact he was born in Brooklyn or Bangladesh, he is likely to remain concealed in the kitchen.

Like hotels, most restaurants are deliberately designed to attract a certain type of customer. Though they may also depend on repeat visits or on local or international reputation, what might be called impulse eating is also sometimes important. Generally, the larger the sign, the more the place counts on walk-in or drive-in trade. A McDonald's may be identifiable from a hundred yards away, while an independent local hangout will be content with a midsized sign. A famous gourmet restaurant, where you must make reservations and casual drop-in customers would merely be a nuisance, will be relatively hard to find. At an expensive New York restaurant called Sidecar, to which the editor of this book was taken, there was once no sign at all, merely a battered-looking old door.

Franchised chain restaurants all look alike. No matter where in the world you are, they promise a familiar experience with no surprises. At every Applebee's or T.G.I. Friday's or Red Lobster the menu is the same, and it usually includes glossy color photographs of available dishes for customers who trust pictures more than words, or cannot read English very well. Independent restaurants, on the other hand, often strive to seem unique. They may have an unusual décor or offer unusual dishes, or disguise familiar dishes with foreign names. As in some examples of postmodern architecture, variety and surprise are offered, occasionally to a disconcerting degree, and items on the menu may combine ingredients that most home cooks might strive to keep apart: (At one such place, for example, I imprudently ordered a dish that combined lamb, beets, ginger, and olives.)

The sign system that identifies an ethnic restaurant is both elaborate and artificial, and may not much resemble its equivalent in the old country. Few upmarket dining places in India, for instance, will be as cluttered with native screens and hangings and statuettes of Hindu gods as the "Taj Mahal" in a midsized American city. The same is true of regional fare. A seafood restaurant that caters almost exclusively to tourists will be littered with old fishnets and colored glass floats and plastic lobsters; one that depends mostly on locals, including actual fishermen, may merely have a drawing of a lobster on its menu. According to comments, there is sometimes a negative correlation between the amount of ethnic or regional kitsch and the quality of the food.

Like hotels, restaurants choose their location and design to attract the customers they want. A casual sandwich shop catering to office employees often opens directly onto a busy street. Restaurants patronized by travelers are on or near highways; those favored by local residents appear in shopping malls at the edge of residential neighborhoods or on the main street downtown.

Even when the location does not provide information, once you enter any restaurant the décor and furniture will tell you what to expect. A small plastic-top table and strip lighting suggest cheap hamburgers and fries; casual checked tablecloths and napkins and shaded lamps predict steak or ribs, fudge sundaes, and apple pie. Carpets, white tablecloths, and padded seats foreshadow fancy sauces and even fancier prices. In what is sometimes referred to as a "temple of gastronomy," the carpets and tablecloths will be even thicker, and the hush almost ecclesiastical. In such places food is worshipped by staff and customers alike. The table is an altar, the chef a kind of high priest surrounded by lesser priests, and waiters serve as acolytes. Dining is a kind of communion, with dishes presented under huge silver covers, and wines decanted and sipped with almost religious reverence.

SEATING

If we are allowed to select our table in a restaurant, we will be affected by the same unconscious messages that are sent by the arrangement of furniture in other public spaces, such as libraries and waiting rooms. Psychologists point out that we have inherited from our remote ancestors a preference for what they call "defensible space." In unfamiliar situations, especially if strangers are present, we like to have our backs against some sort of barrier and a clear area in front of us, so that we can watch for friends or enemies. In restaurants most customers who arrive alone will choose to sit with their back to a wall, and if possible, facing the door, only partly in order to watch for the friend they are meeting. When a couple enters the man will usually offer the woman the presumably safer seat. If customers are of the same sex, the one who takes or is offered the inside seat is likely to be the elder or dominant party.

When there are several empty tables, two friends will often try to take over a four-person table, known in the trade as a "four-top," so that they can sit on adjoining sides and converse more easily. Antagonists, on the other hand, prefer to confront each other across a barricade of flowers and menus and condiments at a "two-top." In many big-city restaurants where rents are high there will be a long row of small tables crowded against a banquette on one or both sides of the room; this arrangement, according to some observers, has a tendency to turn friends and even lovers into antagonists. It often also makes it impossible for any important conversation to take place, since whatever is said can be heard by strangers on each side. When the purpose of the meal is largely ritualistic, or the diners do not like each other very much, this may be an advantage; it is difficult to quarrel seriously while four other people are listening to every word you say.

In large groups the dominant person or host will often be seated at one end of a long table, while those who are being honored (perhaps at a birthday, an engagement or retirement party, or a baby shower) will be assigned a center seat where they are visible to and audible by everyone. The closer the other guests are to the honorees or the host, the more important they are to these persons, and the more central to the occasion.

Whether a restaurant is perceived as crowded or not depends on social and cultural factors. Studies have shown that in general people from a Northern European tradition are more at ease when there is some distance between them and others; people from a Southern European tradition are more comfortable in a crowd. As a result, northerners may feel that southerners are invading their personal space; that they are pushy and threatening—or, on the other hand, overfriendly—while southerners may experience northerners as awkward, cool, or shy. A restaurant with widely spaced tables invites the patronage of northerners; one jammed with furniture attracts those who like to be close to others. Practical considerations also play a part: many people will avoid entering an establishment that is nearly empty, but they may also walk away from one in which every table seems to be taken. Their (often accurate) assumption is that a sparsely occupied place has something wrong with it, while if there are too many other customers they will not get a good table, and it will take a long time to be seated and served.

PLEASURE AND PROFIT

Most restaurants are deeply interested in what is politely called "revenue maximization," and this concern governs even the smallest details of design and operation. Scholars in the hospitality industry, for example, have made detailed studies of "food landscapes" with emphasis on how a plate looks. They know that a very small plate will appear to be piled generously high with food, and that an undersized piece of expensive meat or fish can be disguised by graceful arabesques of sauce or an artful display of vegetables under and around it, and that half a tomato or avocado will seem larger if it is cut in thin slices and fanned out prettily.

In most establishments you order your meal and it is either brought to you or shoved across a counter. In other cases, you help yourself at a buffet. Here, though you may seem to be a free agent, the proprietor has usually employed what is called "managed choice," so as to maximize profits. He will be aware that, as studies have proved, visibility and convenience increase consumption. No matter what our natural preferences, we serve ourselves more from larger and nearer containers. (Even nutrition experts took more ice cream when presented with a 34-ounce bowl instead of a 14-ounce bowl, and did not realize that they had done so.) In most salad bars the plates are small, and the inexpensive tossed greens will be up front in a very large bowl with big serving implements. The tomatoes and cucumbers will be in smaller bowls, while nuts and cheese are farther back in tiny trays that are difficult to reach; they will also have smaller serving spoons, or sometimes none.

Sophisticated restaurant managers are also concerned with what is known as SPM, or "spending per minute," for every table. At a very expensive restaurant customers may linger over a many-course meal for hours; but most places usually count on at least two seatings for lunch or dinner; and look with favor on anyone who wants to arrive unusually early or late. Trouble arises when a couple, or more often a group, stays longer than expected when another reservation has been scheduled for that table. Various methods are employed to hasten the departure of those who linger after they have finished eating and spending. One common ploy is the presentation of the bill before it has been requested. Another method is to turn down the lights slightly, ostensibly to create a more romantic atmosphere, but in fact to suggest that it is getting late and time for people to move on. Studies have also shown that fast, lively contemporary music energizes diners and makes them leave sooner, presumably to do something more active, while slower tempos and classical music encourage people to stay longer.

From the point of view of the restaurant owner, the ideal customer will stay a short time and spend a lot of money, producing the highest possible SPM. This is an ideal that is difficult to achieve, however. People who are seated at agreeable tables, or in the privacy of a booth, tend to report their dining experience as more pleasant and spend more money, but they also stay longer. If they are seated at an undesirable table—for example, one that is too near the kitchen or next to a washroom or a drafty front door—they will leave sooner. Studies have revealed, however, that these bad tables are often the most profitable, since no one wants to be there very long. Unfortunately, customers who are shown to undesirable tables will often not only leave quickly but, feeling slighted, may never return. As a result, some restaurant managers, especially those who depend on local or repeat customers, will remove the bad tables or try to avoid seating anyone they know at them.

Other establishments, however, deliberately work toward rapid turnover, or, as it is known in the trade, "maximum throughput." These restaurants are deliberately designed both to attract customers and to discourage them from staying very long. Big signs, bright colors, and shiny photographs of high-calorie food draw people in; noisy acoustics, glaring and buzzing overhead lights, small, crowded tables, and uncomfortable plastic seats encourage them to leave as soon as they have finished what is appropriately called "fast food." In some cases, especially among those who are used to living well, this combination of factors can produce severe irritation or depression. In London, when a violent rainstorm drove the British writer Alain de Botton to seek shelter in a McDonald's on Victoria Street, he was gradually overcome by existential despair:

> The setting seemed to render all kinds of ideas absurd: that human beings might sometimes be generous to one another without hope of reward; that relationships can on occasion be sincere; that life may be worth enduring. The restaurant's true talent lay in the generation of anxiety. The harsh lighting, the intermittent sounds of frozen fries being sunk into vats of oil and the frenzied behavior of the counter staff invited thoughts of the loneliness and meaninglessness of existence in a random and violent universe.

BARS AND COCKTAIL LOUNGES

Places where the main attraction is alcohol rather than food operate under different guidelines, yet almost all will have some things in common. There will be a counter with stools in front of it and a bartender behind, and the most common colors in the décor will be red, black, brown, and shiny metallic chrome. There will almost always be a mirror behind the counter, fronted by racks of sparkling, colorful bottles.

Other factors will inform potential customers about the kind of activities that will most appropriately occur in this particular bar. They may want to make legitimate or illegitimate business deals, to meet friends, to find possible sexual partners, to avoid going home, to blur a bad mood or amplify a good one, or simply to get drunk. There are sports bars decorated with trophies and bats, where giant TV sets are always tuned to a game with the sound turned up; there are elegant cocktail lounges, all indirect lighting and leather and chrome, where office workers can look each other over during Happy Hour; and there are saloons with long scarred and stained wooden bars and subdued melancholy music for serious drinkers.

In general, a bar is always darker than a restaurant in the same vicinity. But in some cases the difference may be slight, since patrons will want to get a good look at those they are doing business with or trying to pick up. Such places are likely to be relatively easy of access, with large glass doors, or separated from the main space of a hotel lobby or restaurant only by a low wall or planting. The interior of a bar that is primarily designed for dubious transactions such as the purchase of drugs or sex, on the other hand, is likely to be quite dark and often almost invisible from the street. Its windows will be blocked with curtains or screens or with signs advertising brands of alcohol. Even at noon it will always be night inside, or at least a comforting dusk, and most conversations will be made inaudible at a short distance by the blurry noise of a TV set that nobody but the bartender is watching. Often there will be several booths where drinkers cannot be seen from the front door. There may be an atmosphere of tension or depression, often centering on some individual who is growling or cursing under his or her breath, or seems about to pass out.

An establishment where the main drink available is coffee or tea, and many patrons come to read the newspaper, plug in a computer, or meet friends or possible partners (perhaps as a result of previous negotiations on the Internet), will try to look as little like a classic low-down barroom as possible. Their interiors will be easily visible from the street; they will have soft, bright lights, and often many real or artificial plants. (At one time, such institutions were known by the generic term "fern bar.") The impression they attempt to give is one of naturalness, ease, happiness, and health. Simple food may be available, and many of the drinks served will be sweet, fruity, or fluffy. They may come in cheerful, childish colors like pink, orange, and milk chocolate. Although their caffeine count is often high, these concoctions, and the cookies and pastries sold at the same counter, suggest childhood parties. They are the contemporary adult equivalent of the ice-cream parlor or soda shop, which in the past often served as a place to take a date or meet with friends after school.

Today, unfortunately, some of these coffee shops have decided to increase profits by taking out their tables and replacing them with a high counter at which it is possible to drink a cup of coffee, but not to relax, chat, or read for very long without becoming uncomfortable.

CHAPTER 13

Houses of Commerce:
Stores and Offices

The message of any store, from a tiny newspaper kiosk to a terrifyingly large shopping mall, is essentially commercial, and like any language, it can lie. Its signs scream "SAVE!," and if we took this literally we would stay home and put our money in the bank. In fact we act on the real message, which is "SPEND!" The claim that a shiny green umbrella that we do not need can be purchased at a temporary and perhaps imaginary discount transforms itself into a promise that we will have more money; the can of tomatoes we can have *absolutely free* if we buy another one becomes a gift.

To maintain the illusion that we are in a different universe, where ordinary common sense and the usual meanings of words do not apply, most shops, no matter what they sell, block our view of the outside world. Many large stores have no windows, and even when they do these windows are often obstructed by displays of clothing, books, and electronic devices. A modern department or big-box store is usually a completely closed environment, brightly but softly lit to create a kind of trance state in which we will dreamily spend more and more money. Soothing or energizing music, and piped-in odors of flowers, coffee, or baking bread, may reinforce the spell, and there are usually no visible clocks, so that it is easy to lose track of time inside.

One extreme example of the store as a separate universe is the gambling casino. The classic version, as Colin Ellard points out in

You Are Here, has "low ceilings, narrow aisles, and tight spaces so that the visitor is surrounded on all sides by the flashing lights and ringing bells of the slots." There are no clocks, and no exterior windows that might reveal that the weather has changed outside or that day has become night. The goal is "to compel the visitors to spend as much time at the gambling machines as possible and to make it as difficult for them to leave the building as possible." Many casinos are promoted as places where you can have fun and reenter childhood: the décor resembles a circus or amusement park, and words like "games" and "gaming" are used instead of "gambling" or "betting." Not surprisingly, these playground-type casinos cause especially impulsive, highly risky behavior.

The interior design of most so-called "shopping environments" has been carefully calculated. Experts in the field, like Paco Underhill, author of *Why We Buy: The Science of Shopping*, report that even when we take a list to a supermarket, more than 60 percent of what we come out with wasn't on it. He cheerfully admits, "If we went into stores only when we needed to buy something, and if once there we bought only what we needed, the economy would collapse." This was written in 2008, and now that the economy has more or less collapsed, more people may be trying to buy only what they need, but it's an uphill battle. Stores are planned to lure customers in and keep them there, since studies have shown that the longer we stay, the poorer we will be when we leave.

In a supermarket the doors open automatically, making it easy for us to enter. When they do, Americans most often instinctively move to the right, and what they usually see first is a colorful display of flowers and fruit and vegetables. (In countries like Britain, where people drive on the left and instinctively move to the left, flowers and produce are often located there.) Often the front counters will be placed at angles to the entrance, funneling us into the store. Standing displays with large price signs (which may or may not actually indicate a bargain) draw us farther on.

In the average supermarket, less profitable, low-markup merchandise is less prominently displayed, and staples like milk and eggs
and bread are located as far as possible from the entrance. Studies
suggest that though we may plan only to stock up on these necessities, on our way to them and back we will probably put other items
into our shopping cart. This cart will almost always be very large, to
accommodate and encourage extra purchases. Child seats are usually
provided, not only for the convenience of parents, but so that toddlers, while unable to pull things off shelves, will be in the perfect
position to see and demand the sugary cereals and cookies placed at
their eye level. When we get to the checkout line the kids will make
a grab for nearby candy bars, and we ourselves will be next to high-
profit small items like batteries, razor blades, and magazines. We
will probably have to wait a couple of minutes, since lines that move
too fast mean losses for the store (as do those that always move very
slowly, which eventually drive customers away).

Supermarket designers know that if we have too much trouble
getting around a store we will become cross and impatient. On the
other hand, if we can navigate too easily we will buy less. For this reason, shopping carts are constructed so that they will travel smoothly
but not too rapidly, and the width of the aisles is carefully calibrated
so that we are slowed down by other carts and by free-standing displays, but not so often that we become infuriated and leave. Another ploy used by some markets is frequent reorganization of the
merchandise. Necessities will remain in the far back corner, and
fruit and flowers up front, but canned goods and paper products
and salad dressing and soap will be deliberately moved around every
few months so that regular customers cannot find what they want
too easily, and have to spend more time searching, and incidentally
buying things they did not think they needed.

Not all shoppers are aware that manufactures pay for what is
called "product placement," and that a big supermarket may demand
tens of thousands of dollars from a soup or cereal company for a cer-

tain number of feet of shelving at eye level. Supermarket customers rarely choose anything from the highest or lowest shelves, because they cannot reach them, are in a hurry, or are too lazy to stretch or stoop. Since products in choice locations often have the highest markup, and are usually more expensive, a savvy shopper will choose staples like paper towels or rice from the lowest shelf.

Bookshops also charge high fees for product placement. The publisher of a book whose front cover is visible on the shelf has probably paid for this privilege, and there will often be twenty copies of the latest bestseller on a stand near the checkout counter. Even when there has been no up-front payment, most stores use location to increase profits. According to a local bookstore employee, "there is one spot about ten feet from the door, and whatever we put there always sells. It is a great place to display expensive cookbooks." In other locations, such as the lowest shelves next to the door, almost nothing moves.

Most stores that sell clothes, drugs, liquor, toys, and furniture are deliberately designed to attract a certain income level of shoppers. An establishment that carries expensive items at a big markup will try to create a fancy setting for them. In a high-end clothing shop the dressing rooms will be large, with soft, flattering lights. The thick carpets, velvety sofas, floor-length mirrors, and polished wood paneling will have been chosen to create an air of expensive good taste. Some customers, of course, will not have such fancy furnishings at home; in this case, a visit to Bergdorf Goodman in New York or Liberty's in London allows them to enjoy a brief fantasy of wealth and luxury.

A less expensive store will make fewer efforts to flatter its customers. It will provide only a straight chair or two, and may force you to try on garments in a communal dressing room. On an even lower level there may be no place to sit down, and no dressing room at all. Discount stores often go in for dark gray paint and industrial shelving, not only because they are cheap but also to suggest that we are getting warehouse prices from a seller who does not waste his and our money on décor.

One infallible sign of an expensive shop is the amount of empty space it contains. In a low-end clothing store several hundred blouses and skirts and slacks and sweaters will be visible on crowded racks and shelves; a high-end shop may show only a few dozen garments at a time. The message usually gets across; as one friend reported, "If I look into a shop in New York and see only a few items, I'm almost always scared to go in. Chances are I won't be able to afford anything." Especially in a big city, space costs money, and the fewer goods that are on display per cubic foot, the higher prices will be. Tiffany's flagship store in New York usually features only one or two items in each small window, with no price tags. A much cheaper jewelry store will have windows crowded with watches and rings, all with visible prices, often presented as amazing discounts.

As customers we are susceptible to what psychologists call "framing," and just as nineteenth-century paintings were given elaborate gold frames to make them seem more valuable, so store managers will separate and highlight items to make them look especially desirable. Usually, the more isolated an object is, the higher the markup: a scarf or handbag in a glass case will cost more than those hung in a row on hooks, and even more if it is separately spotlit.

Both manufacturers and stores, especially if they are part of a big chain, often try to use their customers as walking billboards. They may not only adopt a special color scheme and typeface for their shopping bags, but also sell visibly branded merchandise, so that our stove, our bag of potato chips, and our T-shirt will continue to serve as advertisements to whoever sees them. (More discreet establishments may use symbols like Ralph Lauren's polo pony or the red-and-white Target logo, but the principle is the same.) Sometimes this ploy is successful. At other times designers overreach themselves;

when one maker of women's underwear began to print its own name repeatedly on the waistband of every pair of briefs and bikinis, many customers, including me, stopped buying them.

Traditionally, shoppers like to feel the merchandise—to stroke sweaters, read a few pages of a book, try out a pair of scissors, and test peaches for ripeness. Store owners deeply dislike this sort of thing, because it makes the goods look untidy or shopworn. They have tried to fight back: supermarket managers have experimented with wrapping fruit in cellophane, and toy stores may encase dolls and trucks in impenetrable plastic. Sometimes it works: we have become accustomed to bagged herbs and boxed tights; but many attempts to prevent all physical contact have resulted in drastically reduced sales and a rash of time-consuming returns. Books and magazines wrapped in plastic, for instance, seldom sell unless their contents are pornographic.

The arrangement of different types of goods within a shop is always carefully calculated. It has been discovered, for instance, that men are often reluctant to enter a large department store, especially if they have to make their way through sections devoted to cosmetics and women's clothes. As a result, some establishments have separate entrances that open directly onto reassuring displays of male slacks and shirts; the window outside this entrance will often feature male mannequins in macho sports gear. Electronics and tools may be nearby, so that it will be possible to buy an electric drill and a pair of jeans without glimpsing a single women's dress, let alone a rack of ruffled panties. Women's departments are usually located next to baby supplies and children's clothes. If the store carries toys, they will be nearby, so that the kid you have taken in to get new shoes and a couple of T-shirts can glom on to a pea-green plastic dinosaur and scream to take it home.

Very often, the interior design of a large store is deliberately confusing. "I'm constantly getting lost in the Bon-Ton," one local friend complained. "There's not a single straight line in the place, and I end up going through every department trying to find the exit." Restrooms, both male and female, also tend to be hard to find, and you must pass a lot of merchandise on your way there and back.

Many large stores with more than one floor deliberately make it easier to rise than to descend. Up escalators are located near the entrance, and large signs direct you to them, while down escalators are harder to find and may even be lacking. When you want to leave you may have to hunt for stairs or an elevator, possibly buying more things on the way out. (A similar situation exists in the Museum of Modern Art in New York, where the up escalators run all the way to the top, and the down escalators stop on the second floor.)

A common stratagem for many stores has been to suggest that what they are selling is not goods, but a "lifestyle." As Sharon Zukin remarks in "The Social Space of Shopping," the idea of a lifestyle is "less crude than price and less cruel than social class." It also encourages the proliferation of choices, and therefore of purchases. Once you decide that you are a jock or Goth or a green, an urban sophisticate or a country gal or a car-pool mom, you will need the clothes and CDs and video games and cell phone that go with that role. As time passes, many people will move from one lifestyle to another, and they will then need to buy new clothes, music, and electronic items. They may also move to a different climate, get a different job, or take up a new hobby or sport. All this is good news for merchandisers.

Even if they cling to a certain lifestyle, people will eventually grow older and need different kinds of clothes and furniture. They may also grow richer—or simply wish to seem richer than they are—a common desire that has been catered to for a long time. More than a hundred years ago the first department stores were already implying that buying their goods could enroll you in a middle- or upper-middle-class way of life, or at least make it seem that you were better off and more sophisticated than was actually the case.

THE MALL

The shopping mall has all the characteristics of a supermarket or a department store, and more. It makes even greater efforts to attract customers, and (especially) to keep them there. This is really big business: as Peter Coleman reports in *Shopping Environments*, in the largest malls there may be more than a thousand visitors a day, and several hundred thousand a year. In these malls, "enclosing and climatizing the public areas" is deliberately planned around the idea "that customers who feel comfortable will stop longer and spend more." Even greater amounts of what mall designers refer to as "dwell time" can be created by adding restaurants, bars, cinemas, seasonal events and displays, craft shows, art shows, children's play areas, and of course Santa Claus at Christmas. Often the end result is the same as that of the playground-type casino: impulsive, risky spending.

A very large shopping mall may be internally diversified, so that different areas will contain stores calculated to appeal to different types of customers: teenagers, families, the somewhat impoverished, and the well-to-do. The most expensive shops, for instance, will be clustered around the most expensive anchor store. Large malls usually have at least one "food court" surrounded by takeout food vendors. It will be colorful and brightly lit—but also often crowded and uncomfortable, with hard metal or plastic chairs and a high noise level. As a result, customers will be encouraged to refuel so that they can continue to shop, but not to linger.

Most large department stores and shopping malls are also equipped with security cameras, mainly to deter theft by both customers and employees. As members of the public become aware of this, they may be either reassured or annoyed. Other, flakier responses are also possible. According to some experts, at times "acts of sexual intimacy or obscenity are performed deliberately by members of the public in front of the security cameras: so much so that tapes of such acts are compiled by security staff for wider distribution."

SURROUNDED BY SHOPPING

Today almost every public destination has its own shop or shops. Museums, libraries, public parks, and tourist attractions offer opportunities for buying; often you cannot exit except through the gift shop. Once upon a time all that was for sale in a museum store were postcards and posters: now you can buy books, toys, clothing, glassware, and china—and, if you lose your head, an original signed painting or a two-thousand-dollar reproduction of an ancient Egyptian gold and jeweled necklace.

Bus stations, train stations, and airports also provide a captive mass of customers and opportunities to purchase. In the case of air travel this opportunity is almost a compulsion, since most flights no longer offer meals. As Peter Coleman points out, "By the late 1990s airport operators worldwide recognized the lucrative revenue generated by retail operations." British Airways, for instance, now gets more than half its income from retail shops at Heathrow, Gatwick, Stansted, and Glasgow airports. Prices in these shops are invariably high, and delays and compulsory early check-in produce even more sales. According to Coleman, "the average time passengers spend in American airports has been identified as an hour and a half—and often much more in bad weather." He also remarks that the route from the check-in area to the gates is deliberately arranged so that you will pass as many shops as possible.

TO SHOP OR NOT TO SHOP?

Some people hate to shop: one friend, for instance, told me that her idea of hell was to be imprisoned in a mall for all eternity. But in spite of the time it takes, and the occasional sense that they are being manipulated, other people actually like to go into a building and spend money. They see it as a recreational activity, or even as a therapeutic one. Experts in the field often encourage this view: Peter Coleman, for instance, declares that "shopping is about transforma-

tion . . . about collecting aspects of a lifestyle or things that con-
tribute to a person's mental well-being." Other enthusiasts go even
further. According to Jim Pooler, shopping, for many people, "gives
life a sense of purpose, value, and a function." At times, for Pooler
and perhaps for others, it seems to be the psychological equivalent
of religion. "It is a solemn rite, a ceremonial act that is an integral
part of every person's life." It may also be the moral equivalent of
war: as Pooler puts it, "everyone has experienced the ecstatic thrill
of the perfect shopping event, and the feelings of victory that can
come from making a successful purchase." If this is true, it may help
to explain why some stores, notably those that sell very expensive
clothing or jewelry or furniture, have the echoing spaces, hushed
air, and almost mystical lighting of a cathedral. Others, like low-end
department and electronics stores during a giant sale, may remind
observers of a battlefield—and indeed, have often produced injuries
and sometimes actual fatalities as maddened shoppers struggle to
be the first to enter and claim a bargain after the doors are opened.

THE OFFICE

Every office, whether it is a multi-story skyscraper or a single room
in a private home, speaks to us clearly, giving information (which
may be true or false) about the business it houses. Depending on the
purpose of the enterprise, we will be silently instructed to feel awe or
ease, or some combination of the two. Ideally, we will be impressed
by the persons who work there and believe that they know what is
best for us.

In general, the décor of any office can be located on a continuum
from the factory to the home. Metallic furniture, rectangular lines,
drab colors, and expanses of bare wall and window suggest the factory; upholstered chairs and sofas, rounded shapes, bright colors,
pictures, and plants suggest a family sitting room. A substantial business will often be designed to produce both awe and ease in different
locations. The reception area will be impressive and even slightly

intimidating, projecting power, prosperity, and stability; a very large firm may have a high lobby in which light filters down from far above, suggesting the presence of some higher authority. The interior office in which we sign a contract to purchase property or insurance, make investments, take out a loan, or engage the services of a lawyer, on the other hand, is apt to be reassuringly informal and comfortable.

The reception areas of some businesses, especially in media and advertising, may have brightly colored walls; but once you get farther in, white, off-white, and beige will predominate. This is in part because studies have shown that office walls in dramatic colors, especially red and black, cause trouble. Red walls have been found to produce anxiety and nervousness, black walls create depression, and the end result is often a marked increase in tardiness, absenteeism, and employee turnover.

In many commercial enterprises our first contact with the people who work there will take place over a counter, and the shape of this counter usually indicates the degree of separation or suspicion that is presumed to exist between employee and client. Government bureaus and theatre ticket offices, for instance, tend to have high counters, often with grilles or sheets of glass across them, and some banks still do. The original reason for this was probably that large amounts of cash change hands in these places, and they must be protected from theft. But when there is no need to guard against theft, a high partition with a small hole in it suggests that the transaction will be formal and limited. Unless you already know the person behind the counter, you will probably not chat with them. In most American post offices, on the other hand, the counters are generally wide and open so that bundles of mail and packages can be passed over them, and friendly conversations often take place there.

Private businesses usually try to project a welcoming aura. An investment advisor or insurance agent, who is usually eager to make friends and sell them something, will probably sit behind a low desk. In a lawyer's office the reception area may be either friendly or intimidating, depending on the nature of the practice. A family firm that deals mainly with wills and real estate transfers tends to have comfortable chairs and many green plants, while corporate or criminal lawyers are more likely to go for a more formal, even at times frightening look.

Variations in counter height within a big organization are always significant. At most universities, for instance, some departments block public access with a tall metal counter, enclosed at both ends; in others there is only a low shelf on which catalogs and campus maps and announcements of lectures and concerts are displayed. Of course, just as the phrase "Can I help you?" may be uttered in a friendly or hostile way, the manner of the receptionist contributes to the general effect.

The appearance of some large enterprises tends to suggest the factory rather than the home. As Professor Jeremy Myerson of the Royal College of Art, London, puts it, the "oldest and most profound conflict in office design . . . [is] between the corporate needs of the organization in terms of output, productivity, and efficiency and the needs of the individual worker in terms of morale, privacy, comfort and health." From the 1920s and 1930s on, many big businesses were redesigned to produce maximum impersonal efficiency. Huge, low-ceilinged, often windowless spaces appeared, and rows of identical desks were laid out in rectilinear patterns. Now every occupant of the room was visible to everyone else, and it was possible for the boss to see at a glance whether you were working or just talking to your neighbor or reading a magazine. It was, in effect, a version of the Panopticon prison surveillance system. Centralized lighting, heating, and air-conditioning also removed individual control, and it was impossible to open most of the windows.

As the principles of factory and prison design were applied to the office, not only was the status and comfort of individual workers gradually eroded; there was also an increase in absenteeism, job turnover, and workplace injuries. The economic disadvantages of this, as well as occasional impulses of empathy and goodwill, eventually resulted in changes. The ranks of identical desks were replaced by individual cubicles, which—depending on their design—provided a certain amount of privacy and light control. Freedom to move about, however, remained limited. In a computerized cubicle today, as Myerson points out, the office worker is "literally tied to the workstation by a tangle of power, data, and communication cable."

In the past, midlevel management workers usually had their own offices. Today they tend merely to be given larger cubicles, partly in order to increase the number of employees who can be housed in a given area. Many businesses now also group "teams" of midlevel or even senior employees into a collection of adjoining cubicles, where each team will have its own small meeting room, coffee machine, and washroom. These cubicles, which mostly lack doors, have the advantage (or disadvantage, depending on one's psychological makeup) of increasing communication and consultation. But because they usually have walls at least five feet high, they have given rise to the phenomenon now known as "gophering," in which the occupant of a cubicle will suddenly stand up to peer into the adjoining ones. In some cases this has caused so much unease and resentment that cubicle walls have been raised to six feet or more, too high for all but the tallest gophers.

Meeting rooms, whatever their size, give immediate information about what it will be like to work in any enterprise. Small rooms with soft furniture suggest not only informality and comfort, but also consultation and consensus. Huge conference rooms with a row of identical chairs on both sides of a long table have an opposite effect. The recognition of this kind of message is not new; back in the sixteenth century, in his essay "Of Counsel," Sir Francis Bacon remarked: "A long table and a square table, or seats about the walls, seem things of form, but are things of substance; for at a long table a few at the upper end, in effect, sway all the business; but in the other form, there is more use of the counsellors' opinions that sit lower."

For those who habitually occupy the upper end of any table, the office environment has always been more agreeable. They will have larger cubicles with higher walls and more comfortable chairs, and their meeting and break rooms will suggest a comfortable hotel lobby. At the top of the organization there will be impressive conference rooms and private offices with designer furniture and panoramic views. As one informant reported, "There is definitely an office hierarchy where I work. You start with a desk in a shared cubicle. Next you get a bigger single cubicle, then you move to a real office that you share with just one person, and then you get your own office. After that you get a window, and finally you get a nice view." The more power you have in an organization the more likely your office is to look like a room in a house, with soft chairs and sofas, plants, artworks, and perhaps even a private bathroom or wet bar. But though a CEO's workplace may contain all these domestic amenities, it will also project authority with the help of massive furniture, indirect lighting, heavy materials, and dark colors.

In the nineteenth and early twentieth centuries, the standard high-end office desk was tall and elaborate, with many drawers and shelves and cubbyholes. It was designed to store documents and papers and thus metaphorically suggest the amount of knowledge its owner possessed. But as data began to be saved invisibly and electronically, the desks of important people changed. Today they tend to be huge, flat, and often almost empty expanses of mahogany or metal, holding only a few pieces of expensive communication equipment and perhaps one or two family photographs to reassure the visitor that the demigod who sits behind them is in some respects human. (If he or she has neglected to acquire an attractive mate or children, there may be the portrait of a favorite dog or cat.) There will also often be one or more large and impressive pictures on the walls, often of neutral outdoorsy subjects: seascapes with or without boats, autumn forests, or snow-covered mountains. A consciously masculine office may have sports trophies and paintings of game fish or birds, or possibly even stuffed examples of these prestigious creatures. If there are plants, they will be large and uniformly dark green. More feminine décor will tend toward pictures of gardens and flowers, and also possibly actual flowering plants. The absence of plants, paintings, or photographs, and of any indication of outside interests or hobbies—such as tennis and golf trophies, views of high-end tourist destinations, or awards for services to the community—is apt to create a cold and even ominous effect. In some cases we will become so uneasy and suspicious of the apparent alien who works there that we will decide not to have anything to do with him or her.

The self-important inhabitant of an important office typically sits in a large and impressive chair behind a large and impressive desk, with a smaller and possibly lower chair in front of it. Someone who wants to win confidence and project friendliness and goodwill, on the other hand, may have a smaller desk and a chair not much larger than yours. There will be lots of photos and often souvenirs or coffee mugs honoring sports teams or civic organizations. When you enter the room this person will probably stand up to greet you. He or she may even come out from behind the desk and guide you to a chair placed beside it rather than in front, suggesting collaboration rather than confrontation.

An official who wants to project power and make you feel small and weak, on the other hand, will remain in his or her seat or immediately return to it. Sometimes the light from a window behind his or her desk will shine directly into your eyes, as at an interrogation. There are, of course, ways for the determined or astute visitor to avoid being placed in this disadvantageous position, especially if you have something the inhabitant of the office wants. You may, for instance, decline to sit down, lean over the desk, or even move your chair out of the glare. It is also possible to make disconcerting remarks about the décor, commenting in a humorous way on the small size of a mounted fish, for instance, or the lack of a good view from the window. ("It's really a shame you can't see the mountains from here"—subliminally implying that the occupant should in fact be ashamed.)

Different professions use their offices to express different types of expertise. Lawyers exhibit shelves of leather-bound law books, investment brokers and managers of mutual funds will have computers displaying current stock prices, and professors will awe us with entire walls of serious-looking books in their chosen field—all of which, it is implied, they have actually read. The architect's office will have a drawing table and one or more elaborate cardboard models of buildings, complete with tiny trees and figures. All this décor is not only impressive, but also reassuring, since it suggests that the person we are consulting is competent and experienced. Framed awards, degrees from good universities, and photographs of the official with recognizable politicians or celebrities increase the effect.

AT THE DOCTOR'S

Medical offices are a special case. There is a complex system of meaning in these places, which patients soon grasp unconsciously. Sometimes the décor is minimalist and bleak: chairs are stiff and uncomfortable, and a high, closed counter creates negative vibrations. As one friend put it, "My new doctor's office has a glass wall between the receptionist and the waiting room. There's even a glass panel they slide shut between signing people in. It gives me the feeling that I'm contaminated and unwelcome." Another friend remarked that, in her experience, when it is difficult to speak to the receptionist it will probably be equally hard to speak to the doctor, who will tend not to hear your questions or will not reply to them in any meaningful way. Studies have also shown that when a waiting room is attractive and well provided with reading material, patients are content to wait longer. When the room is shabby and crowded and the magazines are months out of date, people tend to become discouraged, and sometimes they will actually get up and leave. Often they will not return for another appointment.

According to a recent study, patients expect to receive better care when the waiting room is well lighted, well furnished, and contains artwork. Many doctors' and dentists' reception areas, in fact, have been designed to induce feelings of ease and confidence. There will be comfortable chairs, pictures, and plants. The selection of reading material will provide a ready guide to the clientele and also to probable charges. A small-town family practice will have toys and children's books and copies of homemaking and celebrity-gossip periodicals; a gerontologist will have an outside ramp, flowering plants, and often the *National Geographic*.

All consulting rooms, whether luxurious or homey, will subtly project authority. In earlier centuries doctors would often have an entire articulated skeleton in their offices; this was an effective, if expensive, proof of arcane medical knowledge, but one that also often caused terror, especially in children, and the ploy has now largely been abandoned. Separate three-dimensional plastic models of a foot or an eye or even a spine are still common in the offices of specialists, however.

Whether the doctor you are consulting is rich or poor, his or her examination rooms will usually be fairly bare and functional, designed not to cause relaxation and confidence but to cut down on dust and germs, and also perhaps to induce obedience. Typically, you will be shown into this room and asked to remove your clothing and put on a flimsy cotton or paper gown that resembles an infant's wrapper. The door will then be shut, and you will typically wait for up to fifteen minutes. Symbolically, you have been reduced not only to the status of an infant, but to that of a broken appliance that must stay on its shelf until an expert has time to diagnose the trouble and repair it. If you have forgotten to bring a truly absorbing book or magazine, you will gradually become more and more bored and anxious, especially if there are strange machines and locked cabinets of drugs in the room, or if the walls are covered with large, brightly colored, scary medical charts, to remind you that you are ignorant of the workings of your own body. Medical professionals, whether consciously or not, know this, and count on it to increase your willingness to accept their advice.

In general, the offices of specialists, especially surgeons, will be designed to produce awe. A successful plastic surgeon will have a luxurious office with thick carpeting, exotic fresh flowers and plants, glossy fashion magazines, and possibly the *Wall Street Journal*. Allergists and dermatologists will avoid live vegetation, and sometimes even carpets and curtains. The offices of New Age practitioners and massage therapists, however, tend to concentrate on encouraging trust and confidence, while at the same time suggesting exotic knowledge and expertise. There may be Japanese scrolls, Tibetan mandalas, statues of Hindu or Buddhist gods, and unusual plants such as bamboo and cactus. Often there will be incense and piped-in Eastern music to create an atmosphere of dreamy relaxation.

Patients who enter a doctor's office may feel ill or anxious, but they are not usually in acute pain—if they were, they would be in an emergency room. Visits to dentists, on the other hand, often involve severe toothache. In this case, nothing is gained by making you wait in an examination room; in fact, the longer you stay there, the more angry and miserable and tense you will become, and thus the harder to treat. It is also true that in this society the statement that you are about to go or have just been to the dentist merely arouses sympathy, whereas news of a doctor's appointment is apt to cause both curiosity and anxiety. Possibly for this reason, the doors of dentists' treatment rooms are almost always left open: nobody will be very interested, and you will not be embarrassed to be seen there.

DISTURBANCES OF THE MIND AND SOUL

Practitioners who concern themselves with the mind rather than the body also use design to create awe and confidence in their clients. Often there will be signs of the therapist's extensive training and superior wisdom: framed diplomas and shelves of impressive-looking books. A very expensive and well-known shrink may dispense with these signs, replacing them with a stripped-down décor and authoritarian manner. Certain types of interior design are common at all levels, however. A psychoanalyst or psychiatrist—and sometimes even a successful psychotherapist—is apt to have costly designer furniture. At one time, a black leather Knoll chair and a large, well-upholstered sofa were almost obligatory, and the Oriental carpets and examples of antique and primitive sculpture famous from Freud's Vienna consulting room still appear in the offices of many classic analysts. At the other end of the economic scale, even a newly established psychiatric social worker is apt to display an original painting or print.

Therapists know from experience that during any extended course of treatment, every object in their room will arouse associations and questions from their clients. Some practitioners will deliberately choose dramatic artworks, indicating their willingness to deal with unpleasant and even violent matters; but more often the décor is likely to be as neutral as possible. There are seldom any family photographs, since they are apt to produce, sooner or later, a flood of inquisitive remarks and emotionally loaded assumptions. Even a picture of a pet can trigger angry, suspicious reactions ("I've always hated cats, and yours looks like an evil white demon, so I'm not going to tell you anything").

CHAPTER 14

Personal Space

Most people, no matter what their circumstances, possess some private, unshared space. It may be as large as a house; it may be as small as a gym locker, a bedside cupboard, or a shelf in an office cubicle. But whatever its size it will usually give important information about its owner's age, history, personality, gender, and tastes.

FRIENDS AND FOES

Just as the age of grown men and women can sometimes be ascertained by their use of the popular phrases and slang words of their childhood and youth, so a look at the personal space of someone you have recently met will often give a fairly accurate indication of both their actual and subconscious age. It may also provide an almost archaeological view of their history, in which beloved teddy bears, posters, sports equipment and trophies, and souvenirs of schools and colleges reveal layered strata of meaning. All these things, of course, are also an invitation to comment: in the long run, to a friendship based on common interests.

Another, opposite kind of private space can sometimes be seen in the rooms and offices of those who hope not to reveal anything about themselves to anyone. Here there will be nothing personal: no amusing photos or pictures, no childhood keepsakes, and no visible light reading matter. The furniture will look as if it had been chosen by an anonymous decorator: there will be neutral colors and restrained shapes; dark woods and shiny metals will be prominent. If there is art it will be anonymous: pictures or photographs of landscapes and possibly of those animals and birds and fish that are hunted for sport. In an expensive office or apartment there may be some large, rather threatening abstract paintings and sculptures by currently fashionable artists. But of course the effort to create anonymity can only succeed partially, since such rooms also suggest something about their owners. Their message is cold, formal, and even menacing: watch out, don't expect sympathy or necessarily trust anything I say.

MALE AND FEMALE

Designers who are followers of Eastern philosophy sometimes speak of interiors in terms of a yin or yang effect. A yin room features soft surfaces, rounded shapes, and soft, dim, or neutral colors; it is associated with the feminine principle. A yang room is full of hard, shiny surfaces, rectangular shapes, and bright colors; it expresses the masculine principle. (Ideally, a room that is used by both men and women will combine these aspects, though perhaps in different proportions.)

Though most Westerners do not follow these rules, many personal spaces today, and even more often in the past, were obviously and strongly gendered. When middle- and upper-class females typically stayed home, the typical parlor and drawing room were essentially feminine: they contained slim-legged and curvaceous tables and bureaus, and soft upholstered furniture and curtains whose ruffled and flowered and fringed materials resembled the clothes of the ladies who presided there. Plants and flowers adorned almost every horizontal surface, just as they did female bonnets and hats. Men, who spent much less time in the house, had separate domains: studies or libraries where the furniture, curtains, and carpets were dark and sturdy and long-wearing. As in their clothes, leather and wool predominated. Among the wealthy, the husband and other adult males often had separate, masculine-looking bedrooms.

In the late nineteenth and early twentieth centuries, during the campaign for education and votes for women, the parlor or drawing room, as well as female fashion, began to be less puffy, frilly, and ruffled. Mid-Victorian drawing rooms resembled late Victorian matrons, with heavy damask and brocade hangings and ponderous, curvy, claw-footed furniture. Late-nineteenth- and early-twentieth-century Art Nouveau sitting rooms had light walls and furniture that seemed to have been inspired by plants instead of animals; the young women who sat there often shed both pounds and petticoats and resembled wood nymphs clad in diaphanous silky fabrics.

Even today, in many bedrooms and some offices the décor is feminine. The furniture is covered in soft, velvety materials and heaped with small pillows: flowers and plants are everywhere. There are many variations, of course: a room may suggest a mid-twentieth-century vamp, with shiny satin fabrics and mirrored tables; it may go in for big, soft, squashy furniture and loose bunches of garden flowers, giving us the impression of maternal warmth and comfort and generosity. Sometimes, of course, the owner of such a room has a very different, more neutral, or even masculine bedroom or office. This may be because someone else, possibly a professional interior decorator, has imposed his or her own taste. In a few cases it may suggest that the inhabitant has more than one personality, and we should do well to prepare for this.

HOMES AWAY FROM HOME

When there is no wish to conceal personal matters, the occupant of any office is likely to try to convert it into a kind of symbolic home. Tiny cubicles become galleries of photographs, postcards, posters, cartoons, and framed mottoes—some sentimental and some ironic. Even receptionists or bank clerks, whose working territory is severely limited, may bring in a favorite pillow and an African violet, and paste pictures of and by their children on the side of the nearest file cabinet. These things are proofs that they have a real life outside of routine office duties—and also, perhaps, an invitation to visitors to treat them as a human being rather than an appliance.

Employees who have their own offices, including many school-teachers and college instructors, tend to decorate their doors with items that give information about their interests and attitudes. A sports enthusiast will post the schedule of a favorite team; a specialist in medieval literature or art may put up a reproduction of a medie-val manuscript; an engineer a diagram of an invention, a musician a brochure for a concert series. Most common of all are cartoons and signs that make ironic fun of the type of institution for which these people are working, suggesting, not always accurately, that they are relaxed, friendly people who are on the side of their clients or students.

Today, of course, a lot of work is done off-site: at home, in hotels, and even while in transit. Airport lounges, planes, and commuter trains, which used to be places to read a newspaper, chat, or nap, are now full of well-dressed, anxious-looking people hunched over lap-tops or explaining themselves into cell phones. Electronic communication has made it unnecessary for us to report to the office every day, and there are now organizations in which many employees no longer have a cubicle or even a desk of their own, but simply connect their computer to any available wireless terminal when they stop by. According to interviews, some people find such working conditions liberating and even agreeable, but for most it is disorienting. Perhaps that is why many of us now carry around small electronic devices loaded with our favorite music and photos of our favorite people, in a desperate attempt to provide ourselves with the equiva-lent of private personal space.

WHO LIVES HERE?

Any space that belongs to an individual speaks to us instantly and loudly. When we enter or even glance into it, we will have an instinctive reaction, just as we do when we first meet someone. In most cases, it will always be interesting and sometimes useful to become aware of the message we are getting. We might, for instance, ask ourselves whether, considering any differences in age, gender, class, and occupation, we would be content to occupy this bedroom or office—and, if not, what changes we would want. If nothing could make us willing to live or work there, we would do well to be wary of any possible close relationship with this person. If we would be happy to occupy this space, we may have just met a potential friend and ally, or even a future life partner.

Of course, such first impressions may be corrected later, when we know more, but they are always significant in some way. A friend's new office may turn out to contain a picture or a plant that its owner dislikes but cannot remove because her boss has put it there. Soon we may learn that she hates this painting of exhaustingly cute kittens or that huge prickly cactus—but in the process we will also learn that she cannot choose her own décor because she is afraid of her boss.

As time goes on, one of our friend's first priorities will probably be to get rid of these unwelcome objects. If she is prevented from doing this, she will never enjoy working there, and may eventually quit. But more often, as she becomes secure in her job, she will be able to replace the kittens and the cactus with pictures and plants she really likes, ones that express her own history, tastes, and interests. She will begin to enjoy her work more, and feel safe and comfortable there. And why not? After all, we are a territorial species.

Afterword

This book owes a lot to all the people who took the time to tell me how they felt about the places that they had lived, worked, learned, played, prayed, shopped, and found shelter in. I am especially grateful to my friends and family, and to the research assistants who discovered books and articles that I had never heard of, surveyed their own friends and families and fellow students, and reported with wit and originality on the buildings in their own lives: Rhian Ellis, Hannah Steinberg, and Alex Wolf. I also want to thank my colleagues at Cornell University for giving me their reading lists and allowing me to sit in on their courses: Gary Evans and Jan Jennings of the Department of Design and Environmental Analysis, and Bonnie Mac-Dougall of the School of Architecture.

A book like this cannot take permanent shape without the help of those who, like good architects, know how to turn a collection of sparks on a computer into a useful three-dimensional object. My brilliant editor, Joe Olshan, and my skilled copyeditor, Tom Pitoniak, have this ability; without them this would be a much more confused and flawed construction. I am also grateful to Greg Mortimer, designer at Delphinium Books, and especially to Karen Sung, the gifted and original young artist whose drawings head each chapter of the book. And, as always, I want to thank my agent and friend, Melanie Jackson, for her good advice and expert knowledge of the publishing world.

It can be hard to share a house with other people, who are sure to have their own ideas about what they want it to look like and say to the world. I am fortunate that for many years my husband, Edward Hower, has made this process both easy and enjoyable.

Bibliography

Allen, Edward. *How Buildings Work: The Natural Order of Architecture*. New York: Oxford University Press, 1995.

Anson, Peter F. *The Building of Churches*. London: Burns & Oates, 1964.

Arneill, Allison B., and Ann Sloan Devlin. "Perceived Quality of Care: The Influence of the Waiting Room Environment." *Journal of Environmental Psychology* 22, no. 4 (December 2002): 345–60.

Austen, Jane. *Northanger Abbey*. London: John Murray, 1818.

Bachelard, Gaston. *The Poetics of Space*. Boston: Beacon Press,1969.

Bacon, Sir Francis. *Essays Civil and Moral*. Chapter XX: "Of Counsel." New York: P. F. Collier & Son, 1909.

Bailey, W. H. *Defining Edges: A New Look at Picture Frames*. Foreword by Adam Gopnik. New York: Harry N. Abrams, 2002.

Barker, Emma, ed. *Contemporary Cultures of Display*. New Haven: Yale University Press, 1999.

Belkin, Lisa. *First, Do No Harm*. New York: Simon & Schuster, 1993.

Bennett, Alan. *Untold Stories*. London: Faber & Faber, 2005.

Bettelheim, Bruno. *Surviving and Other Essays*. New York: Vintage, 1980.

Block, Libbie. *The Hills of Beverly*. Garden City, New York: Doubleday, 1957

Brand, Stewart. *How Buildings Learn: What Happens After They're Built*. New York: Viking, 1994.

Bronner, Simon J., ed. *Consuming Visions: Accumulation and Display of Goods in America, 1880–1920*. New York: Norton, 1989.

Brontë, Charlotte. *Jane Eyre*, 1847; reprint, New York: Knopf, 1991.

Brooks, Charles J., and James L. Rebeta. "College Classroom Ecology: The Relation of Sex of Student to Classroom Performance and Seating Preference." *Environment and Behavior* 23 (May 1991): 305–13.

Burke, Catherine, and Ian Grosvenor. *School*. London: Reaktion Books, 2008.

Carlson, Marvin. *Places of Performance*. Ithaca: Cornell University Press, 1989.

Chiat, Marilyn J. *America's Religious Architecture: Sacred Places for Every Community*. New York: Wiley, 1997.

Christensen, Julia. *Big Box Reuse*. Cambridge, Mass.: MIT Press, 2008.

Cohen, Deborah. *Household Gods: The British and Their Possessions*. New Haven: Yale University Press, 2006.

Coleman, Peter. *Shopping Environments: Evolution, Planning and Design*. London: Architectural Press, 2006.

Collins, Jim, ed. *High-Pop: Making Culture into Popular Entertainment*. Oxford: Blackwell, 2002.

Cotterell, John L. "Effects of School Architectural Design on Student and Teacher Anxiety." *Environment and Behavior* 16 (July 1984): 455–79.

Crosbie, Michael J. *Architecture for the Gods*. New York: Watson-Guptill, 2000.

Cuno, James, ed. *Whose Muse? Art Museums and the Public Trust*. Cambridge, Mass.: Harvard University Press, 2004.

Dale, Karen, and Gibson Burrell. *The Spaces of Organization and the Organization of Space: Power, Identity and Materiality at Work*. New York: Palgrave Macmillan, 2008.

de Botton, Alain. *The Architecture of Happiness*. New York: Penguin, 2006.

DeSanctis, Michael. *Building from Belief: Advance, Retreat, and Compromise in the Remaking of Catholic Church Architecture*. Collegeville, Minn.: Liturgical Press, 2002.

de Swaan, Abram. "Constraints and Challenges in Designing Hospitals: The Sociological View." In Cor Wagenaar, ed., *The Architecture of Hospitals*. Rotterdam: NAi, 2006.

Devlin, Ann Sloan, and Allison B. Arneill. "Health Care Environments and Patient Outcomes." *Environment and Behavior* 33, no. 5 (September 2003): 665–94.

Dewan, Shaila. "Using Crayons to Exorcise Katrina." *New York Times*, September 17, 2007, sec. E, p. 1.

de Wolfe, Elsie. *The House in Good Taste*. New York: Century, 1931.

Dickens, Charles. *Little Dorrit*. London: Bradbury & Evans, 1857.

Dober, Richard P. *Campus Design*. New York: Wiley, 1992.

———. *Campus Heritage: An Appreciation of the History and Traditions of College and University Architecture*. Ann Arbor: Society for College and University Planning, 2005.

———. *Campus Landscape: Functions, Forms, Features*. New York: Wiley, 2000.

Dudek, Mark, ed. *Children's Spaces*. New York: Oxford University Press, 2005.

Duncan, Carol. *Civilizing Rituals: Inside Public Art Museums*. London: Routledge, 1995.

Dykman, Benjamin M., and Harry T. Reis. "Personality Correlates of Classroom Seating Position." *Journal of Educational Psychology* 71, no. 3 (1972): 352–56.

Ellard, Colin. *You Are Here: Why We Can Find Our Way to the Moon, but Get Lost in the Mall*. New York: Doubleday, 2009.

Feinberg, Susan G. "The Genesis of Sir John Soane's Museum Idea: 1801–1810." *Journal of the Society of Architectural Historians* 43 (October 1984): 225–37.

Ford, Alan. *Designing the Sustainable School*. Mulgrave, Victoria, Australia: Images, 2007.

Ford, Richard. "The Shore." *New Yorker*, August 2, 2004.

Forster, E. M. *Howards End*. London: Edward Arnold, 1910.

Gallagher, Winifred. *House Thinking: A Room-by-Room Look at How We Live*. New York: HarperCollins, 2006.

Garland, David. *The Culture of Control: Crime and Social Order in Contemporary Society*. Chicago: University of Chicago Press, 2001.

Giles, Richard. *Re-Pitching the Tent: Re-ordering the Church Building for Worship and Mission*. Collegeville, Minn.: Liturgical Press, 1999.

Glazer, Nathan. *From a Cause to a Style: Modernist Architecture's Encounter with the American City*. Princeton: Princeton University Press, 2007.

Goffman, Erving. *Asylums: Essays on the Social Situation of Mental Patients and Other Inmates*. Garden City, N.Y.: Anchor Books,1961.

———. *The Goffman Reader*. Edited with introductory essays by Charles Lemert and Ann Branaman. Malden, Mass.: Blackwell, 1977.

Goldberger, Paul. "Art Houses: New Museums in Milwaukee and St. Louis." *New Yorker*, November 5, 2001.

Grandin, Temple. *Animals in Translation*. New York: Scribner's, 2005.

Greenblatt, Stephen. "Resonance and Wonder." In Ivan Karp and Steven Lavine, eds., *Exhibiting Cultures: The Poetics and Politics of Museum Display*. Washington, D.C.: Smithsonian Institution Press, 1991, pp. 377–415.

Greenman, Jim. *Caring Spaces, Learning Places: Children's Environments That Work*. Redmond, Wash.: Exchange Press, 2005.

Griswold, Jerry. *Feeling Like a Kid: Childhood and Children's Literature*. Baltimore: Johns Hopkins University Press, 2006.

Harris, Cyril M., ed. *Illustrated Dictionary of Historic Architecture*. New York: Dover, 1977.

Harris, Neal. *Cultural Excursions: Marketing Appetites and Cultural Tastes in North America*. Chicago: University of Chicago Press, 1990.

Harsanyi, David. *Nanny State: How Food Fascists, Teetotaling Do-Gooders, Priggish Moralists, and Other Boneheaded Bureaucrats Are Turning America into a Nation of Children*. New York: Broadway, 2007.

Hawthorne, Nathaniel. *The House of the Seven Gables*. Boston: Ticknor, Reed, & Fields, 1851.

Haxthausen, Charles W., ed. *The Two Art Histories: The Museum and the University*. New Haven: Yale University Press, 2002.

Hayward, Cynthia. *Healthcare Facility Planning*. Chicago: Health Administration Press, 2006.

Hein, Hilde S. *The Museum in Transition: A Philosophical Perspective*. Washington, D.C.: Smithsonian Institution Press, 2000.

Herivel, Tara, and Paul Wright, eds. *Prison Profiteers: Who Makes Money from Mass Incarceration?* New York: Norton, 2007.

Hosking, Sarah, and Liz Haggard. *Healing the Hospital Environment: Design, Management and Maintenance of Healthcare Premises*. London and New York: E. & F. N. Spon, 1999.

Howells, William Dean. *A Hazard of New Fortunes*. New York: Boni & Liveright, 1889.

Humphrey, Caroline, and Piers Vitebsky. *Sacred Architecture*. Boston: Little, Brown, 1997.

Jackson, Shirley. *The Haunting of Hill House*. New York: Viking Press, 1959.

James, Henry. *The American*. Boston: J. R. Osgood, 1877.

———. *The Spoils of Poynton*. 1896; reprint, Norfolk, Conn.: New Directions, 1945.

Kachur, Lewis. *Displaying the Marvelous: Marcel Duchamp, Salvador Dali, and Surrealist Exhibition Installations*. Cambridge, Mass.: MIT Press, 2001.

Karp, Ivan, and Steven D. Lavine, ed. *Exhibiting Cultures: The Poetics and Politics of Museum Display*. Washington, D.C.: Smithsonian Institution Press, 1991.

Kieckhefer, Richard. *Theology in Stone: Church Architecture from Byzantium to Berkeley*. Oxford: Oxford University Press, 2004.

Kilde, Jeanne Halgren. *When Church Became Theatre: The Transformation of Evangelical Architecture and Worship in Nineteenth-Century America*. Oxford and New York: Oxford University Press, 2002.

Kimball, Fiske. "The Modern Museum of Art." *Architectural Record*, December 1929, pp. 559–80.

Kohl, Herbert R. *The Open Classroom: A Practical Guide to a New Way of Teaching*. New York: Random House, 1969.

Kunstler, James Howard. *Home from Nowhere: Remaking Our Everyday World for the 21st Century*. New York: Simon & Schuster, 1998.

Lancaster, John. *Mr. Phillips*. London: Faber & Faber, 2000.

Langdon, Philip. *A Better Place to Live: Reshaping the American Suburb*. Amherst: University of Massachusetts Press, 1994.

Laver, James. *Taste and Fashion from the French Revolution to the Present Day*. London: Harrap, 1945.

Lewis, Michael. "The Mansion: A Subprime Parable." *Best American Essays 2009*. New York: Mariner Books, 2009.

Macdonald, Ross. "Gone Girl." In Tony Hillerman, ed., *Best American Mystery Stories of the Century*. New York: Mariner Books, 2001.

McAlester, Virginia, and Lee McAlester. *A Field Guide to American Houses*. New York: Knopf, 1984.

Mead, Rebecca. "State of Play: How Tot Lots Became Places to Build Children's Brains." *New Yorker*, July 5, 2010, pp. 32–37.

Miller, Richard L., and Earl S. Swensson. *Hospital and Healthcare Facility Design*. New York: Norton, 2002.

Myerson, Jeremy. "After Modernism: The Contemporary Office Environment." In Susie McKellar and Penny Sparke, eds., *Interior Design and Identity*. Manchester, England, and New York: Manchester University Press, 2004.

Nair, Prakash, and Randall Fielding. *The Language of School Design: Design Patterns for 21st Century Schools*. Minneapolis: DesignShare, 2007.

Newhouse, Victoria. *Art and the Power of Placement*. New York: Monacelli Press, 2005.

Oates, Joyce Carol. "They All Went Away." In Joyce Carol Oates and Robert Atwan, eds., *The Best American Essays of the Century*. Boston: Houghton Mifflin, 2002.

O'Doherty, Brian. *Inside the White Cube: The Ideology of the Gallery Space*. Berkeley: University of California Press, 1999.

Pevsner, Nikolaus. "Market Halls, Conservatories, and Exhibition Buildings" and "Museums." In *A History of Building Types*. Princeton: Princeton University Press, 1976, pp. 111–38, 235–57.

Pooler, Jim. *Why We Shop: Emotional Rewards and Retail Strategies*. Westport, Conn.: Praeger, 2003.

Putnam, James. *Art and Artifact: The Museum as Medium*. London: Thames & Hudson, 2001.

"Rescaling the Guggenheim." Editorial, *New York Times*, January 5, 2003.

Rifkind, Carole. "Art Museums." In *A Field Guide to Contemporary American Architecture*. New York: Dutton, 1998.

Rose, Michael S. *Ugly as Sin: Why They Changed Our Churches from Sacred Places to Meeting Spaces—and How We Can Change Them Back Again*. Manchester, N.H.: Sophia Institute Press, 2001.

Schjeldahl, Peter. "Art Houses: Why a White Box in Munich Succeeds as a Museum." *New Yorker*, January 13, 2003, pp. 87–89.

Schlereth, Thomas J. "History Museums and Material Culture." In *Cultural History and Material Culture: Everyday Life, Landscapes, Museums*. Ann Arbor: UMI Research Press, 1990, pp. 337–415.

Sedaris, David. "This Old House." In Adam Gopnik and Robert Atwan, eds., *Best American Essays 2008*. New York: Mariner Books, 2008.

Smith, Lee. *Cakewalk*. New York: Putnam, 1981.

Sobal, Jeffrey, and Brian Wansink. "Kitchenscapes, Tablescapes, Platescapes, and Foodscapes: Influence of Microscale Built Environments on Food Intake." *Environment and Behavior* 39, no. 1 (2007): 124–42.

Sommer, Robert. *Personal Space: The Behavioral Basis of Design*. Englewood Cliffs, N.J.: Prentice-Hall, 1969.

———. *Social Design: Creating Buildings with People in Mind*. Englewood Cliffs, N.J.: Prentice-Hall, 1983.

———. *Tight Spaces: Hard Architecture and How to Humanize It*. Englewood Cliffs, N.J.: Prentice-Hall, 1974.

Staniszewski, Mary Anne. *The Power of Display: A History of Exhibition Installations at the Museum of Modern Art*. Cambridge, Mass.: MIT Press, 1998.

Stephens, Suzanne. "Small Museums: Identity with Integrity." *Architectural Record*, January 2003, pp. 127–46.

Stires, Lloyd. "Classroom Seating Location, Student Grades, and Attitudes: Environment or Self-Selection." *Environment and Behavior* 23 (May 1991): 305–313.

Sutton, Sharon E. *Weaving a Tapestry of Resistance: The Places, Power, and Poetry of a Sustainable Society*. Westport, Conn.: Bergin & Garvey, 1996.

Tilden, Scott J. *Architecture for Art: American Art Museums, 1938–2008.* New York: Harry N. Abrams, 2004.

Topp, Leslie, et al., eds. *Madness, Architecture and the Built Environment.* New York and London: Routledge, 2007.

Underhill, Paco. *Why We Buy: The Science of Shopping.* New York: Simon & Schuster, 2009.

Wagenaar, Cor. "Five Revolutions: A Short History of Hospital Architecture." In Cor Wagenaar, ed., *The Architecture of Hospitals.* Rotterdam: NAi, 2006.

Wallis, Allan D. *Wheel Estate: The Rise and Decline of Mobile Homes.* New York: Oxford University Press, 1997.

Weil, Elizabeth. "Teaching to the Testosterone." *New York Times Magazine,* March 2, 2008.

Wickersham, Joan. "Bricks & Politics." *Harvard Magazine,* September/October 2007.

Williams, Peter W. *Houses of God: Region, Religion, and Architecture in the United States.* Urbana: University of Illinois Press, 1997.

Wolfe, Tom. *The Kandy-Kolored Tangerine-Flake Streamline Baby.* New York: Farrar, Straus & Giroux, 1965.

Wollin, Dorothy D., and Mary Montagne. "College Classroom Environment: Effects of Sterility Versus Amiability on Student and Teacher Performance." *Environment and Behavior* 13 (November 1981): 707–716.

Zepp, Ira G., Jr. *The New Religious Image of Urban America: The Shopping Mall as Ceremonial Center.* Niwot: University Press of Colorado, 1997.

Zimmerman, Jonathan. *Small Wonder: The Little Red Schoolhouse in History and Memory.* New Haven: Yale University Press, 2009.

Zukin, Sharon. *Point of Purchase: How Shopping Changed American Culture.* New York: Routledge, 2004.

Notes

CHAPTER 1: WHAT BUILDINGS SAY

6   "the 'Happy House'": Gaston Bachelard, *The Poetics of Space*, pp. 72–73.

8   "decorative statues, frescos or carvings": Alain de Botton, *The Architecture of Happiness*, p. 53.

11   "In institutional buildings, it means power": Stewart Brand, *How Buildings Learn*, p. 23.

15   "can sleep or nap undisturbed": Jerry Griswold, *Feeling Like a Kid*, p. 18.

15   "A child's sense of security": Ibid., p. 22.

22   "that odious and abominable Past, with all its bad influences": Nathaniel Hawthorne, *The House of the Seven Gables*, p. 45.

CHAPTER 2: ARCHITECTURAL LANGUAGES

28   "half-baked versions of Scarlett O'Hara's Tara": James Howard Kunstler, *Home from Nowhere*, p. 31.

30   "[It was a] middle-class motel room": Ross Macdonald, "Gone Girl," in *Best American Mystery Stories of the Century*, p. 377.

31   "supermarkets in cities around the United States": Robert Sommer, *Social Design: Creating Buildings with People in Mind*, pp. 42–43.

34   The buildings we admire": Alain de Botton, *The Architecture of Happiness*, p. 98.

35   "a house with prison-like windows": Ibid., p. 154.

37   "Attractive architecture was held to be a version of goodness": Ibid., p. 13.

37   "a structure was correct and honest": Ibid., p. 53

38   "Present-day modernism expresses itself": Nathan Glazer, *From a Cause to a Style*, p. 291.

38   " walls that cant and lean": Ibid., p. 111.

38   "Every space in the building is a pain to work with": Stewart Brand, *How Buildings Learn*, pp. 58–59.

CHAPTER 3: MATERIALS AND STYLES

50   "low in thermal capacity": Edward Allen: *How Buildings Work*, p. 62.

50   "a room-temperature surface of metal": Ibid., p. 62.

53   "designed to be strong and resistant": Robert Sommer, *Tight Spaces*, p 2.

59   "siding with a wood grain pattern printed on it": Allan D. Wallis, *Wheel Estate*, p. 30.

59   "constructed with the fully conscious certainty that they will disintegrate": James Howard Kunstler, *Home from Nowhere*, p. 89.

59   "cartoon decoration": Ibid., p. 89

59   "a house that is built like a television set": Ibid., p. 101.

CHAPTER 4: OUTSIDE THE HOUSE

64 "The mansion was not satisfied with making us uneasy": Michael Lewis, "The Mansion: A Subprime Parable," p. 92.

64 "two squad cars with lights flashing": Ibid., p. 83.

64 "we are quite obviously, a nation of financial impostors": Ibid., p. 82.

69 "mighty old thorn trees": Charlotte Brontë, *Jane Eyre*, p. 125.

69 "The hallway is painted": Tom Wolfe, *The Kandy-Kolored Tangerine-Flake Streamline Baby*, p. 282.

71 "fashions in clothes go through a cycle": James Laver, *Taste and Fashion*, p. 255

76 "a mostly vertical, isosceles-angled, multi-windowed": Richard Ford, "The Shore," p. 67.

76 "a white farmhouse and willows": Ibid., p. 75.

77 "a house may be large or small": Karl Marx, *Wage-labour and Capital*, New York: International Publishers, 1976, p. 42.

79 "this circle is surrounded by lowlife": Lee Smith, *Cakewalk*, p. 139.

CHAPTER 5: INSIDE THE HOUSE

85 "small prey animals": Temple Grandin, *Animals in Translation*, p. 208.

91 "We walk into a sort of kitchen": Tom Wolfe, *The Kandy-Kolored Tangerine-Flake Streamline Baby*, pp. 282–83.

91 "We attribute vulgar qualities": Elsie de Wolfe, *The House in Good Taste*, p. 34.

96 "There were antiquities from Central Italy": Charles Dickens, *Little Dorrit*, p. 201.

96 "an inlaid chest from Bombay": Alan Bennett, *Untold Stories*, p. 72.

97 "The front door opened onto a living room": David Sedaris, "This Old House," p. 196.

97 "Scandinavian, we learned, was the name of a region": Ibid., p. 193.

99 "Urged on by clergymen": Deborah Cohen, *Household Gods*, p. x.

99 "morally injurious to keep company with bad things": Ibid., p. 25.

CHAPTER 6: INSIDE THE ROOM

125 "there were houses which made for laughter": Libbie Block, *The Hills of Beverly*, p. 184.

125 "the walls seemed always in one direction a fraction longer": Shirley Jackson, *The Haunting of Hill House*, p. 30.

125 "The house contains the home": Joyce Carol Oates, "They All Just Went Away," p. 558.

CHAPTER 7: HOUSES OF GOD

130 "exert a subtle but real influence": Michael DeSanctis, *Building from Belief*, p. 25.

130 "Every house represents a self-portrait": Ibid., p. 33.

132   "more ecclesiastical worship practices and worship spaces": Jeanne
      Halgren Kilde, *When Church Became Theatre*, p. 56.
133   "movement takes place along a processional path": Richard Kieckhefer,
      Theology in Stone, p. 60.
134   "Rapt far from New York": William Dean Howells, *A Hazard of New
      Fortunes*, p. 66.
135   "used to create an appearance of impregnability": *Illustrated Dictionary of
      Historic Architecture*, p. 474.
136   "The church is not a hive for drones": M. M. Dana, "A Congregational
      Corner Stone," quoted in Kilde, *When Church Became Theatre*, p. 110.
143   "often so sacred that it can be reached only by degrees": Caroline
      Humphrey and Piers Vitebsky, *Sacred Architecture*, p. 130.
143   "usually shelters the altar behind a screen of icons": Ibid., p. 73.
145   "Christians are to be found worshipping in long Gothic tunnels": Richard
      Giles, *Re-Pitching the Tent*, p. 5.
145   "Churches should be machines specially designed": Peter F. Anson, *The
      Building of Churches*, p.1003.
146   "a home, a worship workshop, a source of inspiration": Giles, *Re-Pitching
      the Tent*, p. 5.
146   "ceased to appeal to customers": Ibid., p. 75.
147   "a sense of ordinariness and cheapness": Michael S. Rose, *Ugly as Sin*, p.
      111.
147   "a giant clam": Ibid., p. 171.
147   "ever since Christians have established holy places for sacred worship":
      Ibid., p. 146.
147   "an extinct form of Christianity": Giles, *Re-Pitching the Tent*, pp. 7–8

CHAPTER 8: HOUSES OF ART AND SCIENCE

156   "the very sight of art could improve the morals": Carol Duncan, *Civilizing
      Rituals*, p. 43.
157   "to dazzle and overwhelm": Ibid., p. 90.
161   "it is doubtful that they represent any period": Ibid.
161   "related to past structures": Ibid., p. 91.
162   "were our religion, they were our life": Henry James, *The Spoils of Poynton*,
      p. 35.
162   "to read all behavior in the light of some fancied relation": Ibid., p. 27.
162   "ideal spaces that, more than any single picture, may be the archetypal image
      of twentieth century art": Brian O'Doherty, *Inside the White Cube*, p. 14.
163   "there was only really one path through the collection": James Hall,
      "Choice Without Voice," *Times Literary Supplement*, February 25, 2005, p.
      18.
163   "despite all the extra floor space hardly any more work can be shown":
      Ibid., p. 19.
166   "in the history of indoor looking up, we rank low": O'Doherty, *Inside the
      White Cube*, p. 66.
166   "Modern architecture simply ran the blank wall into the blank ceiling":
      Ibid., p. 67.

168 "seats are absent": James Cuno, ed., *Whose Muse?*, p. 95.

169 "they seem to glow of their own accord": Emma Barker, ed., *Contemporary Cultures of Display*, p. 15.

175 "brings the pages of the Bible to life": Creation Museum website, http://creationmuseum.org.

CHAPTER 9: HOUSES OF LEARNING I: GRADE SCHOOLS

185 "there was a moral panic about war children": Catherine Burke and Ian Grosvenor, *School*, p. 93.

185 "not one single piece of soft material anywhere": Ibid., p. 112.

185 "there is an utter and refreshing absence of conscious detailing": Ibid., p. 105.

188 "walls of the boys' classroom": Elizabeth Weil, "Teaching to the Testosterone," p. 38.

190 "public space teaches children their roles in society": Sharon Sutton, *Weaving a Tapestry of Resistance*, p. 2.

192 "rooms represent in physical form the spirit and soul of places and institutions": Herbert R. Kohl, *The Open Classroom*, p. 35.

192 "they teach people to be silent": Ibid., p. 116.

192 "was obsessed by control": Ibid., p. 13.

197 "when conservatives imagine a schoolhouse of quiet obedience": Jonathan Zimmerman, *Small Wonder*, p. 175.

201 "A recent poll of schoolchildren": Burke, *School*, p. 22.

201 "nothing like the playgrounds I so fondly remember": David Harsanyi, *Nanny State*, p. 139.

CHAPTER 10: HOUSES OF LEARNING II: HIGH SCHOOLS AND COLLEGES

207 "Countless public high school and middle schools slunk out of the center of town": Philip Langdon, *A Better Place to Live*, p. 134.

211 "regular, symmetrical, rectilinear": Richard P. Dober, *Campus Design*, p. 41.

211 "a separation of the world of the mind": Ibid., p. 77.

212 "remove the mind of the student": Ibid., p. 79.

213 "The pride of using modern materials": Ibid., p. 106.

213 "a 1960s-vintage monstrosity": James Howard Kunstler, *Home from Nowhere*, p. 40.

214 "massive gently sloping walls, high indented windows": Dober, *Campus Design*, p. 71.

215 "a university needs to have its own brand": Joan Wickersham, "Bricks & Politics," p. 56.

218 "Students with the most positive self-concepts": Lloyd Stires, "Classroom Seating Location, Student Grades, and Attitudes: Environment or Self-Selection."

218 "women sat in the front of the classroom more often than men": Benjamin M. Dykman and Harry T. Reis, "Personality Correlates of Classroom Seating Position," p. 352.

219   "The students in the "soft" classroom" Dorothy D. Wollin and Mary
       Montagne, "College Classroom Environment," pp. 707–716.

CHAPTER 11: HOUSES OF CONFINEMENT: PRISONS, HOSPITALS, ASYLUMS, NURSING HOMES

227   "dangerous others who threaten our safety": David Garland, *The Culture
       of Control*, p. 184.
232   "garages where people are taken to be checked and repaired": Sarah
       Hosking and Liz Haggard, *Healing the Hospital Environment*, p.1.
235   "depression, passivity, . . . and reduced immune system functioning": Ann
       Sloan Devlin and Allison B. Arneill, "Health Care Environments and
       Patient Outcomes," p. 672.
235   "the bad patient is angry and resistant": Ibid.
235   "prison guards do more time than the inmates": Ibid., p. 678.
237   "Undersized and inappropriate visitor support space": Cynthia Hayward,
       Healthcare Facility Planning, p. 99.
238   "hospitals, hotels, and prison pose similar problems": Abram de Swaan,
       "Constraints and Challenges in Designing Hospitals: The Sociological
       View," in Cor Wagenaar, ed., *Architecture of Hospitals*, p. 11.
240   "to rest immobile in bed": Erving Goffman, *Asylums*, p. 347.

CHAPTER 12: HOUSES OF HOSPITALITY: HOTELS AND RESTAURANTS

255   "it is virtually impossible for two people sitting down to converse
       comfortably": Robert Sommer, *Personal Space*, p. 121.
261   "The setting seemed to render all kinds of ideas absurd": Alain de Botton,
       The Art of Happiness, p. 108.

CHAPTER 13: HOUSES OF COMMERCE: STORES AND OFFICES

268   "low ceilings, narrow aisles, and tight spaces": Colin Ellard, *You Are Here*,
       p. 173.
268   "to compel the visitors to spend as much time at the gambling machines
       as possible": Ibid., p. 173.
268   "If we went into stores only when we needed to buy something": Paco
       Underhill, *Why We Buy: The Science of Shopping*, p. 24.
273   "less crude than price and less cruel than social class": Sharon Zukin,
       "The Social Space of Shopping," p. 213.
274   "enclosing and climatizing the public areas": Peter Coleman, *Shopping
       Environments*, p. 43.
274   " acts of sexual intimacy or obscenity are performed": Karen Dale and
       Gibson Burrell, *The Spaces of Organization and the Organization of Space*, p.
       47.
275   "By the late 1990s airport operators worldwide": Coleman, *Shopping
       Environments*, p. 244.
275   "the average time passengers spend in American airports": Ibid., p. 242.

275   "shopping is about transformation": Ibid., p. 5.

276   "gives life a sense of purpose": Jim Pooler, *Why We Shop*, p. 6.

276   "It is a solemn rite, a ceremonial act": Ibid., p. 5.

276   "everyone has experienced the ecstatic thrill of the perfect shopping event": Ibid., p. 3.

278   "oldest and most profound conflict in office design": Jeremy Myerson, "After Modernism: The Contemporary Office Environment," p. 196.

279   "literally tied to the workstation": Ibid., p. 202.

279   "A long table and a square table": Sir Francis Bacon, "Of Counsel," in *Essays Civil and Moral*, Chapter XX.

ABOUT THE AUTHOR

Alison Lurie, who won the Pulitzer Prize for her novel *Foreign Affairs*, has published ten books of fiction, four works of non-fiction, and three collections of tales for children. She is a former professor of English at Cornell University, and lives in an old house in upstate New York with her husband, the writer Edward Hower.

So here cometh
"Delphinium Books"
To recognize excellence in writing
And bring it to the attention
Of the careful reader
Being a book of the heart
Wherein is an attempt to body forth
Ideas and ideals for the betterment
Of men, eke women
Who are preparing for life
By living. . . .

(In the manner of Elbert Hubbard,
        "White Hyacinths," 1907)